DATE DUE

Demco, Inc. 38-293

Neville Chamberlain
and Appeasement

Neville Chamberlain and Appeasement

Robert J. Caputi

SUP

Selinsgrove: Susquehanna University Press
London: Associated University Presses

Associated University Presses
440 Forsgate Drive
Cranbury, NJ 08512

Associated University Presses
16 Barter Street
London WC1A 2AH, England

Associated University Presses
P.O. Box 338, Port Credit
Mississauga, Ontario
Canada L5G 4L8

The paper used in this publication meets the requirements of the American National Standard for Permanence of Paper for Printed Library Materials Z39.48-1984.

Library of Congress Cataloging-in-Publication Data

Caputi, Robert J., 1953–
    Neville Chamberlain and appeasement / Robert J. Caputi.
        p.   cm.
    Includes bibliographical references (p.   ) and index.
    ISBN 1-57591-027-6 (alk. paper)
    1. Great Britain—Foreign relations—Germany.   2. Chamberlain, Neville, 1869–1940—Views on Germany.   3. Great Britain—Politics and government—1936–1945.   4. Great Britain—Foreign relations—1936–1945.   5. Germany—Foreign relations—Great Britain. 6. World War, 1939–1945—Causes.   7. World politics—1900–1945. I. Title.
DA47.2.C36   2000
941.084—dc21
                                                                    99-23975
                                                                        CIP

PRINTED IN THE UNITED STATES OF AMERICA

To my Father and my Mother

Contents

Acknowledgments

ANY ENDEAVOR OF THIS SCALE COULD NOT POSSIBLY BE BROUGHT TO publication without a great deal of assistance generously given to its author. At the State University of New York at Buffalo, to the staff of Lockwood Library, especially Karen Senglaup, Mike Pasternak, and Paul Ryan, many thanks. Lockwood's interlibrary loan was very helpful in the obtaining of scarce source materials. To the SUNY Buffalo Department of History, Drs. John Milligan and Paul Guinn, for your cogent suggestions, which strengthened the manuscript. To Dr. R. J. Q. Adams of Texas A & M, heartfelt gratitude for your contribution.

Thanks also to the Public Record Office, Kew Gardens, London, for assistance in the early stages of my research. The staff of the Heslop Room at the University of Birmingham Library, where the Chamberlain archives are housed, was very congenial, especially Dr. B. S. Benedikz. Incidentally, the excerpts from Neville Chamberlain's letters within the text appear with the kind permission of Dr. Benedikz. To Colin and Maura Judges of Edgbaston, Birmingham, for their hospitality during my research sojourn in England, thanks. To Director Hans Feldmann of Susquehanna University Press, for his faith in the finished product, my gratitude.

A true debt of appreciation is owed to the good people at Associated University Presses in Cranbury, New Jersey. To Director Julien Yoseloff, many thanks. I feel obligated in the best sense of the word to offer my plaudits for your efforts and those of your superlative staff; Production Editors Melody Sadighi and Mr. Brian Haskell, Copy Editor Laura Ann Starrett, and finally, the indispensable element in the entire equation, my phenomenal Managing Editor and friend, Christine Retz. Your staff's professionalism and attention to detail has made the finished product much the better, and I thank you warmly.

To Dr. John F. Naylor of SUNY-Buffalo, the entirety of my efforts, in a positive sense, can only reflect his brilliance as a scholar, and his humanity as a friend.

Finally, to Mary and Elizabeth, who in many ways have wrestled nearly as much with Chamberlain's ghost as I have in the recent past, thanks for everything.

Introduction

SEPTEMBER 1988 MARKED THE FIFTIETH ANNIVERSARY OF THE INFA-
mous Four-Power Pact of the Munich Conference, which ceded
the Sudetenland to Nazi Germany and led to the liquidation of
Czechoslovakia as an independent state. For the British, it was
one in a long series of fifty-year remembrances associated with the
inexorable outbreak of the Second World War. It is rather ironic
that at the time of Munich the agreement was perceived as a last-
ditch, even providential, maintenance of the European peace. With
a righteous hindsight a majority of historians and politicians have
since regarded the pact as another sad step on the road to war.
Munich was arguably the apogee of Prime Minister Neville Chamberlain's prewar policy of appeasement of the dictator states. The
recent anniversary of this watershed event again brought into
focus the fifty-year historiographic debate on the efficacy of this
policy.

Why, after all, more discussion of appeasement? Arthur Neville
Chamberlain has been at eternal rest since 9 November 1940, and
his demise, coming as it did in the midst of nine months of the
relentless destruction of British cities by the Luftwaffe, evoked little overall mourning from his countrymen. Indeed, the positioning
of his crypt in Westminster Abbey, as I discovered during a recent
visit, spoke volumes about his popularity among Britain's twentieth-century worthies. Half-hidden by a pew, which necessitated
removal for a view, his memorial lay isolated and forlorn, a poignant metaphor of his failed policies, which were to lead to the
cataclysm that had been his deadliest fear. His successor, Winston
Churchill, was to lead the nation through its "finest hour" of 1940,
and on to ultimate victory. No mean historian himself, Churchill
perceived that as a victor he would have the final word on appeasement when he noted, "Poor Neville, he will come badly out of history. . . . I know, because I will write the history."[1] Indeed he did,
at great length, but therein lies the rub. It would be comforting to
believe that the greatest Englishman of the twentieth century had
eliminated every trace of ambiguity and had the definitive last

11

word on Chamberlain and his deserved place in history. Many were ready to accept his redoubtable six volumes on the war as the "Gospel According to Saint Winston." History, however, is an active process, an ongoing search for enlightenment that more often leads to a muddying of the waters than any irrefutable answers. Some twenty-five years ago, British historian Robert Skidelsky quoted the great German dramatist Goethe on historical revisionism and the words are apropos today:

> the history of the world must be rewritten from time to time not because many events of the past are being rediscovered, but because new vistas are opening up, new ways of looking at things, which show the past in a different light.[2]

Fortunately for most historians, there are no easy answers, and new ideas, reinforced by research, help to keep the story of the past alive and vital, with the Chamberlain debate being no exception.

Sources dealing with Chamberlain and appeasement from the 1930s and 1940s up to the present will be discussed chronologically. At the same time, critical events in the Chamberlain premiership will be examined for the divergence of the respective analyses throughout the years. This format is designed to afford the desired width and breadth to the scholarship, bringing the efforts of the last half-century into a tighter focus.

The initial chapter details the bitter exchanges between pro-Chamberlain supporters and the antiappeasers, whose voices were well-nigh unheard and certainly unheeded in Britain until after the March 1939 Nazi seizure of Prague. Sources from this period include the memoirs of many significant British political figures. Later chapters include in-depth analyses of the authorized biographies of Chamberlain by Sir Keith Feiling and Iain Macleod, discussion of the Churchillian postwar influence that characterized the incipient Cold War, and the beginnings of "revisionist" tendencies led by D. C. Watt's 1965 clarion call, developed below. Other topics cover ancillary themes; for example, the economic efficacy of appeasement, the military aspects of rearmament and defensive planning, and finally the reciprocal relationship between the British print media and the Chamberlain administration, which had hopes for an overall European pacification through appeasement.

Perhaps a greater understanding, an alleviation of some of the historiographic confusion surrounding the appeasement years, an objective analysis of a variety of sources, should be my optimal goal. I offer, then, if not the last word, at least a more contemporary one.

Neville Chamberlain
and Appeasement

1

Beginnings of Conflict, 1938–1940

THE ATTEMPTS OF GREAT BRITAIN TO FORESTALL A EUROPEAN WAR IN 1938 by appeasing the dictator states seemed, to a grateful world, to bear fruit that September, with the signing of the Four-Power Pact in Munich. The integrity and independence of a lesser power was sacrificed to avoid the catastrophe of war. Never was the debate over the efficacy of appeasement more spirited than in the eighteen months following Munich. The luckless Neville Chamberlain saw his efforts at conciliation wrecked by the German seizure of Prague in March 1939, when both Bohemia and Moravia were perfunctorily subsumed into the Nazi maw. Eleven months after returning to London bearing that fateful scrap of paper fluttering in the wind that symbolized his tenuous "peace with honour," Chamberlain issued an ultimatum to Berlin that passed unheeded, and Britain went to war a generation after Versailles. He who had stated, "I am a man of peace to the depths of my soul,"[1] was forced to lead His Majesty's government into world war. After the slaughter of the betrayed and overmatched Poles and the six months of *Sitzkrieg*, the disaster of Norway marked the endgame for Chamberlain's tenure, and Churchill took office the day of the Nazi attack on France and the Low Countries. Six months later Neville Chamberlain was dead, his policies disgraced, his legacy reviled as the essence of weakness and fear in the face of forceful aggression.

In the space of that eighteen months the man once hailed as the "world's greatest peacemaker" would, because of the failure of his policies, have his administration accused of the most spineless conduct, in the most negative account of a negligence and cowardice tantamount to treason. The passage of time has enabled historians to render judgment on a far more balanced and dispassionate level just not possible under the circumstances that existed in the denouement of Munich. The work that came to symbolize the entire genre that cast blame on the Chamberlain government for Britain's unreadiness was *Guilty Men*. Written by CATO, a collective pseudonym for Peter Howard, Michael Foot, and Frank Owen, this rather brief philippic was published in July 1940 by Victor Gollancz, Ltd. Gollancz had created the Left Book Club in 1936 to resist, if only in print, the rise of European Fascism and German Nazism. The "Guilty Men" school of literature on appeasement was to remain influential well into the 1960s, when historical judgment would be challenged by a more sophisticated scholarship. In 1940, after the humiliation of Dunkirk and the fall of France, CATO's thesis was widely accepted, and its tone was condemnatory. Chamberlain's immediate predecessors as Prime Minister, National Labour's Ramsay MacDonald and the Tory Stanley Baldwin, were charged with heavy responsibility for the destruction of Britain's military capabilities, which to CATO led to defeat in battle. From May 1923 to May 1937 either Baldwin or MacDonald was Premier; indeed, from late 1931 until the 1935 election they shared power in a National Government. The widespread dread of war and armaments that characterized Britain in this era was a legacy of the carnage and waste of the Great War. The idea that a comprehensive European disarmament would eliminate the danger of military conflict was, as we now know, rather illusory, but represented the ultimate hope of the Western democracies. The disarmament policies were reflected in the British Treasury's slashing of military expenditures throughout the 1920s and early 1930s. Throughout *Guilty Men*, the authors effectively condemned the malfeasance of the "guilty" by employing the actual words of a governmental figure to attack that individual. Reflecting on the near-disaster of the Dunkirk evacuation, when the trapped British Expeditionary Force was mercilessly pounded by the seemingly unopposed Luftwaffe, CATO invoked a 1934 speech by former Prime Minister Baldwin. At that time, the P.M. had solemnly declared that "His Majesty's Government are determined in no conditions to accept any position of inferiority with regard to what air force may be raised in Germany in the future."[2] This causal link between governmental negligence and battlefield disaster was a crucial theme of CATO's efforts. Although Chamberlain must take blame for being part of this process as the Chancellor of the Exchequer from 1931 to 1937, it is fair to say that many of his problems were inherited from his predecessors. To that end, CATO charged, "MacDonald and Lord Baldwin took over a great empire, supreme in arms and secure in liberty. They conducted it to the edge of national annihilation."[3] The analysis was of the political and diplomatic misjudgments that led to the "betrayal" of the Czechs and the descent into war. Although the authors credited Mr. Chamberlain for being a nominal supporter of rearmament, they denigrated both the level and speed of those efforts. They did not share Chamberlain's sanguine belief in Britain's military strength in December 1937, when he stated, six months after becoming Premier: "The country is strong. She is getting stronger every day. Our strength makes it easier for us to appeal to others to join us in applying our common sense to these problems."[4] When war did come in spite of Chamberlain's best efforts at appeasement, CATO chided the P.M. for his decision to continue with peacetime methods and limited rearmament, so that the Germans were spending nearly double the British total in war preparation.[5] In reference to the Prime Minister's failed attempts at conciliation leading to the "betrayal" of Czechoslovakia, the authors noted the high cost of that tragedy when they reflected on the battle for France in May 1940. In that battle, the French destroyed *"hundreds of the thousands of tanks opposing them. . . . Those that fell into their hands bore a familiar sign upon them. They had been made, according to French design, in the Skoda Works of Czechoslovakia."*[6] CATO's conclusion included a strong recommendation to sweep the malefactors responsible for this dangerous situation out of power, and with all possible speed. The authors stated:

> One final and absolute guarantee is still imperatively demanded by a people determined to resist and conquer; namely, that the men who are now repairing the breaches in our walls should not carry along with them those who let the walls fall into ruin. . . . Let the Guilty Men retire then, of their own volition, and so make an essential contribution to the victory upon which all are implacably resolved.[7]

Those hard, vengeful words served to establish *Guilty Men* as a classic polemic against appeasement. The specter of Britain at the edge of the abyss in the summer of 1940 after having been one of the victors of 1919 led to a rush for a scapegoat on whom to pin the blame. In the face of future histories, multidimensional efforts that would offer many reasons for Britain's unreadiness, *Guilty Men* seems simplistic in its stark portrayal of good and evil, its lack of ambiguity and high moral tone. Indeed, Gollancz Publishing would later advertise the book, then out of print in 1945, as "probably the most famous British pamphlet for a hundred years."[8] Whatever the verdict on that score, it lent the signature to the entire genre of anti-Chamberlain literature of the era. In a recent article, a historian of Britain stressed his view that *Guilty Men* "enshrined the disillusion of a generation . . . and set the tone of debate for the study of appeasement for twenty years after the war."[9]

There were other attacks on the Conservative leadership in the immediate wake of Munich, stridently partisan, very often vituperative in tone. These aimed to exploit the shame of Britain's betrayal of the Czechs as a club with which to beat the Tories and manufacture political advantage to boot. Several attacked the Chamberlain government for its perceived pro-Nazi sentiment. One of these, published before *Guilty Men*, was Simon Haxey's 1939 tome, *England's Money Lords, Tory M.P.* Its venomous tone and accusatory content had the flavor of class warfare, from an overly bitter and cynical perspective. The author suggested that only Labour's rise to power could ensure a democratic Britain. He stressed that the object of his work was to show the true character of Toryism, and to answer the question "to what extent is the oligarchy still in power today . . . rank, property, the employment of labour still exist, but how far are they represented in Parliament?"[10] His chapter titles mirrored his sentiments, as with *Business Men as Politicians*, *Makers of Munitions as Members of Parliament*, and *Property and Patriotism*. Government by rich men, he stated, was the fundamental aim and object of Conservative politics.[11] Going a step further, he opined that "no man is welcome among the upper ranks of the Conservative Party unless he is either wealthy or aristocratic,"[12] and that while the Conservatives are in power the class of the major employers of this country direct the nation's destinies. This class, he added, uses Parliament as a weapon to facilitate the pursuit of profit and as a means to fortify its power and authority.[13] The author was directing his criticism at the political and economic misjudgments of the Tories, while simultaneously calling for social and political change.

The book's most strident passages of partisanship were in the chapter entitled "The Tory Right Wing." Haxey indisputably accused the minority of ardent Nazi sympathizers in the Tory Party of dominating the government. He cited the number as "very considerable" and argued "what are we to think of the promises of Conservative leaders to defend us against the encroachments of Fascism, when they cannot even exclude Fascists from among their members of Parliament?"[14] The Anglo-German fellowship provided a platform for Nazi propaganda in Britain, and included among its members nearly thirty M.P.s from the House of Commons listed by the author, and another thirty from the House of

Lords. Haxey made it clear that even though the activities of the Anglo-German Fellowship were limited in scope, they did show the section of British society that desired to befriend the Nazis and for whom the Fellowship provided a suitable meeting place.[15] To that end, he described a few of the more influential members, among them Lord Mount Temple, Sir Barry Domvile, and the Lord Londonderry, as fully supporting the Munich agreement, and claiming it as a victory for their policy. A letter from this group to *The Times* of 12 October 1938 was quoted for dramatic effect. The Munich agreement "took nothing from Czechoslovakia to which that country could rightfully lay claim and gave nothing to Germany which could have been rightfully withheld."[16] Haxey also commented on the strategic losses suffered by Britain and France at Munich, not the least of which was the famous Skoda armament works of Czechoslovakia, whose loss the critic CATO would later mourn.

On appeasement and Munich, the author insisted that "the policy which led to the destruction of this last democratic country in Central Europe, to the loss by Britain of its only ally in Central Europe, and to the great accession to the military strength of Nazi Germany was welcomed by leading Conservatives."[17] Haxey assessed the virulent anti-Communist sentiments in the Chamberlain government as the reason behind Britain's rejection of the Soviet Union as a potential ally. Inherent in the reasoning was the notion that influential Tories actually preferred the rise of Nazi power to that of the specter of Moscow. He argued as much when he stated, "without Austria, Czechoslovakia, and Franco-Spain, Nazi Germany had no chance of winning a war against the united strength of the British Empire, France, and Russia . . . a united stand against Nazi encroachment three or four years ago would have been immediately successful and there and there would have been no danger of war."[18] Haxey's most outrageous claim, however, was that concerning the nature of the Tory party in relation to European fascism. Tory sympathy for Fascism, he wrote:

is the result of their fear of democracy . . . they believe that unless Fascism succeeds in Europe, the privileged position of Britain's wealthy governing class may be irretrievably lost. Their policy of retreat before Fascism is the instinctive act of self-preservation of a wealthy oligarchy. . . . In order to preserve the power of their particular political party, they have been willing to jeopardise the safety of this country and of the Empire, and to condone a neo-Napoleonic hegemony in Europe by German Fascism.[19]

While calling on the Labour Party to turn out the appeasers, Haxey concluded that the record of His Majesty's government in foreign affairs had been one of disastrous capitulation and even open support for the Fascist aggressors, and that the Britain that would react to threats from Nazi Germany would be a democratic and not a Fascist Britain.[20] At least on that point alone, the events of 1940, during Britain's "finest hour," would prove the sagacity of Haxey's judgment. At the time of its publication, however, a leading British literary source charged *Tory M.P.* as being "narrowly partisan in spirit,"[21] a not uncommon trait among literature in the turbulent summer of 1939.

Another class-laden polemic published in 1939 was Steven Macgregor's pamphlet, *Truth and Mr. Chamberlain*. Like Haxey, Macgregor attacked what he perceived as the disastrous results of the Chamberlain foreign policy, but he aimed his criticisms at the privileged elites of the Conservative Party as well. Chamberlain's parliamentary opposition were scarcely in a position to criticize the speed or level of rearmament, since Labour support for it had not been in any way forthcoming until the dangerous days of late 1938. However, Macgregor derided Chamberlain for allowing the arms profits of private manufacturers to reach levels unequaled in peace time, twelve firms having nearly quadrupled their profits from 1935 to 1938.[22] Macgregor stated, "at home, Mr. Chamberlain's policy, whether consciously or not, has worked with admirable consistency to the advantage of the wealthy minority."[23] Nearly in lockstep with what Haxey had stressed, Macgregor intimated that the Tories would rather see the growth of Fascism in Britain than fight a war for a truly democratic Britain. He declared that when Mr. Chamberlain speaks of the good of the nation, he really means the "welfare of five percent who own ninety-five percent of the national wealth and not the requirements, just and simple though they are, of the great masses."[24] The preservation of the status quo was imperative for the Conservative majority.

Macgregor took the Prime Minister to task for being less than forthright with his parliamentary colleagues. He alluded to a luncheon meeting of 10 May 1938 hosted by Lady Astor, where Chamberlain reportedly communicated to twelve American journalists his secret plans concerning a Four-Power Pact in Europe, with the exclusion of Russia. The Premier also stated at that time that he was in favor of ceding the Sudeten region of Czechoslovakia to the Germans. When opposition members of Parliament heard of these statements through the Canadian and American press, the Prime Minister attempted, according to the author, to evade and then to obfuscate the issue. "Plainly," Macgregor insisted, "Mr. Chamberlain's policy was to create an imperialist bloc to revive the exploitation of weaker countries."[25] In reference to the actual settlement at Munich, the author cited a speech of 7 March 1938, when Chamberlain had stated that His Majesty's government's international efforts did not signify a willingness to purchase peace today at the price of peace hereafter.[26] With a sense of cruel irony, the author concluded, "the tragic events which have since darkened the political future of the world all bore the hallmark of abject surrender or of some short, even shameful, respite."[27] Only if Britain's leadership radically modified its policies would the freedoms of Englishmen be preserved at home and around the world in the perilous summer of 1939.

Along with the rather extremist viewpoints of Macgregor and Haxey, there existed in the eighteen months after Munich several other accounts critical of Chamberlain and appeasement that were far more balanced and of a less hectoring tone. One such work was R. W. Seton-Watson's *From Munich to Danzig* (1939), a larger version of his earlier *Munich and the Dictators* (1938). Seton-Watson viewed with abhorrence what he perceived as the stranglehold that the Prime Minister had on Parliament and the British nation; he saw that the domination of the appeasers could lead to a loss of liberties at home. "Most of all," he stressed, "it is necessary to protest against the totalitarian tendencies inside our own government, which lead the P.M. himself to accuse anyone who dares to criticise his policy, of 'fouling his own nest,' and to unite with the Nazis in denouncing as war-mongers, and 'war-at-any-price men' men who have been his close colleagues in the past and might in the future be called to replace him."[28] In reference to the government's foreign policy, Seton-Watson noted:

> appeasement . . . is unfortunately a phrase that is vague and open to miscalculation, for it does not face up to the fundamental issue, that peace can neither be attained by yielding to dictation nor by suppression of awkward facts. We must first have the certainty that the State with which we are bargaining respects law, order, and justice at home, and in the foreign sphere puts the Rule of Law above the Rule of Force.[29]

Certainly Germany in the first six months of 1939 fulfilled neither of these criteria. Chamberlain's hopes had been based on his ability to "reason" and "do business" with the dictators, but Seton-Watson believed those hopes to be more illusion than reality. Referring to *Kristallnacht*, when in November 1938 the world first witnessed the murderous violence of Nazi Germany's widespread anti-Semitism, he stated: "This far-reaching policy of Pogrom and extermination . . . affords that the Berlin Government, so far from aiming at 'appeasement,' is more than ever wedded to methods of naked force at home and abroad."[30] He added the opinion that "we must not renounce our goal of Anglo-German understanding, but we must at the same time make it clear that there are limits not only to territorial concessions, but to the condonation of crime."[31] Business as usual under the circumstances was not only futile, but dangerous.

In conclusion, Seton-Watson insisted that there was a middle course between surrender and aggression. He recommended a clear definition of aims and a stern warning of "thus far and no farther," along with continued attempts to construct a "Democratic Front" for defensive purposes only. He advocated the buildup of healthy relations with America and Russia, which would serve as a deterrent against the adventurism of the dictators, and noted rather eloquently that "the price of peace cannot be paid vicariously, and so far [circa February 1939] we have shown no sign of readiness to make any sacrifice of our own in its cause."[32] For the British, as with all of their allies, that sacrifice would surely come soon enough.

An opinion critical of appeasement that was published after the outbreak of war in 1939 was Sir Norman Angell's *For What Do We Fight?* Angell had been a strong force in the pacifist efforts in Britain between the wars. In 1910, before the Great War, he had published the best-seller *The Great Illusion*. This influential work had proclaimed that armed aggression would not pay, and was the initial practical discussion on the possibility of preventing war.[33] Angell had also been one of the pioneers pressing for the creation of a League of Nations, and he had received the Nobel Peace Prize in 1933 for his peacemaking efforts. In the aforementioned *For What Do We Fight?*, the author pondered how a British victory in the present conflict would be any more permanent than that of the Great War; how would it leave the world a safer, more secure place? He admonished the supporters of appeasement for insisting on the "absolute blamelessness of Great Britain in the events of the last seven or eight years . . . because such failure as there has been of the world order has been the fault of others, due to forces beyond our control."[34] Angell called for the British people to face the truth about the international situation, to recognize that the strategy of appeasement had not been "completely sound and fully vindicated," and that the public were not totally blameless for their current troubles. The ultimate indictment, he stressed, "is not of Mr. Chamberlain, or his Government, but of the nation, the electorate, the public as a whole. If it be true that Mr. Chamberlain or his predecessors were leading us along a path the end of which was war, then it was the nation's business to get rid of him."[35] Angell voiced the need for Britain to strengthen its moral position in the world as it sought allies as war began. To that end, regarding appeasement, his view was that the British ought "to admit with some decent humility that we were mistaken in this line during those long years of retreat; that we ought to have taken the lesser risks to resist the earlier aggressions to the end that the later ones would not be attempted."[36] This view would years later be argued eloquently by Churchill in his six-volume history of the war.

Perhaps a critique of the British foreign policy that led to Munich would not be complete without a source from Czechoslovakia, the final ally of the West in Eastern Europe, and the last democracy east of the Rhine. Hubert Ripka, a close colleague of Czech President Eduard Benes, published his *Munich: Before and After* in mid-1939. A witness to those fateful months encompassing the Munich settlement, Ripka wrote with dignified restraint of the events that led to the destruction of his country. He referred to an impassioned speech given on 22 September 1938 by President Benes, who during the midst of the crisis, stated: "If such an understanding is achieved, provided that it is an honourable one, it will be to the advantage also of our nation. It will mean a general appeasement between England, France, and Germany, and between our country and Germany."[37] Benes and his Czechs had placed their trust in the better judgment of Britain and France, and they would pay dearly as a result.

Ripka brought into clear focus one of the chief factors for the tragedy wrought upon the Czechs at Munich, namely that the Western powers, in their desire to do business, did not recognize the true nature of their adversary. As Seton-Watson stated earlier, Neville Chamberlain stood little chance of "doing business" at Munich, for his rivals were criminals and not businessmen. Every mistake of tactics or of principle that was committed by Prague or by the Western powers in seeking a "just, reasonable settlement" of the Sudeten-German question was due "to one and the same fundamental misconception: they were looking for reconciliation with a partner who desired, not reconciliation, but domination."[38] Whether it was negligence, naivete, or cowardice on the part of the democracies, the pill was just as bitter to the Czech people. The

Lord Mayor of Prague, Dr. Zenkl, summed up the fate of his nation when he opined that Britain and France "have considered the rights of a small nation as of less importance than the brutal might of one which is great and powerful. . . . We have found ourselves at a crisis in history when might has taken precedence over right."[39] What, then, was to be done in the aftermath of Munich? Was Munich a sign of the "general capitulation" or of the recovery of the Western democracies? Ripka was perhaps more sanguine than most concerning his erstwhile Western allies. In Britain, he concluded, there is "ample evidence of growing disgust with the policy pursued by the dictatorships . . . the moral forces of British democracy are still strong, and it is only necessary that they should be mobilised and dynamised."[40] In the six-year world war that would soon follow the publication of Ripka's book, Britain's moral forces would oftentimes be stretched to their limits.

Another source critical of the appeasement policies of the Chamberlain administration was Eleanor Rathbone's 1938 publication, *War Can Be Averted*. The author, a renowned social reformer, one of the leaders of the women's suffrage movement in Britain, as well as a longtime Independent M.P., believed that collective security could yet be achieved by the West. She declared that Britain's ability to lead this effort was hindered only by a "lack of faith and will among ourselves and in these other nations."[41] She attacked appeasement as being untenable in those dangerous times as a betrayal of the Covenant of the League, and charged that it served only to whet the appetites of aggressors. In rather Churchillian tones, she stated:

> What is more likely to foster the delusions of a would-be Caesar or Napoleon than to find the most powerful nations suing for his friendship and the less powerful for his protection? . . . Is any course of action more likely to encourage the gambler's temperament than the uncertainty of Great Britain's present policy, which keeps all Europe guessing as to how much we will put up with and where, if anywhere, we will make a stand?[42]

Rathbone took the entirety of the British political establishment to task for their inability to construct a viable policy to further Britain's security while simultaneously obviating the chances of war. The Tory leadership, the "Peace Movement," and the "Defeatist Left" all came under the author's withering criticism, and each was dispensed their share of the blame for the danger of Britain's situation. On the Conservative Party's fear of Soviet influence crippling their chances of a rapprochement with Moscow, Rathbone noted, "Easy indeed is the descent to Hell and to the War which is Hell, when all resolute action to deter aggression and cruelty is paralysed by fear and by the prejudices of class and creed."[43] Written as it was before the *Anschluss* or Munich had occurred, Rathbone's analysis of the international situation was cogent and insightful, and more than a little prescient as to the future course of European affairs. She rejected the conciliatory policies of the past in favor of a more effective defensive alignment that would serve to discourage aggression. Her conclusion eloquently illuminated her views:

> War has been averted—so far . . . but have we, or any other peace-loving nation, purchased security even for ourselves, or is not the war menace greater and nearer than it has ever been since 1914? . . . Although they [Nazi demands] may be temporarily bought off by the sacrifice of Czechoslovakia—how long will they be postponed? And if that price is paid, what will be the next demand? Where is it going to stop? Is it not time to try another path—the path of collective defence of peace—or at least to explore the possibilities of it more persistently and realistically than has yet been done?[44]

In order to obtain the historical balance and objectivity that is necessary for a proper perspective, the supporters of Chamberlain and appeasement must have their due, and, for the eighteen months after Munich until May 1940 they were numerous and influential. The truly pejorative stigma of the "Guilty Men" school would develop to a greater extent in the postwar years, when peace brought time and opportunity for reflection, and with it, condemnation. One account that must be described as a hagiography was the 1940 effort, *Neville Chamberlain: Man of Peace*, by Derek Walker-Smith. The author perceived his famous subject as a very "rational" man, who had the ability to deal with anyone to ensure the peace of Europe. It is quite interesting to note tnat while Chamberlain's critics hectored him for "doing business" with the dictators, his own supporters saw this personal diplomacy and hands-on foreign policy as one of the Prime Minister's strengths. The author outlined clearly Chamberlain's perception of the meaning of his policy of appeasement. The Prime Minister described how he meant by that term a settlement within the framework of a European agreement. In Chamberlain's own words:

> The peace of Europe must depend upon the attitude of the four major Powers—Germany, Italy, France and ourselves. Should these Powers

be content simply to form themselves into two rival blocs a conflict would be the inevitable result—conflict which many think would mark the end of civilisation. . . . If we can bring these nations into friendly discussion, into a settling of their differences we shall have saved the peace of Europe for a generation.[45]

Perhaps the negative aspect of the Prime Minister's astute business sense was that he perceived foreign "statesmen" (and there were precious few to be found at Munich), to be as rational as he. Walker-Smith commented on this when he reflected on the decision to put Plan Z, that is, the plan for Chamberlain's personal physical intervention in the Czech crisis of September 1938, into practice. On Plan Z, he noted, "then came the revelation of Mr. Chamberlain . . . breaking down the barriers by action breathtaking in its simplicity and courage . . . to undertake the rigours of a difficult journey in order . . . to put the whole issue on a frank man to man basis, had about it the quality of genius."[46] A personal letter from Chamberlain to his sister Ida on 3 September 1938, referred to the selfsame plan and offered evidence of the Premier's courage and sincerity in leaving no stone unturned in his desperate search for a European peace. He alluded to Lord Halifax, at that time Foreign Secretary, and Nevile Henderson, British Ambassador to Berlin, in that dispatch. On Plan Z, Chamberlain remarked to his sister:

Is it not positively horrible to think that the fate of hundreds of millions depends on the man and he is half mad. I keep racking my brain to try and devise some means of averting a catastrophe if it should seem to be upon us. I thought of one so unconventional and daring that it rather took Halifax's breath away. But since Henderson thought it might save the situation at the eleventh hour I haven't abandoned it though I hope all the time that it won't be necessary to try it.[47]

As fate would have it, the Prime Minister made not one but three trips to Germany in search of a settlement of the Czech question, and the final result was the Munich agreement. The author shared with Chamberlain the belief that war should be averted at all costs, that a European war would be the ultimate disaster for "civilisation." Even as war began with the Nazi invasion of Poland on 1 September 1939, and scores of his colleagues were attacking the Prime Minister for an evident lack of nerve in serving an ultimatum to Berlin, Walker-Smith would congratulate Chamberlain for his behavior. Of that fateful weekend, the author remarked, "in holding out the hope of peace on September 2nd, and showing readiness to meet a wholly new situation if Germany gave the word and took the action necessary, Mr. Chamberlain gave evidence of a breadth of vision and greatness of mind truly Olympian."[48] As supportive as Walker-Smith's account was, he certainly chose the correct title when he characterized Chamberlain as the "Man of Peace." When war did come it is understandable that this peacemaker's legacy would suffer, and his historical standing would plummet.

A source of strong support for the Prime Minister came from Duncan Keith-Shaw's 1939 publication, *Prime Minister Neville Chamberlain*. Essentially an apologia for the Tory Party leadership, it was both well written and argued. The author contended that Neville was certainly the greatest of the Chamberlains, that his restraining of the "dogs of war" in September 1938 was enough to cement his position for immortality. Keith-Shaw stressed, "Even if the madness of war is ultimately loosed upon us, to Chamberlain is due the credit of giving the world one last year before civilisation plunged into what might prove its catastrophic doom."[49] The Premier was lauded for his diplomatic efforts, in phrases chosen carefully and argued with characteristic Tory sentiment. Keith-Shaw stated it with an almost poetic eloquence:

> Chamberlain pursues today the same end he sought at Munich—but that end is not peace! . . . Though he may use the term "peace" as convenient to the understanding of the multitude, it is significant that he has more often used the term "appeasement" . . . the implications of his whole life suggest that what he seeks, the objective he has pursued with unwavering devotion, and the goal he still tenaciously strives for, is *understanding*. When none seek war there will be peace, and none would seek war if there were understanding. Chamberlain knows that with understanding there would be no thought either of peace or its negation, war, but a new state, harmony, with its inseparable counterpart, goodwill.[50]

The inference is again that Conservative supporters felt that foreign statesmen, no matter the ideology, could be counted on to be as rational as the British Prime Minister, to do business as if they were rival commercial interests in turn-of-the-century Birmingham instead of power-crazed Fascists preparing for war.

In response to Steven Macgregor's criticism of Chamberlain's "plan" for an alleged four-power imperialist bloc to exploit weaker countries, Keith-Shaw argued forcefully in defense of the Prime Minister, when he stressed that all his experience has taught Chamberlain that generous concession to the other point of view is essential to understanding. It is also conceivable . . . that ultimate European peace could best be secured by a four-power bloc living peacefully alongside a self-contained Russia. There is nothing very unreasonable in such a plan and if in the existing circumstances, he saw in it the best possible means of achieving his ultimate end of appeasement, then there was nothing to his discredit in the rumoured association with the "Cliveden group."[51]

Ideology be damned, the Prime Minister would see his way through to do business. On the Sudeten crisis of the same summer, the author credited Chamberlain for his adherence to a modern version of what could be called realpolitik. He insisted that the Prime Minister "could see no reason why a balancing reconciliation should not be struck between the aims and ideals of the so-called democratic and totalitarian states."[52] As Simon Haxey had written, this was a notion dear to the leadership of the Conservative Party. Keith-Shaw did remind his readership that the heinous wrongs perpetrated at Versailles were partially the fault of Britain. On the Nazi regime, he noted, "it is a terrible thought that civilisation should be at the mercy of a handful of madmen. It must not be forgotten that the German people are responsible for giving these madmen that power and it would also be well for us to remember upon whom rests the responsibility for reducing the German people to such a state of desperation that they were willing to commit their fates into the hands of anyone who promised them redemption."[53] Among many Tories, particularly the right wing, this "mea maxima culpa" attitude toward the Versailles Treaty was very common. In an epilogue ostensibly written on 5 September 1939, Keith-Shaw summarily and indisputably recorded his perception of the Chamberlain legacy. He concluded: "after it is all over . . . if there is an audience to listen, one thing is certain—none will be able to establish with truth that if Chamberlain had done this or that, war could have been averted. He did everything that mortal man could do to save humanity from the disaster which now envelops it."[54] This viewpoint remains as plausible and defensible a position in the historical debate today as it was more than fifty years ago, despite the long list of particulars for which Neville Chamberlain has since been indicted.

Among the works that supported the Conservative leadership, Stuart Hodgson's *The Man Who Made the Peace: Neville Chamberlain*, was more balanced than many of the accounts of the time. Written by a former editor at the London *Daily News*, published almost immediately after Munich, his effort was characteristically factual and less ideological than most of the genre. He did, however, espouse a popular Tory belief in the unjust nature of Versailles when he commented on the Czech crisis: "The real responsibility for the situation in 1938 lay with the founders of Czechoslovakia twenty years before. The harvest had been long ripening, but it was bound to ripen in the end."[55] Duncan Keith-Shaw stated above Chamberlain's belief in the reconciliation of democratic and totalitarian states, and Hodgson held much the same view. He argued that the fact "that dictatorships and democracies cannot in any circumstances live peacefully together is a fallacy clearly disputed by history . . . it is not true that dictatorships are necessarily warlike and democracies necessarily peaceful."[56] Hodgson defended Chamberlain for his conduct during the Czech crisis, which he felt was above reproach. In a legalistic tone the author insisted that the three steps the crisis demanded were accomplished by the Prime Minister. To that end, Hodgson noted: "He warned Germany . . . short of actually threatening her he could not have warned her more plainly. . . . He kept in the closest touch with France. . . . He made urgent representations to the Prague Government of the danger ahead and the necessity of leaving nothing undone to forestall it."[57] Finally, Hodgson recapitulated the "saving of the peace" at Munich and commended the Prime Minister's restraint in a very trying situation. He concluded that the real victory that Chamberlain won at Munich was the "definite assertion of the forms of international law as against the claims of any nation to assert its rights . . . by naked voice."[58] Regrettably for the Chamberlain government, this obeisance to the parameters of international law would quickly be dashed by Berlin's seizure of Bohemia and Moravia six months later.

Edward Hallett Carr lent another voice of support to the Tory leadership with an overarching analysis of British foreign policy for a generation after the Great War. His 1939 *Britain: A Study of Foreign Policy from the Versailles Treaty to the Outbreak of War* was much more akin to a historical treatise than an ideological broadside, which made it somewhat exceptional in those emotionally overheated days. Carr, who would later become an internationally renowned historian of the highest caliber and one of the leading scholars of Soviet history in the twentieth century, had joined the Foreign Office in 1916 as a young man. His various postings included time in Paris and Riga, and he later became an assistant advisor on League of Nations affairs. He eventually rose to the position of first secretary in the Foreign Office, so that his trained opinion probably accounted for the lack of invective and demagoguery in his written work, which not surprisingly added to its worth. Carr believed that any foreign policy was always dependent on the possession of military strength, or rather, on the ratio between military strength of one's own country and that of others. In that vein, all policy ultimately entailed some element of risk of war, and the prudent statesman, in this case Chamberlain, must "balance the chances, and not pursue a policy which is likely to expose his country to war against equal or superior odds."[59] Carr expounded on Britain's weakened economic position in 1939, which in reality was the most accurate gauge of political power. He noted that Britain in the nineteenth century was an "imperialist" and "expansionist" power, and had, in the twentieth century, become a "pacific" and "satisfied" power, finding her "greatest good in the maintenance of the status quo, and defending herself against the imperialism and expansionism of others."[60] In this analysis is the logical raison d'être of appeasement. The author quoted the Prime Minister himself on this point, when he alluded to a Chamberlain speech of 24 June 1938. The Premier insisted that British opposition is not to change, "for in a changing world there must be adjustments from time to time . . . but what we are resolved to resist is an attempt to bring about by force changes which should be determined by discussion and co-operation."[61] In the light of the relative weakness of Britain's war machine, Carr pondered whether any other policies could have been followed. "It may well be felt," he stated, "that, right down to 1938, the armament situation made a policy of conciliation the only practical one . . . the alternative was a policy of hostile words which could not be reinforced by military action."[62] Britain was fighting in late 1939, Carr concluded, as she had fought many times before, to keep the independent nations of Europe free from the brutal domination of a single overwhelming power,[63] whether that be the Armada of 1588, Louis XIV at Blenheim, Napoleon's *Grand Armée*, or Nazi Germany.

When Simon Haxey attacked the "Tory Right Wing" in his *Tory M.P.*, he charged that Nazi sympathizers were in control of His Majesty's government. The quintessential example of a member of this group was Charles Stuart, Lord Londonderry. The eldest son of a distinguished aristocratic family, he had succeeded to the peerage in 1915, and was a leading member of the Anglo-German fellowship in the 1930s. His book, *Ourselves and Germany*, was published in late March 1938, within days of the *Anschluss*. Like many of Britain's Conservatives, the author had a robust hatred of

Communism and all its works, and saw Nazi Germany as a possible bulwark against Soviet expansionism in Eastern Europe. As a colleague of Neville Chamberlain, Londonderry was characteristic of his class and creed, which included a disgust for the Treaty of Versailles and a certain tinge of anti-Semitism. A letter that he wrote to then-German Ambassador to London von Ribbentrop in 1936 exhibited some of this sentiment, none too uncommon for the circumstances: "As I told you, I have no great affection for the Jews. It is possible to trace their participation in most of those international disturbances which have created so much havoc in different countries."[64] Londonderry believed the most important issue was to achieve an understanding that would make a world war improbable. On Britain and Germany, he wrote, "there are many points of similarity between our two countries, and there is a racial connection which in itself establishes a primary friendly feeling between us which cannot be said to exist between us and the French."[65] Londonderry became well acquainted with most of the Nazi high command through his two visits to Germany in 1936 and 1937, and was a gracious host to von Ribbentrop for an extended holiday in his country home. The author, much like the Prime Minister, felt that nothing should stand in the way of "doing business" in order to secure a European peace. Londonderry stated:

> The time has come to rid the diplomatic atmosphere of suspicions and recriminations, and to extend the hand of true friendship to the Third Reich. . . . Let us frankly accept the fact of Germany's rehabilitation as a World Power and try, if we can, to work in harmony with her in European affairs, for on our mutual goodwill, I am convinced, depends the assurance of peace in the years which lie ahead.[66]

In all probability, whether deliberately or not, the message that Lord Londonderry and his many influential supporters were advancing was well nigh the same as Dr. Goebbels' infamous rag the *Volkischer Beobachter*. The author was also willing to accept without question Nazi assurances that their immense stockpiling of armaments were purely defensive in nature.[67] Much has already been discussed above concerning Chamberlain's plans for a Four-Power agreement that would ensure the peace of Europe. Londonderry concluded in much the same fashion, his final paragraphs radiating the optimism of one who called for understanding on a decidedly dire world stage. His words bear a haunting similarity to those of the pride of Birmingham:

> But if, on the other hand, we can sink our differences with Germany and come to some permanent understanding with her, I am convinced

that France and Italy could be persuaded to join in, and that between them these four Great Powers would have a real opportunity of realizing those great but hitherto elusive ideals of international security and peace.[68]

A balanced account that deflected much of the blame for the descent into war from the shoulders of Chamberlain was the work of the young American collegian John F. Kennedy, whose *Why England Slept* was published after the fall of France in mid-1940. Kennedy paraphrased an earlier title from Winston Churchill and attempted to analyze the decade of the 1930s to deduce why the British were so slow to rearm in the face of the Nazi threat. Henry Luce, the *Time* magazine magnate, wrote the foreword to the book, and his words were illustrative. Luce offered: "The book is remarkable for having been written by one so young. I cannot recall a single man of my college generation who could have written such an adult book on such a vitally important subject during his Senior year at college."[69] It was indeed a rather sophisticated, multidimensional vehicle for a man so young to have written, but Kennedy stated his case well. On the Prime Minister's leadership capabilities, he noted:

> Chamberlain's policy was motivated by two factors; he, first of all, honestly believed that some sort of solution could be worked out for Europe's problems. . . . Having himself an essentially business mentality, he could not understand how any problems could possibly be settled by a war . . . at the same time his policy was realistic, in that England in 1937 was in very poor condition in regard to armaments.[70]

Kennedy analyzed and examined the economic aspects of rearming Britain in the 1930s, and he mused that the British really did not think in terms of emergency situations until after the war scare that surrounded the Munich Conference. On the ramifications of Munich, he stated, "the policy of appeasement, while it was partly based on a sincere belief that a permanent basis could be built for peace, was also formulated on the realization that Britain's defense, due to its tardiness in getting started, would not come to harvest until 1939. Munich was to be the price she had to pay for this year of grace."[71] This perception of a year's "breathing-space" won by Chamberlain at Munich would later evolve into one of the chief justifications of appeasement's defenders, and Kennedy was one of the first to be fully cognizant of its future importance. To charges that Chamberlain was totally unrealistic in trusting the destiny of Czechoslovakia to the tender mercies of Berlin, Kennedy felt that Britain may have been, at that point, out of options. "In light of the Munich Pact," he added, "it shows that appeasement did have some realism; it was the inevitable result of conditions that permitted no other decision."[72] In Kennedy's estimation, war in 1938 would have been an utter disaster for Britain. He believed that it was simplistic to place all the blame for what turned out to be a diplomatic defeat at Munich on the shoulders of the head of government. His conclusion was thus rather objective in nature, when he offered, "this has not been merely a pro-Baldwin or anti Baldwin, pro-Chamberlain or anti-Chamberlain discussion. I believe it is one of democracy's failings that it seeks to make scapegoats for its own weaknesses."[73] Perhaps just because history is oftentimes written by the victors is such a debate on the efficacy of appeasement so vital an exercise.

Sir Charles Petrie's *The Chamberlain Tradition*, released in November of 1938, was a favorable commentary on not only the Prime Minister, but also dealt with his renowned father and his half-brother, Austen. Like Neville Chamberlain, Petrie advanced the notion that he perceived the Munich Conference as a preliminary to an overall redress of European grievances from which a stable peace could realistically be forged. After Munich, Petrie stressed,

> It remains to be seen whether an agreement with Germany is possible, but if it is it will not be at the price of sacrificing others—a course which would lose us the few friends in the world whom we still possess . . . nor will Mr. Chamberlain consent even to discuss any German request for Treaty revision save as part of some scheme of general pacification . . . a policy of sops does not appeal to him, and he knows that paying Danegeld does not get rid of the Dane.[74]

Certainly the events of March 1939 would prove the truth of Sir Charles' words. In support of the Prime Minister, he cautioned his readership about a rush to judgment on the Four-Power Pact of 1938.

> "We are," he concluded, "as yet too near the Munich agreement to be able to view it in the proper perspective . . . if it was merely an end, then peace was bought at too great a price; but if it was a beginning, then generations yet unborn will have cause to bless the name of Neville Chamberlain."[75]

In the final months of 1938, when it appeared to a stricken world that a catastrophic war had been averted, many millions all over the globe would indeed invoke the name of that enigmatic figure from Birmingham.

2

The Feiling and Macleod Biographies

MORE THAN HALF A CENTURY HAS ELAPSED SINCE NEVILLE CHAMBER-lain's political downfall in May 1940. The commencement of Germany's *Sieg im Westem*, concurrent with Britain's Norwegian debacle at Narvik, shattered the Prime Minister's ability to continue as a war leader, and prefaced Churchill's rise and the "finest hour" of 1940. Chamberlain met his demise soon afterward; he went to his grave convinced that his conduct at Munich had been fully justified by the circumstances. It would be a long six years before any "authorized" biography could be researched and published. It is illuminating that the initial effort is still perceived by many to be the best of the genre. That work is Sir Keith Grahame Feiling's *The Life of Neville Chamberlain*, published by Macmillan in 1946. This section will analyze the influence of Feiling's efforts on the postwar legacy of Chamberlain and appeasement, and also weigh the relative importance of Iain Macleod's *Neville Chamberlain*, published in 1961. This exercise will serve well to clear the literary stage for the 1950s debate spurred by the arguably formidable efforts of Sir Winston Churchill and many of his contemporaries.

The reference to an "authorized" biography implies the favor and generous assistance of the Chamberlain estate to the prospective author of the work. This included free access to Chamberlain's personal letters and diaries as well as the blessing of Birmingham's first family. Ironically, Sir Keith Feiling was not the family's initial choice for the task. An Oxford Fellow, Feiling was hard-pressed for time as the onset of the European war had added to his work load at Christ Church. Neville's widow, Mrs. Annie Chamberlain, had entrusted many of her late husband's close associates to assist her in the search for a suitable biographer. Sir Horace Wilson, the former Chief Industrial Advisor to the government, and former *Times* editor Geoffrey Dawson were two in particular. A letter from Dawson to Mrs.Chamberlain in January 1941 offered a few suggestions on the matter: "it is vital from every point of view, that the book should be written by someone who is both informed and sympathetic . . . to that end, first is *Arthur Bryant*, secondly *G. M. Young*."[1] Dawson continued with some personal remarks on Young, who would later write a critical but "authorized" biography of Stanley Baldwin: "He is a curious creature; but he is brilliantly clever and quite incapable of writing badly. I believe that if he could be inspired with the idea that there was *not only a Life to be written but a case to be set out*, he might perhaps be attracted.[2]

For whatever reason, Young declined, as did Arthur Bryant, an eminent historian. It was not until 11 June 1941 that Sir Horace Wilson suggested to Mrs. Chamberlain that Keith Feiling might be the man for the job. After a subsequent interview with Feiling, Wilson, in a letter of 25 June to Mrs. Chamberlain, outlined Feiling's "intense interest" in doing the work, although present responsibilities at Oxford would mean that the book could take only one-third of his available time. A Feiling letter to Wilson on 31 July corroborated the earlier communication on that point. Feiling added that in his own estimation, necessary access to Foreign Office and War Cabinet papers would not be a terribly difficult problem due to his acquaintance with Lord Halifax and Cabinet Secretary Edward Bridges.[3] Another point that "weighed heavily" with Feiling as he pondered the task ahead read as follows:

> So far I have always written my own books in my own way and should have to do so again; wherever what seemed to me the truth may lead me. Lord Baldwin has written of bias in history, and we all have it; on the last ten years mine leaned hard to an effort to reconciliation with Germany. Moreover, I could point you to a good many places where I have written one of my strongest feelings; on the unfairness of putting all responsibility on one man in our system.[4]

In that vein, Feiling was unknowingly in concert with the earlier Dawson dicta of "someone who is both informed and sympathetic." Feiling concluded the letter with a suggestion for a personal meeting between himself and Mrs. Chamberlain, anytime after 5 August. Evidently all went well, for the surviving evidence infers that by 22 August 1941 Mrs. Chamberlain had made her decision in favor of Keith Feiling.

Progress was rather slow on the project, and it was not until late

December 1943 that Feiling, freed from his responsibilities at Christ Church, determined to devote the entirety of 1944 to the book.[5] A September 1944 communication between the author and Mrs. Chamberlain illuminated Feiling's perception of his famous subject. In Feiling's words, "I have tried throughout to write this as a historian. . . . I am right, am I not, that there is nothing Neville would have hated more, with his soul of candour and integrity, than the 'stained glass window' type of biography?"[6] There would soon be weightier problems for Feiling to address over and above the preservation of his historical objectivity. Cabinet Secretary Edward Bridges ruled in March 1945 that Feiling's completed manuscript could not possibly be published until two or three years after the cessation of war. The ostensible rationale was that certain allusions in Neville's letters, etc., to some of Britain's present allies might cause "grave embarrassment" if published.[7] Any possible publication before Bridges' two- to three-year ukase would entail the evisceration of central portions of the book, a task Feiling felt was impossible for him, as he explained to Neville's widow:

> For how can Neville's policy and position be explained or defended except by giving the whole set of overwhelming difficulties he had to face, and those must include, for example, the hopeless attitude of America as to Japan, the wooden obstinacy of the Czechs for many years, and the suspicious egoism of Russia in 1939.[8]

He advised Mrs. Chamberlain that he would "play for time" with the government in the attempt to wear them down later; perhaps after the British election circumstances might be different. Earlier than he anticipated, in April 1946, permission to publish was given. On that occasion, Feiling wrote to Mrs. Chamberlain explicitly delineating the three principles he had adhered to in the creation of the biography. He noted:

> I feel my responsibility, for the wonderful freedom that you have given me involves that. But I anchor myself to three principles; that this is an independent book, giving however inadequately a historian's point of view; that it is a provisional book, since the whole truth cannot be told, or known; and that, though I seek to avoid giving pain to living men, I have believed it right, in these terrible and testing times, to err on the side of giving candidly Neville's expressed opinions. Through such balances of duty I have tried to move.[9]

Such were the rather byzantine processes employed in the creation of Feiling's *Life of Chamberlain*; now, an examination of the contents.

Although Feiling covered Chamberlain's life from his birth in March 1869 to his untimely end, a discussion of appeasement suggests that a concentration on the second half of the book would be more relevant to our purposes. However, much of Chamberlain the man was forged in those early days, and one can only understand the man in the context of his upbringing. Feiling alluded to the seven years Chamberlain spent in the Bahamas as a young man in a disastrous attempt to grow sisal as time spent that put some steel into his soul, to wit:

> This experience surely drove in deeper the moralities of his temperament, of progress dependent on labour, and a duty, indistinguishable from discipline, to his neighbour . . . we must conclude it over-sharpened some sides of his virtue, . . . over-darkening for him the incompetence of humanity en masse, and imparting to his energy an unreflective turn, so that a day without incessant action seemed a day wasted.[10]

Indeed, many of the personality traits that would hamstring Chamberlain's later career were formulated from that early business fiasco. The self-reliance, dogged determination, and unwillingness to change once a plan had been charted may have have served a young Neville well thousands of miles from home in the 1890s, but would scarcely ease his burdens as a head of government in the late 1930s. He was to become a rather unique politician. Ill at ease in the company of strangers, naturally shy, with a speaking style that could hardly be considered eloquent, he focused on issues rather than people. He had none of the glad-handing bonhomie that seems to be second nature for most public figures. Feiling discussed his adult personality in the following terms:

> On the whole his mentality must be called sensitive, proud, and sanguine. Having taken infinite pains, his decision, once reached, was hard to shake, yet he respected reasoned opposition and was never found obstinate by colleagues, civil servants, or financiers; if, on the other hand, he were attacked, as he conceived, unjustly or unreasonably resisted, his hand went to his sword.[11]

Certainly the Labour Party's judgment of Chamberlain's obstinacy in the eventful days of his premiership would prove less complimentary then Feiling's assessment.

Feiling traced a good portion of Chamberlain's early life in Birmingham business, and his eventual decision to enter public service out of a sincere desire to better the fate of his fellow men. His appointment in January 1917 as Minister of National Service was pivotal in view of his later career. The nebulous responsibilities of the position, never clearly enunciated by then-Premier Lloyd George, led to Neville's utter humiliation and resignation in August of the same year. The author stated that Chamberlain reached two determined conclusions in the light of that debacle, "to enter Parliament, but never to serve with Lloyd George again."[12] This desire to set right his reputation after 1917 would drive Chamberlain to the summit of British politics, 10 Downing Street, in 1937. As for Neville's failure at National Service, Lloyd George tendered his feelings on that issue years later, in 1934, and Feiling dutifully reported on those comments. The task, stated Lloyd George, called for "a great breadth and boldness of conception, a remorseless energy and thoroughness of execution, and for the exercise of supreme tact, indeed, for a man of exceptional gifts."[13] But Mr. Chamberlain, he stressed, "is a man of rigid competency, lost in an emergency or in creative tasks at any time . . . with a vein of self-sufficient obstinacy. . . . Only when he retired did the Ministry work smoothly and efficiently."[14] That reciprocal animosity between the former and future prime ministers would last for the remainder of their careers. Chamberlain went on to serve as both Minister of Health in the Government of 1924–1929, and twice as the Chancellor of the Exchequer in 1923 and from 1931 to May 1937. In these capacities he proved a very able administrator and a dynamic presence, holding himself both physically and mentally to exalted standards of performance. In contrast with the phlegmatic Stanley Baldwin's premiership of 1935–1937, Chamberlain possessed nearly workaholic tendencies, as was made clear in a letter to his sister Hilda in July 1936. On Baldwin, he remarked: "For so far as I can see he is doing no work at all and as I slave over my papers into the small hours I think a little bitterly of him snoozing comfortably away next door . . . but I must not pursue that train of thought."[15] Chamberlain was perceived as the nominal heir apparent to Baldwin by a majority of the Conservative Party from the mid-1930s on. His tireless work at the Treasury, where he had been a consistent advocate of a limited rearmament in the face of the Fascist threat, made him the clear choice upon Baldwin's retirement. As Feiling recounted, defense expenditures rose from a low of £102 million in 1932 to £280 million in 1937 and some 700 million in 1939. Chamberlain's personal estimates from August 1935, when he reasoned that £120 million would be suitable for the next few years, to February 1937 when his White Paper mentioned totals of £1,500 million pounds, evidenced his growing concern for the nation's defences.[16]

It was only upon Baldwin's retirement that Chamberlain could begin to shape his vision of a peaceful European future. On 28 May 1937, Chamberlain at last became Prime Minister, and sought to combine his steady rearmament with a policy of European "appeasement," that is, a redress of legitimate grievances through Great Power consultation and peaceful means. Added to the mix must be his strong abhorrence of war, a sentiment common enough to Englishmen who had experienced the Great War and its senseless slaughter. Feiling noted that the technology of modern warfare and the horrors it held for civilians made it the ultimate evil for Chamberlain, who stated: "No such war must be asked of the people, unless you feel yourself, and can make them feel, that the cause for which they are going to fight is a vital cause, a cause that transcends all the human values . . . a cause to which you can point, if some day you win the victory, and say, "the cause is safe."[17] To Neville Chamberlain, who meant to end the dangerous drift of British foreign policy that had existed under Baldwin, there were few causes that could justify an apocalyptic war. The revision of the Treaty of Versailles, thought among many Britons to have been unjust from its creation, was one of many German grievances perceived as legitimate, subject to negotiation as part of the appeasement process. During the course of the mid- and late-1930s, the record rather spoke for itself in European international affairs. The German violation of Versailles by the introduction of rearmament and conscription in the mid-1930s, the remilitarization of the Rhineland in March 1936, the *Anschluss*, and the Czech crisis were viewed to some extent as legitimate grievances that were summarily redressed by force or threat of force. However, no military reaction was forthcoming from the Western powers, for the tenet of self-determination, among other reasons, was critical to their philosophies. After all, was not Germany simply incorporating German-speaking populations into their new Reich? What right did Britain and France have to stand in the way of self-determination? Certainly military weakness or the widespread perception of the same had much to do with Britain's rather timid acquiescence to German hegemony in Central Europe. Feiling reasoned that Chamberlain, in his efforts to promote a general European peace, would not stand against German aggrandizement as long as it came in a peaceful fashion. He quoted the P.M. on 26

November 1937: "But I don't see why we shouldn't say to Germany, 'give us satisfactory assurances that you won't use force to deal with the Austrians and Czechoslovakians, and we will give you similar assurances that we won't use force to prevent the changes you want, if you can get them by peaceful means.' "[18] Certainly one can ascertain the logic of appeasement, at least through March 1939, for Chamberlain felt strongly that he would be able to construct a lasting peace by removal of the obstacles to peace. His split with Foreign Secretary Anthony Eden, ostensibly over the timing of Anglo-Italian conversations, preceded Eden's resignation in February 1938, and signaled the Prime Minister's growing estrangement from the Foreign Office. His own personal diplomacy during the Czech crisis would ignore Foreign Secretary Halifax and utilize the expertise of the shadowy Horace Wilson in his stead.

On Munich itself, Feiling stated that many have written as if Chamberlain's first object at Munich was to gain time to arm against an inevitable war.[19] However, he continued:

> It was never his first motive, which was plain enough, simply the rightness of peace and the wrongness of war. . . . "Even if it were to fail," Chamberlain said, "I should still say that it was right to attempt it, for the only alternative was war, and I would never take that awful responsibility upon my shoulders unless it were forced upon me by the madness of others."[20]

Feiling stated unequivocally that Chamberlain saw the Munich settlement as just the prelude to a comprehensive European peace. Rather eloquently the author outlined Chamberlain's *mentalité* during the days that encompassed Munich:

> From this fiery passion for peace came both his great strength in those days, and his weakness thereafter. He made himself the champion of common humanity . . . believing that all men in all nations must desire peace, he took too large comfort from every token that reached him, and failed by a noble infirmity, of hoping too much from human nature.[21]

Certainly the turning point of Chamberlain's premiership, the nadir of appeasement, was March 1939 and the Nazi seizure of the rump of Czechoslovakia. Self-determination was proven to be nothing but a sham after all, and Nazi treachery was well evident to even the most myopic. Feiling commented on the combination of Chamberlain and Lord Halifax, and on their shattered hopes after the German seizure of Prague. He noted, "in truth, when and if they failed, it was in some incapacity or unwillingness . . . to generalise or to comprehend racial and national passion. They were too insular, not at all in their objective but in their code, too inelastic, both for good and ill, to adapt themselves to revolutionary situations."[22] All of the acrimony, the righteous indignation that Chamberlain's opposition was forced to swallow upon his Munich triumph was now to overflow in resentment for the failure of his policies. Feiling astutely remarked on the shades of difference between Neville and his domestic rivals:

> The difference between his critics and himself, though now much narrowed and changed from a clash of ideal to a difference of judgment, was still there, turning on one plain fact; that, come what may, he would never accept war as inevitable. Neither abroad nor at home would he do anything that might bring it nearer, nor leave anything undone that might stave it off. War, he believed, might be stopped, if Germany could be convinced not merely that her abuse of force would be instantly resisted, but that she would get consideration for any rational demand by the way of peace.[23]

On 31 March 1939, Chamberlain announced to the House of Commons the details of the Polish Guarantee, specifying that in the face of any action that clearly threatened Polish independence and that Poland felt the need to resist militarily, His Majesty's government would be bound at once to lend the Poles all the support it was in their power to give.[24] Chamberlain characterized this guarantee in the following terms, as Feiling related:

> This was no policy of encirclement but one of self-defence, against that challenge which, as he held, at Munich had been offset by the German pledges, now thrown to the wind. "I am no more a man of war today than I was in September; I trust that our actions, begun but not concluded, will prove to be the turning-point not towards war, which wins nothing, cures nothing, ends nothing, but towards a more wholesome era, when reason will take the place of force."[25]

Alas, within five months the dogs of war would be loosed, and Chamberlain's world would indeed crumble. The man of peace, Feiling noted, would have done well to have left office at the outbreak of the World War. A 17 May 1940 Chamberlain letter well illustrated this theme:

> I used to say to Annie before war came that, if such a thing happened, I thought I should have to hand over to someone else, for I know what

agony of mind it would mean for me to give directions that would bring death and mutilation and misery to so many. But the war was so different from what I expected that I found the strain bearable, and perhaps it was providential that the revolution which overturned me coincided with the entry of the real thing.[26]

Indeed, the "phony war" of late 1939 and early 1940 would end with the German strike in the West, and so would Neville's tenure as Prime Minister. Feiling recounted Chamberlain's testament to his own actions in a letter from May 1940, after his resignation.

Whatever the outcome, it is as clear as daylight that, if we had had to fight in 1938, the result would have been far worse. It would be rash to prophesy the verdict of history, but if full access is obtained to all the records, it will be seen that I realised from the beginning our military weakness, and did my best to postpone, if I could not avert, the war.[27]

So he did, in all sincerity. In what seemed a denouement well nigh to a Greek tragedy, Chamberlain fell deathly ill almost immediately that summer. His stomach cancer was diagnosed as terminal, and he prepared for the end with valor. Feiling noted how Chamberlain was fond of Eliot's *Middlemarch*, and had a passage of that book marked by his bedside. In that passage, the character Caleb spoke: "I call it improper pride to let fools' notions hinder you from doing a good action . . . there's no sort of work that could ever be done well, if you minded what fools say. You must have it inside you that your plan is right, and that plan you must follow."[28] From his early experience in the Bahamas, to his late entry into Parliament, and on to his ill-starred efforts to save the European peace, Neville Chamberlain followed his own plan. Feiling concluded with a sanguine opinion on the future of the Chamberlain legacy when he stated, "for a short time, measured by the long scale of history, the standards by which he marched have been cast down and trampled on by brute force. But they will be raised again."[29]

After an extended analysis of a seminal work such as Feiling's, it may well be illustrative to examine what a few contemporaries thought of the "authorized" biography when it was initially published. The *Times* review of 10 December 1946 was written by Dr. Thomas Jones, confidant to Premiers Lloyd George and Baldwin and an ardent advocate of the policy of appeasement. He offered that Feiling's book was "a highly competent and sympathetic study of a straight-forward character . . . a peace Prime Minister of the second rank, called to guide the ship of State in a gathering storm and then, as the darkness thickened, to make way for the greatest of our war pilots."[30] Jones congratulated the author for his "impartial approach" to his subject, and his admirable sense of proportion throughout the book. He concluded that Feiling would be the standard against which others would be judged:

> Its biographical value lies not in any new unpublished facts dealing with the double policy of conciliation and rearmament—these are few—but in the self-revelation and unfolding of the character of a statesman of simple goodness, complete integrity, but limited perspective who collides with a dictator of powerful intuition, exceptional will, and extreme evil. Each was the head of a great State: the one loathed war, the other planned war.[31]

A compelling counterpoise to the Jones review was the commentary of Richard Law, in the 1 February 1947 edition of *Time and Tide*. Law, who unlike Jones was a critic of appeasement, had voted against Chamberlain during the Munich debate of 3–6 October 1938. In his column, "Notes on the Way," he lauded Feiling for drawing the portrait, for "no public man of our day has been so completely misunderstood as Neville Chamberlain."[32] Feiling's book, he added, revealed for the first time the wholeness of Chamberlain's personality: "It lays bare not only the strength of his character but its terrible infirmity . . . his pride, that overwhelming confidence on the rightness of his own judgment, a confidence which brought him to ruin, which nothing could shake and which remained with him to the end."[33] In conclusion, Law stressed that the picture was still incomplete; it was too soon to anticipate the judgment of history on these terrible events, but in his view, Professor Feiling had not tried to influence the verdict of history.[34]

> He has tried to give a picture, faithful and complete, of a man of the highest intentions, of remarkable ability and of quite unusual integrity. And he has succeeded. Neville Chamberlain fell, like Lucifer, because of his pride, because he had a confidence in the value of his own judgment which no mortal judgment could justify.[35]

Keith Feiling's efforts reflected the high caliber of his scholarship, and clearly delineated the reasons why his book was widely perceived as the standard for its time.

We now advance nearly a generation to consider the other renowned biography, Iain Macleod's *Neville Chamberlain*, published in 1961 by Frederick Muller, Ltd. In 1961, Iain Macleod was Leader of the House of Commons and Chairman of the Conservative Party, one of the brighter lights in Harold Macmillan's administration. Like Chamberlain before him, Macleod had done duty as both the Minister of Health (beginning in 1952) and as Director of National Service, when in 1955 the Ministry of Labour and National Service were under one roof. Macleod explained in his preface his motivation for writing another life of Neville Chamberlain. "From my study of earlier social legislation," he wrote, "I began to form of this man I never knew a mental picture that seemed to me utterly different from the public image which all but his friends seemed to accept."[36] It does bear mentioning that the Churchillian literary efforts of the immediate postwar years, especially his initial volume, *The Gathering Storm*, had colored that image of Chamberlain in a largely negative manner. The "men of Munich" would be repeatedly flayed for their misjudgments, lack of leadership at a critical juncture, and baseless truckling under in the face of aggression. Feiling had written his *Life of Chamberlain* during the war, and in 1946 it held the high ground in support of Chamberlain's actions. In 1961, after over a decade of the Churchillian influence, bolstered by the various memoirs of his wartime comrades, the defense of Chamberlain would be much more problematical. Lord Avon, who had as Foreign Secretary resigned from Chamberlain's Cabinet in February 1938, offered his opinion on Macleod's biography in a *Times Literary Supplement* review from December 1961. Eden noted:

> It is not perhaps a very happy time to bring out a defence of appeasement as it was practiced by Mr. Chamberlain, because, whatever the opinions in this country about it, Europe has condemned that kind of appeasement, and in the present international situation it is certainly not a policy the West can pursue if it intends to survive.[37]

With all Europe in the shadow of the newly constructed Berlin Wall, the hoary Munich analogy about "standing tall against aggression" would dominate the 1960s and make the defense of Chamberlain's reputation a difficult prospect. Despite the daunting circumstances, Macleod desired to afford to a new generation of Conservatives, and, in a larger sense, to the world, a "better understanding" of the man and his times; it was along this line, in spite of the unpopularity of appeasement, that he set about to the completion of his task.

In many ways, Macleod followed the path successfully trod by Keith Feiling in 1946, in his utilization of Chamberlain's personal letters and diaries for his documentation. He would later draw criticism from certain circles for his alleged failure to unearth any new information of importance. Again like his predecessor, Macleod used a rather straightforward chronology to highlight the life of his subject, leading to the apogee of his triumphal return from Munich and on to his untimely death just over two years later. Our review of Iain Macleod's work begins with the early 1930s, during Chamberlain's second tour as Chancellor of the Exchequer, with his advocacy of slow but steady rearmament. Neville's rather "activist" sense of duty and service prompted the author to quote the then Chancellor of the Exchequer: "The amount of work you have to do . . . largely depends on what you make for yourself. Unhappily it is part of my nature that I cannot contemplate any problem without trying to find a solution for it."[38] This attitude was in stark contrast to Stanley Baldwin, whose lassitude toward governmental affairs (save perhaps King Edward VIII's!) was of near-legendary scope. Chamberlain's disdain for unsolved tasks would lead his foreign policy into rather treacherous waters after his assumption of the premiership in May 1937. On rearmament, Macleod credited Chamberlain for being one of the earliest and most consistent supporters of a gradual campaign to rearm against the Fascist threat. Macleod noted that throughout 1934, with each succeeding month, "the strength of Chamberlain's convictions about rearmament grew . . . his speeches hammered home the truth," that " 'we shall not make peace certain by leaving ourselves so weak, that we become a temptation to other powers to bully us.' "[39] The operative term here, however, in reference to the rearmament efforts, is *gradual*. One of the factors that limited the speed of Britain's military buildup was Chamberlain's fear of the deleterious effects that such a process would have on the domestic fiber, indeed, the very quality of the British way of life. In the wake of the March 1936 German remilitarization of the Rhineland, the issue gained an impetus of its own. Macleod noted how Chamberlain, in November 1936, spoke out against a quick and total rearmament: "It would be rash and panicky to follow Churchill's advice that we 'must lay aside every impediment in raising our own strength,' for the sacrifices demanded would injure trade for generations, destroy confidence, and cripple the revenue."[40] In short, a balanced budget was a higher priority item than the buildup of a war machine for a conflict that, in Chamberlain's eyes, might never occur. In Macleod's estimation, it was not "at Munich but at the 'locust years,' 1934 and 1935, that the finger of criticism should be pointed. Too little was done in that period, even though Chamberlain was the most valiant for rearmament in the Government."[41] This statement itself belies the common mythology of Chamberlain as a weak-kneed technocrat singularly obsessed with the preservation of his social class and standing.

Macleod considered another cruel aspect of Chamberlain's legacy, namely the rumor that he had pro-Nazi sympathies. To that end, Macleod stated: "It is in a sense an irony of pre-war history that a man of Chamberlain's temperament and opinions should have become the archpriest of appeasement. Throughout his life he had disliked and distrusted Germany . . . a phrase he used when on holiday in the Black Forest in 1930 was 'on the whole I hate Germans.'[42] This, too, before the onset of the Nazi regime! A letter from Chamberlain to his sister Hilda in July 1934 commented on the cruel murder of Austrian Chancellor Englebert Dollfuss by Nazi sympathizers. In Chamberlain's own anguished words:

> That these beasts should have got him at last and they should have treated him with such callous brutality makes me hate Nazi-ism and all its works with a greater loathing than ever . . . I was glad to hear of Mussolini's movements of troops. It's the only thing Germans understand.[43]

One can only wonder at the makeup of a man, who, with the sentiments voiced above, had such utter faith in his own judgment that peace was the only option that he would submit thrice to travel to Germany in September 1938. That situation could only have been made more personally torturous for the Prime Minister because of the perception, in the eyes of many, that his role in the drama was one of a supplicant, pleading for peace with the Nazi despot.

This considerable pride that some saw as arrogance was to hamper Chamberlain more than a little during his career of public service. Macleod recounted Chamberlain's own illuminating assessment after watching a film of himself in 1937: "I suppose it is a good thing to see oneself as others see us, but it is a very painful process . . . if I had not previously seen the person who addressed us from the screen, I should call him pompous, insufferably slow in diction and unspeakably repellent in person!"[44] Unquestionably the Labour opposition felt something close to the above during Chamberlain's premiership, particularly after March 1939, when it was clear that European appeasement had failed miserably, and Chamberlain was much more vulnerable to criticism. Macleod noted that Stanley Baldwin once related to Chamberlain that Neville gave the impression that when he spoke in the House of Commons, he "looked upon the Labour Party as dirt."[45] It is certain also that Chamberlain's resolute stance of non-intervention in the Spanish Civil War did much to antagonize the Labour and Liberal opposition into what Macleod referred to as "a bitter personal animosity."[46] This rancor was to redound to the Prime Minister's disadvantage in May 1940, when Labour refused to participate in a coalition under his leadership, and the resultant loss of face obligated him to resign.

What of Macleod and appeasement? The author fully supported Chamberlain's ill-fated efforts to forge a European peace, and disavowed any allegedly dictatorial behavior on the Prime Minister's part. Rather, Macleod argued,

Appeasement was not Chamberlain's personal policy. Not only was it supported by his colleagues; it expressed the general desire of the British people . . . nothing was further from the truth than the myth that has been invented of his intolerant omnipotence . . . whilst the prime mover, he was never the dictator of the Government's policy.[47]

Macleod added that history has since exposed to posterity that the Nazis were "insatiable" and war thus "inevitable," but never in Chamberlain's estimation. On the contrary, he wrote:

Since those who pursued appeasement lacked the benefit of hindsight, it was neither a foolish nor an ignoble hope. The case for appeasement thus rested on the proposition not merely that it would have been folly to incur war without adequate defences or reliable allies, but morally wrong to accept it as inevitable unless every attempt had been made to redress legitimate grievances peacefully.[48]

The shattering irony for Chamberlain was that a policy carefully designed to avoid war at all costs systematically drove Britain into war anyway. On appeasement and rearmament, the author felt strongly that the year's respite gained by Chamberlain at Munich gave Britain a critical "breathing space" to retool and strengthen her war machine, which in turn saved her fortunes during the Battle of Britain.[49] On the Churchillian charges from *The Gathering Storm* (1948), that Britain would have been better off fighting in September 1938, Macleod did not agree. He admitted that the German rearmament preparations were already in their third or fourth year by 1938, while in contrast, Britain's had really just begun in earnest. The logical conclusion for Macleod therefore, was the following:

> We should have fought Germany much earlier before their rearmament programme had got under way, or else that we should have avoided fighting them until much later when the full flood of our own rearmament programme had reduced the ratios of German superiority. Strategically 1938 was about two years too late and 1939 was about two years too soon.[50]

To Neville Chamberlain, however, war as the ultimate human catastrophe would be disastrous no matter the year. Therefore he persevered in the five agonizing months following his guarantee to Poland in a desperate attempt to ward off the seemingly inevitable. The Nazi-Soviet Pact of 23 August 1939 relieved German fears of a two-front war, sealed Poland's fate, and shattered the peace of the world.

In his conclusion, Macleod stressed his feelings on what Chamberlain should have done when the war began on Sunday, 3 September 1939, and they dovetailed neatly with Feiling's: "He should have resigned on the outbreak of war. He was too much a man of peace to lead a nation and an Empire effectively in war. Different qualities are needed and it is inevitable that the Lloyd Georges should succeed the Asquiths, and the Churchills the Chamberlains."[51] Perhaps Macleod was correct, as for his entire life war had been anathema to Chamberlain; it is little surprise that he would have no zest for death and destruction, or any talent to inflict the same. His passing from the scene and untimely death that same year, then, appeared as a demarcation between the failed policies of the peacemaker and the glory of 1940, Britain's "finest hour." Allow Macleod to deliver his own brief eulogy:

> Like his father, he had failed in his lifetime to realise the dearest of all his hopes. Yet the hope could not have been more noble, nor could it have been pursued with greater courage or capacity; it was frustrated by evil, but it won at least a respite, if not for reason to prevail, then for strength to be gathered.[52]

Such was Iain Macleod's testament to Neville Chamberlain, an uncommon voice of support in those years when the "Guilty Men" school of appeasement historiography still reigned supreme.

As with Keith Feiling's earlier effort, Iain Macleod's *Neville Chamberlain* was immediately reviewed upon its release in late 1961, by the *Times Literary Supplement* of 1 December. In a rather harsh comparison with Feiling's biography, the *TLS'* anonymous reviewer stressed that: "Macleod adds nothing to the early portrait. Mr. Macleod, a leading Tory radical himself, obviously has a sense that in the postwar years it has fallen to him to take up the torch from Neville Chamberlain and bear it forward on the next lap into the unseen future."[53] The review, having noted that while Macleod rather "regrettably" retraced the territory covered so very thoroughly by Feiling the first time,[54] did give the author credit for the manner in which he updated the lessons of the 1930s into the present. The analysis of the work was as follows:

> It is rather a timely revival of the lesson that, after the case for Munich has been stated with skill and full force, there are still elements in it that pain, shock and shame by the revelation of the weakness of the good man against evil and the peril in which democracies live out their days when honourable men too easily assume that their own ethics are valid at all times in all places.[55]

Another rather critical review emanated from A. J. P. Taylor in the *New Statesman* of 1 December 1961. Taylor described Neville Chamberlain as a statesman who suffered more than his fair share of bad luck in life, from his early disaster in the tropics to the fiasco over the Ministry of National Service in 1917, and then to the failure of appeasement and his resultant fall from office in May 1940. On Macleod, Taylor remarked, "It is excessive even in Chamberlain's run of bad luck that a biography claiming to vindicate him should neither vindicate him in any serious sense nor contain new information of importance."[56] On Macleod's assertion that Chamberlain's efforts at Munich bought needed time for Britain's rearmament, Taylor insisted that it was indeed "too simple to say that Chamberlain merely aimed to buy time. He did this, but also hoped, and even believed, that appeasement might succeed."[57] In conclusion, Taylor remarked rather coldly that his own perception of Chamberlain was that

> The Prime Minister's aim was to avert war. . . . He failed, and failure on this scale cannot be excused by a plea of good intentions. Chamberlain is now beyond defence or condemnation. He needs a biographer who will try to understand him, and probably none will be found. Neville Chamberlain is fated to go on being the man of no luck.[58]

The rather negative response of these reviewers to the Macleod book must be analyzed in view of the knowledge that the decade of the 1950s was dominated by the Churchillian literature of the postwar era, buttressed by a fair bit of anti-Communist hysteria in the West. The Munich analogy of crumbling before aggression had been employed often during the decade, a few examples having been Korea and the Suez debacle of 1956. Because of the fact that the "Munich Analogy" so dominated the "Cold War" years, venues of conflict such as Korea, Suez, and later Vietnam were thought to be *crucial* to Western freedom, which we now know that they were of little danger—or at least a much less grave danger than German aggression in Central Europe was in the 1930s. Many young men were to perish needlessly because of the faulty analogy. The influence of the "Guilty Men" genre had yet to be diminished as the 1960s began. This influence weighed heavily on the appeasement debate, and is our next main focus.

3

Churchill and the "Guilty Men" Genre

THE MOST IMPORTANT PUBLICATION TO FOLLOW FEILING'S BIOGRA-
phy of Chamberlain was the initial volume of Winston Churchill's
History of the Second World War, published in 1948 and entitled
The Gathering Storm. This effort had indeed been anticipated, as
an author and historian of Churchill's caliber could always be expected to write history on a grand scale, with masterful insights on
world events and his own grandiloquent phrasing evoking the style
of a Macaulay. That its creator also happened to be the greatest
Englishman of the twentieth century, the savior of Britain through
his toils as the "indispensable man" of 1940, and the perceived ar-
chitect of victory, gave his opinions and commentary an enormous
weight. Logically the influence of *The Gathering Storm* would oc-
cupy center stage in the appeasement debate for an extended period of the postwar epoch. Its antiappeasement sentiments were
corroborated by various and sundry collections of political memoirs from the Prime Minister's wartime colleagues, effectively for-
tifying the "Guilty Men" school of the debate well into the 1960s.
It is again understandable that Churchill, out of power during his
"Wilderness Years" of 1929–1939, would desire to settle accounts
once he had the opportunity against his erstwhile political adversaries, namely MacDonald, Baldwin, and Chamberlain, and their
advisors. The old cliché that offers that "history is often written by
the victors" is once more applicable in the case of *The Gathering
Storm*. Freed from the weight of executive duties by the astound-
ing, and at the same time, wounding, Labour victory of July 1945,
Churchill commenced to create his version of the "locust years,"
with posterity, that is, future historians, as the ultimate arbiter of
his veracity. In his own words: "I do not describe it as history, for
that belongs to another generation. But I claim with confidence
that it is a contribution to history which will be of service to the
future."[1] To be sure, the exalted reputation of the author eventually led the public to regard *The Gathering Storm*—in reality an

outsider's account, covering the years Churchill was a political pariah—as an insider's version of actual events.

One can hardly help reflecting upon the great difference in tone between Churchill's heartfelt eulogy on the occasion of Chamberlain's passing in November 1940, and, conversely, his rather thorough critique of the "Men of Munich" that permeated his powerfully scripted account. In that eulogy, delivered on 12 November 1940, Churchill eloquently lauded his immediate predecessor:

> Whatever else history may or may not say about these terrible tremendous years, we can be sure that Neville Chamberlain acted with perfect sincerity according to his lights and strove to the utmost of his capacity and authority, which were powerful, to save the world from the awful, devastating struggle in which we are now engaged. This alone will stand him in good stead as far as what is called the verdict of history is concerned.[2]

As for the Churchillian critique, our analysis begins with a descriptive observation on the Chamberlain legacy. Churchill contrasted the restless activism of the new Prime Minister (who had succeeded upon Baldwin's retirement on 28 May 1937), with his phlegmatic ex-chief. In an illustrative paragraph, Churchill remarked:

> Both as Chancellor of the Exchequer and as Prime Minister he kept the tightest and most rigid control upon military expenditure. He was throughout this period the masterful opponent of all emergency measures. He had formed decided judgments about all the political figures of the day, both at home and abroad, and felt himself capable of dealing with them. His all-pervading hope was to go down to history as the Great Peacemaker; and for this he was prepared to strive continually in the teeth of facts, and face great risks for himself and his country. Unhappily, he ran into tides the force of which he could not measure, and met hurricanes from which he did not flinch, but with which he could not cope.[3]

Churchill cited the P.M.'s efforts in the summer of 1937 to divide the dictator states by coming to agreement with the Italians over points of contention between London and Rome. Negotiations with the mercurial and ever obnoxious Il Duce continued in fits and starts, however, and the fragile solidarity of the Stresa Front could not be replicated. Churchill commented on the results of the Nyon Conference of September 1937, when a resolute stand by

Britain and France against Italian piracy in the Mediterranean actually ended that foul behavior, by decree:

> The Nyon Conference, although an incident, is a proof of how powerful the combined influence of Britain and France, if expressed with conviction and a readiness to use force, would have been upon the mood and policy of the Dictators. That such a policy would have prevented war at this stage cannot be asserted. It might easily have delayed it. It is the fact that whereas "appeasement" in all its forms only encouraged their aggression and gave the Dictators more power with their own peoples, any sign of a positive counter-offensive by the Western Democracies immediately produced an abatement of tension.[4]

This feeling of palpable regret, of lost opportunities that generated a forlorn perception of what might have been, was a major leitmotif of Churchill's effort. Another illustrative example of this theme concerned the January 1938 offer of U.S. President Roosevelt to sponsor a conference of world powers, ostensibly to alleviate the European tension, while at the same time attempting to draft the criteria for a lasting European peace.[5] In Churchill's opinion, this proposal was summarily dismissed by Chamberlain as at cross purposes with his own strategy of personal intervention with the dictators. Churchill was incredulous in his observations of the rejection of this potentially crucial opportunity to galvanize the Anglo-American relationship. In his analysis, he remarked:

> That Mr. Chamberlain, with his limited outlook and inexperience of the European scene, should have possessed the self-sufficiency to wave away the proferred hand stretched out across the Atlantic leaves one, even at this date, breathless with amazement. The lack of all sense of proportion, and even of self-preservation, which the episode reveals in an upright, competent, well-meaning man, charged with the destinies of our country and all who depended on it, is appalling. One cannot today even reconstruct the state of mind which would render such gestures possible.[6]

The resignation of Foreign Secretary Anthony Eden a month later would only add to Churchill's chagrin, as Eden could likewise fathom the importance of Britain's cultivation of the United States as a potential ally, a perception seemingly lost on the Prime Minister. Some three weeks after Eden's 20 February resignation, Nazi troops occupied Vienna, and both London and Paris were obligated to accept the *Anschluss* as a fait accompli. Churchill had been urging for the formation of a Grand Alliance of Britain,

France, and the Soviet Union to keep alive, as he put it, the "only hope of checking the Nazi onrush."[7] Churchill later quoted a 20 March 1938 letter from Chamberlain to his sister, in which the Premier stated that "nothing that France or we could do could possibly save Czechoslovakia from being overrun by the Germans. . . . I have, therefore, abandoned any idea of giving a guarantee to Czechoslovakia, or to the French in connection with her obligations to that country."[8] Churchill then expostulated harshly on the later guarantee of March 1939 to Poland, in the face of Chamberlain's admitted abandonment of Czechoslovakia:

> How erroneous Mr. Chamberlain's private and earnest reasoning appears when we cast our minds forward to the guarantee he was to give to Poland within a year, after all the strategic value of Czechoslovakia had been cast away, and Hitler's power and prestige had almost doubled.[9]

In his considerations of the tense summer and autumn of 1938, as events had advanced steadily toward the denouement of the Czech crisis, Churchill pondered why the Russian presence was of so little consequence to the Prime Minister in his diplomacy. He quoted Soviet Foreign Minister Maxim Litvinov, who, in a League of Nations address of 21 September 1938, had stated that just two days prior, the Czech government had formally inquired as to whether the Soviet Union was ready to aid Czechoslovakia if it were attacked. Litvinov stressed that if France intended to honor its obligations to Prague, so too would Moscow.[10] Churchill's analysis followed:

> It is indeed astonishing that this public and unqualified declaration by one of the greatest Powers concerned should not have played its part in Mr. Chamberlain's negotiations . . . They (the Russians) were treated with an indifference . . . which left a mark in Stalin's mind. Events took their course as if Soviet Russia did not exist, and for this we afterwards paid dearly.[11]

On the aftermath of the Munich settlement, after Chamberlain's policy had been emphatically endorsed in the parliamentary debate by a 366–144 margin, the notion of "peace in our time" was lauded by a majority of Britons. Churchill registered his dissenting opinion in an article of 17 November 1938, when he commented on the governmental policy of European appeasement: "By this time next year we shall know whether the Prime Minister's view of Herr Hitler and the German Nazi Party is right or wrong. By this time next year we shall know whether the policy of appease-ment has appeased, or whether it has only stimulated a more fero-cious appetite."[12]

On the very significant question of the timing of the war, that is, would Britain have been better off fighting the Nazi war machine in September 1938 rather than a year later, Churchill stressed his opinion forcefully and with persuasive logic. He cited the loss of thirty-five Czech divisions without a shot fired after Munich, and the relative disintegration of the French martial vigor as the 1930s drew to a close. He stated that because the Germans had begun their rearmament before Britain's, the "year of breathing space" that so many heralded as Chamberlain's main achievement from Munich was illusory, that it had assisted the Nazi efforts much more than Britain's.[13] Most importantly, he cited German military weakness in 1938 as a reason for a resolute stand against Berlin. No effective bombing campaign could have been waged in 1938, as France had yet to be conquered and the Nazis needed the English Channel ports to supply their bombers against London and all points north. In support of this thesis of German weakness, he quoted from the Nuremberg trial documents, when Nazi Marshal Keitel was directly asked whether Germany would have attacked Czechoslovakia in 1938 if the Western powers had supported Prague; Keitel answered: "Certainly not. We were not strong enough militarily. The object of Munich was to get Russia out of Europe, to gain time, and to complete the German armaments."[14] In Churchill's estimation, war in September 1938, despite the rather sorry state of British defenses and the limited offensive capabilities of her war machine, would have been much more ad-vantageous at that time than later on, as in 1940, when the Nazi horde would be deadlier if only because it would be armed to the teeth and spoiling for conquest.

On the March 1939 Nazi seizure of Prague and the consequent abandonment of European appeasement, Churchill expressed his personal response (which incidentally was rather self-righteous in tone) to the Prime Minister's hardening attitude vis-à-vis Nazi Germany:

His reaction surprised me . . . responsible as he was for grave misjudg-ments of facts, having deluded himself and imposed his errors on his subservient colleagues and upon the unhappy British public opinion, he none the less between night and morning turned his back abruptly upon his past. If Chamberlain failed to understand Hitler, Hitler com-pletely underrated the nature of the British Prime Minister. He mistook his civilian aspect and passionate desire for peace for a complete explanation of his personality, and thought that his umbrella was his symbol. He did not realize that Neville Chamberlain had a very hard core, and that he did not like being cheated.[15]

The subsequent British guarantee to Poland was hurriedly drawn up, and by 31 March 1939 Chamberlain detailed that agreement to the House of Commons. It was in essence more of a palpable deterrent to Nazi aggression than a solemn vow to protect the Poles, who were clearly militarily indefensible, at least from London's view.

Six months later, the war that all save the guilty had feared came to fruition. What were Churchill's conclusions on appeasement? Let his words register the verdict: "That we should all have come to this pass makes those responsible, however honourable their motives, blameworthy before history."[16] Churchill continued to stress the litany of the advantages thrown away by the democracies, for example, the Versailles Treaty violation, the reoccupation of the Rhineland, the *Anschluss*, the loss of Czechoslovakia with her thirty-five divisions and the Skoda munitions works, the Roosevelt offer of American intervention, and the Russian desire to join the Western powers in defense of Prague. To make matters worse, Chamberlain's policy was next to insist upon defending the indefensible, Poland.

> There was some sense in fighting for Czechoslovakia in 1938 when the German Army could scarcely put half a dozen trained divisions on the Western Front, when the French with nearly sixty or seventy divisions could most certainly have rolled forward across the Rhine or into the Ruhr.[17]

On the Polish guarantee:

> History . . . may be scoured and ransacked to find a parallel to this sudden and complete reversal of five or six years' policy of easy-going placatory appeasement, and its transformation almost overnight into a readiness to accept an obviously imminent war on far worse conditions and on the greatest scale.[18]

And, in conclusion, a full dose of Churchillian moralizing:

> Moreover, how could we protect Poland and make good our guarantee? Only by declaring war on Germany and attacking a stronger Western Wall and a more powerful German Army than those from which

we had recoiled in September 1938. Here was the righteous cause deliberately and with a refinement of inverted artistry committed to mortal battle after its assets and advantages had been so improvidently squandered. Still, if you will not fight for the right when you can easily win without bloodshed; if you will not fight when your victory will be sure and not too costly; you may come to the moment when you will have to fight with all the odds against you and only a precarious chance of survival. There may even be a worse case. You may have to fight when there is no hope of victory, because it is better to perish than to live as slaves.[19]

So marked the substance and style of *The Gathering Storm*, which carried a formidable weight because of the colossal stature of its author. Was it accepted as gospel truth by the British public and the world at large? Judging the times, and the reputation of the Great Man, it is quite understandable that Churchill's contribution could have been perceived as the "last word" on the subject. This reverence for the man, which in many ways was justified, would serve to strengthen the influence of the "Guilty Men" school of appeasement historiography.

Another influential contributor to the field was Anthony Eden, with his memoirs of the Chamberlain years entitled *Facing the Dictators*, which although not published until 1962, bore all the characteristics of the Churchillian genre. As Foreign Secretary from December 1935 to February 1938, Eden was intimately involved in the formulation of the Chamberlain administration's policies. Eden related that he was initially relieved that Neville Chamberlain was to assume the premiership, because of Stanley Baldwin's diffidence toward foreign policy. Eden felt that having a chief who had an interest in European affairs would be a welcome change that would help to ease his own toil at the Foreign Office. It was only when Chamberlain commenced his aggressive policy of courting Rome that Eden, angered at the way Il Duce had exploited the weaknesses of the League of Nations during the Abyssinian crisis, began to have problems with the Prime Minister. An Eden memorandum from 7 January 1937, nearly five months before the accession of Chamberlain, spoke of the dangers from the Nazi intervention in the Spanish Civil War. Eden's remarks were to have an ironic prescience in light of future events.

It is therefore my conviction that unless we cry a halt in Spain, we shall have trouble this year in one or other of the danger points I have

58 NEVILLE CHAMBERLAIN AND APPEASEMENT

referred to. . . . It is to be remembered that in the language of the Nazi Party any adventure is a minor adventure. They spoke thus of the Rhineland last year, they are speaking thus of Spain today, they will speak thus of Memel, Danzig or Czechoslovakia tomorrow. It is only by showing them that these dangerous distinctions are false that we can hope to avert a greater calamity.[20]

When Chamberlain sent a personal note to Mussolini in July 1937 expressing a readiness to begin Anglo-Italian conversations, he curiously bypassed his Foreign Secretary, because of concern about Eden's potential objection.[21] Eden contrasted the episode with his later close collaboration in Churchill's wartime administration, where the Prime Minister was at all times very solicitous of Eden's judgment. On the Chamberlain faux pas, he remarked: "Complete confidence and candour between Prime Minister and Foreign Secretary are indispensable conditions for conduct of a successful foreign policy under our parliamentary system. Evidently they were already fading from Mr. Chamberlain's mind."[22] Churchill alluded in *The Gathering Storm* to the great advantages that could be gained by standing up to the dictator states, and he utilized the Nyon Conference of September 1937 as an example. Eden possessed a similar attitude, giving evidence of his sentiments in a note on Nyon for the Foreign Office.

There are those who say that at all costs we must avoid being brought into opposition with Germany, Japan, and Italy. This is certainly true, but it is not true that the best way to avoid such a state of affairs is continually to retreat before all three of them. To do so is to invite their converging upon us. In any retreat, there must on occasion be counterattack, and the correct method of counter-attack is to do so against the weakest member of the three in overwhelming force. That is the justification of Nyon.[23]

Although much in Eden's account would have the reader believe that he was distanced from the ignominy of Chamberlain's appeasement policy, and stood resolutely, as "Horatius at the Bridge," against the outrages of the dictator states, the reality may have been far less heroic. Sir Samuel Hoare, Foreign Secretary in 1935 at the time of the Hoare-Laval fiasco and later member of Chamberlain's inner circle, claimed that Eden "fully accepted Chamberlain's programme of European appeasement, and until the beginning of 1938 actively worked for it."[24] It is only natural that Eden, writing a quarter century after those events occurred, fully aware of how the "men of Munich" had been demonized by the "Guilty Men" school, would want to distance himself from the Chamberlain circle so as to appear in the best light. To that end, he commented on the selection in early 1937 of a new British ambassador to Berlin, Sir Nevile Henderson. Eden frankly admitted that he bore full responsibility for the appointment, as disastrous as it would prove to be. Speaking of Henderson, Eden remarked:

> It was an international misfortune that we should have been represented in Berlin at this time by a man who, so far from warning the Nazis, was constantly making excuses for them. . . . He grew to see himself as the man predestined to make peace with the Nazis. Sincerely believing this to be possible, he came to regard me, and others at the Foreign Office who shared my opinions, as obstacles to his purpose. . . . I had to warn him against the recurring habit of interpreting my instructions in a fashion too friendly to the Nazis.[25]

It was indicative of the times that after Eden's departure from the Foreign Office, Henderson would often circumvent his nominal bosses completely, reporting solely to Prime Minister Chamberlain himself, and becoming rather more a personal envoy than a formal ambassador. This would duly aggravate the civil servants at the Foreign Office, and exacerbate the split between them and 10 Downing Street to a greater extent.

Toward the end of 1937 Eden again gave evidence of a remarkable ability to foresee the course of European events. In a communication to his principal colleagues and the Chiefs of Staff in December 1937 he unerringly predicted Russia's future behavior, to wit:

> The outstanding feature of the present political situation is its extreme fluidity. It is impossible to foretell what the international alignment will be in a year's time. Who, for example, can say what Stalin's reorientation of Russian policy will be? If it should result in a Moscow-Berlin Axis, will not this be a more formidable combination than the existing Rome-Berlin Axis? In these circumstances it is clear that we should make every possible effort to come to terms with each or all of our potential enemies, but not by conduct which would lose us our friends, both actual and potential.[26]

Among Britain's actual and potential allies, the United States had a crucial role. On 11 January 1938, as we have seen, FDR offered to sponsor a worldwide conference to alleviate the European tension while simultaneously beginning the process of building a durable European peace. Eden related how very aghast he was when

Neville Chamberlain refused the offer out of hand, made worse because Eden was on holiday in Southern France at the time and was not consulted by the Premier. In a personal meeting with Chamberlain on 16 January, Eden let his feelings be known:

> I told him that I resented his action in sending a reply to Roosevelt without consultation, when he knew I could be home in twenty-four hours. Chamberlain apparently believed with increasing conviction that our approaches to the dictators were likely to lead very soon to genuine settlements. Even if the initiative did fail, we should have gained immeasurably from this first American intervention in Europe and another might follow. I said I agreed with Roosevelt's appreciation of the European situation and that I did not feel optimistic about our discussions with the dictators, though we should have a better chance if Roosevelt were also dealing with them. My view was that we should work on parallel lines, doing our best to improve Anglo-American relations while preparing for discussion with Germany and Italy.[27]

Chamberlain disagreed, and Eden related that he felt that this was the initial time that his relations with Chamberlain were seriously at odds. This episode indisputably played a part in Eden's resignation one month later, although Anglo-Italian relations were the ostensible cause for that event. On Tuesday 18 January, after further unsuccessful wrangling with Chamberlain, Eden wrote in his diary:

> I fear that fundamentally the difficulty is that Neville believes that he is a man with a mission to come to terms with the dictators. Indeed, one of his chief objections to Roosevelt's initiative was that with its strong reference to International Law it would greatly irritate the dictator powers.[28]

Later, Eden was even more critical when dealing with the denouement of this affair, whose end result was that the proposed American initiative never came to pass.

> The Prime Minister, and most of his Cabinet, did not look beyond the Roosevelt plan itself, which admittedly might have failed, to the beneficent consequences which might have flowed from it, even in failure. This was exactly the situation which Chamberlain's mind, accustomed to plans on the short view, was unable to master.[29]

This tension between Eden and Chamberlain would only be worsened by a difference of opinion regarding the timing of Anglo-Italian conversations, and by a rather degrading scene of the Prime

Minister scolding his Foreign Secretary in the immediate presence of a foreign diplomat, the Italian Ambassador Dino Grandi. Inevitably, Eden found himself without support in the Cabinet, and he resigned on 20 February 1938. On his differences with the Prime Minister and his policy of European appeasement, he would later duly expostulate in the House of Commons:

> I do not believe that we can make progress in European appeasement, more particularly in the light of the events of the past few days and those events must surely be present in all our minds—if we allow the impression to gain currency abroad that we yield to constant pressure. I am certain in my own mind that progress depends above all on the temper of the nation, and that temper must find expression in a firm spirit.[30]

That firm spirit, unfortunately, would not be found until the outbreak of the Second World War, some eighteen months later, but would serve the British nation well in its fight for survival during the dark days of 1940–1941. Eden, fairly unscathed by the opprobrium heaped on the "appeasers," would return to the Foreign Office in late 1940 for the duration of the war in Churchill's coalition government.

An account quite critical of Chamberlain's years in power was Leo Amery's *The Unforgiving Years, 1929–1940*, the third volume of his memoirs, which were entitled *My Political Life*. First published in 1955, they were the remembrances of a man who was a longtime Conservative member of Parliament, one of the few who were active antiappeasers in the late 1930s.[31] In a dramatic vignette, Amery recalled the scene when Chamberlain announced the news to the House of Commons that he was returning to Germany a third time to attempt a settlement of the Czech crisis in late September 1938. Among the riotous tumult of the happy moment, as he related, there were three Tory members seated together who were "conspicuously silent and glum." Those three were Churchill, Eden, and Amery.[32] Amery would indeed be the figure who employed the words of Oliver Cromwell to the Long Parliament when, in May 1940, he summarily dismissed Neville Chamberlain with "in the name of God, go!" Amery's rather emotional outburst in the House of Commons belied the somewhat cool detachment of his memoirs. His was a careful and reasoned perspective, from which he analyzed the maelstrom of events. On Chamberlain's foreign policy, he mused:

> His heart was set on "appeasement" to use the word that appeared so often in his speeches and in his letters. A fine and generous word in itself, since tarnished by the failure of the policies which he pursued with a curious simplicity of outlook and a missionary fervour, which is, I believe, the key to understanding Chamberlain's whole policy almost up to the end. It was not, indeed, in the last resort, a policy of peace at any price. He regarded it, rather, as a necessary policy to gain time for rearmament pursued steadily but without creating undue alarm at home or abroad.[33]

Amery agreed wholeheartedly with Churchill that Chamberlain should have employed the potential weapon of Russian assistance at the time of Munich against the aggressive posturing of Berlin.

> Litvinov had consistently backed the conception of collective security—in effect an alliance between Russia and the Western Powers to meet the growing danger from Germany . . . only sheer infatuation with appeasement at almost any price can explain the cold shouldering of Russian offers of help when things were already on the eve of war.[34]

On the aftermath of Munich, when the idea of "peace for our time" lasted only eleven months, Amery had his own conclusion, and this he revealed in a telling paragraph. Of the Prime Minister, he wrote:

> The congratulations showered on him by the whole world on the morrow of Munich were a well-deserved tribute to the sincerity of his striving for peace. Where he failed was in his inability, or unwillingness, to realize the kind of men and forces he was up against in the world, in his touching faith in his own powers of friendly persuasion, in his belief that greedy and unscrupulous men of bound less ambitions could be appeased or bought off by instalments of surrender, in his reluctance to face the ultimate issue of force which alone could, in the long run, have avoided war.[35]

An additional Amery judgment will strengthen his perspective, which is quite close to the tenor of Churchill's characterization. In Amery's words:

> Our judgment of Munich is necessarily a judgment of Neville Chamberlain. Inflexibly dedicated to his self-imposed mission at all costs to avert the risks of a world war he ignored the warnings of the Foreign

Office, dominated his colleagues . . . and, to the last moment, refused to acknowledge failure. . . . He claimed for himself, as against the "illusionists" of collective security, that he was a realist. But "appeasement," as he pursued it, was no less of an illusion, and his passionate pursuit of peace and horror of war, in themselves noble, blinded him to the practical realities and even more to the moral imponderables of a terribly difficult situation.[36]

In short, he was not the man for the time, as were none of the "men of Munich": the generalization that Chamberlain and his coterie were "unworthy of leadership" is a very consistent theme of the works in the "Guilty Men" genre.

A fourth memoir of those turbulent times was that of Alfred Duff Cooper, whose 1954 publication, *Old Men Forget*, was the remembrance of Chamberlain's First Lord of the Admiralty from May 1937 to October 1938. Duff Cooper gained nationwide fame and was lauded by the Prime Minister's political opponents because he was the first to resign his office in protest of the Munich agreement. He was never a favorite of Chamberlain's, ostensibly because of his rather nonchalant attitude toward his job, and it is true that Duff Cooper would probably have enjoyed a position in the House of Lords, where ease was a way of life.[37] Still, as a contemporary, his criticisms carry weight, but of course one must judge them on their own merit. On Chamberlain's characteristics as a "businessman," he wrote:

Chamberlain had many good qualities but he lacked experience of the world, and he lacked also the imagination which can fill the gaps of inexperience. . . . He had been a successful Lord Mayor of Birmingham, and for him the Dictators of Germany and of Italy were like the Lord Mayors of Liverpool and Manchester, who might belong to different political parties and have different interests, but who must desire the welfare of humanity, and be fundamentally reasonable, decent men like himself. This profound misconception lay at the root of his policy and explains his mistakes.[38]

Duff Cooper took his onetime chief to task for dismissing the offer of prospective American assistance in January 1938. As he put it, "the offer by the President of the United States of direct intervention in European affairs presented an immense opportunity which, if it had been seized upon, might have proved one of the turning-points in European history and would probably have averted the coming war."[39] Not even Churchill, the champion of Anglo-American solidarity, was that sanguine. It was during the Munich debate in the House of Commons that Duff Cooper made his points against the government's policy. On Monday 3 October, because of his recent resignation from Chamberlain's cabinet, he was allowed to begin the debate in the House of Commons in the following fashion:

> I said that I could well understand the reluctance of people in this country to go to war on account of Czecho-Slovakia. . . . Had we gone to war, as we so nearly did, it would not have been for Czecho-Slovakia that we should have been fighting any more than it was for Serbia or Belgium that we fought in 1914. . . . We should have been fighting, I said, in accordance with the sound, traditional foreign policy of England, in order to prevent one Great Power, in defiance of treaty obligations, of the laws of nations and the decrees of morality, dominating by brute force the continent of Europe.[40]

In the peroration of his speech, he made his final comment on the Munich agreement, which he had not been able to stomach and which caused him essentially to commit political suicide.

> I remember when we were discussing the Godesberg ultimatum that I said that if I were a party to persuading, or even to suggesting to, the Czecho-Slovak Government that they should accept that ultimatum, I should never be able to hold up my head again. . . . I have ruined, perhaps, my political career. But that is a little matter; I have retained something which is to me of greater value—I can still walk about the world with my head erect.[41]

As much notoriety as Duff Cooper received for his resignation on a matter of principle, the genuine opposition to appeasement was still, at the time of Munich, splintered and at cross-purposes. Only the Nazi seizure of Prague would allow opposition to coalesce against the government's failed policy.

A final account in the Churchillian genre that was rather more balanced than were those of his contemporaries was Robert Boothby's 1947 publication, *I Fight to Live*. Boothby, a onetime Parliamentary Private Secretary to Churchill in the late 1920s, was, like the great man, an antiappeaser during Chamberlain's tenure, but his work was of a palpably less condemnatory nature. He stressed that Chamberlain, upon his accession to the premiership in May 1937, was faced with a series of intractable problems that would necessarily lead the Prime Minister on a perilous course of action to avoid a cataclysmic European war. Chamberlain's options were few, noted the author:

> So he fell back on appeasement. Hence the failure to build the Grand Alliance in time. Hence Munich. Hence the war. No use to cast blame or reproaches. . . . Mr. Chamberlain happened to be a genuine pacifist—one of the few I have ever known. He found himself confronted by a frantic and ferocious madman, with a destructive genius that can have few parallels in history. . . . It was just bad luck that he happened to be Leader of the Conservative Party at this particular moment in history.[42]

Through the dangerous summer of 1938, Boothby continued, the Prime Minister walked a precarious tightrope in his foreign policy, in an attempt to split the dictator states, and then later to achieve an overall pacification of Europe by the conclusion of an agreement with Germany. Boothby asserted that the later stigma associated with the appeasement of Berlin and Rome belied the policy's popular approval at the time.

> The truth is that the vast majority of the British people were behind the Prime Minister. Like him, they viewed the possibility of another war with horror. And, with him, they shared an invincible reluctance to face the realities and brutalities of the situation. In the state of public opinion that then prevailed, I doubt if any man, with the exception of Mr. Chamberlain himself, could have decisively altered the fatal course of events.[43]

On the Munich agreement, which sacrificed Czechoslovakia's integrity in the hope of averting a world war, Boothby assumed a much more uncompromising stance. He noted that even though a great majority of the British public supported it at the time as a disagreeable necessity,[44] this attitude would be dramatically altered in the face of unfolding events.

> It soon became clear, however, that, far from regarding it as an enforced and regrettable humiliation, Mr. Chamberlain looked upon Munich as a diplomatic triumph which would inaugurate a new era of prosperity and peace. His principal Ministers vied with each other in fulsome praise of their chief, and in continued and wholehearted support of the policy of appeasement. It was with difficulty that I could

bring myself to believe that these men had succeeded in deceiving themselves to the point that they sincerely believed in the good intentions of the dictators.[45]

On the personal side, Boothby contended adamantly that the best of all possible decisions Chamberlain could have made was the one that was not made, the decision to stand and fight. "I am even more convinced to-day than I was then that we could have saved the world from an ocean of blood, and European civilization from virtual destruction, if we had stood up to Hitler at that moment."[46] In any case, the Munich agreement would buy only six months of "peace in our time," and the Nazi seizure of Prague and the remainder of the Czech state would rapidly follow. Boothby wrote an article in the *Daily Telegraph* of 19 March 1939, just four days after the Nazi annexation, and he extracted a few telling paragraphs from the same: "What are the facts of the present situation? Let us face them at last. We began to rearm two years too late. The 'policy of appeasement' was a desperate gamble, out of weakness, on the good faith of the dictators. . . . The attempt has failed. The policy is in ashes."[47] Boothby concluded with his analysis of the worth of the policy of appeasement in those dangerous times, with war and peace in the balance:

What are the lessons of the past six months? That you cannot do business with the Nazis, because their signature is not worth the paper upon which it is written. To them treaties and agreements are simply instruments of policy. They are out for world domination, and can be checked only by superior strength and iron resolution.[48]

In his conclusion, Boothby wrote movingly of Chamberlain and his futile campaign to obviate a second European war. His literary effort, although part of the Churchillian genre, was more empathetic and understanding of the burdens that Chamberlain and his supporters worked under, the burdens that would eventually lead to the Prime Minister's fall from power.

He fought for the policy of appeasement with ruthless tenacity because he knew that another world war would bring about the final collapse of the world he had tried, with no small success, to create. And, apart from his hatred of war, no other kind of world seemed to him to be worth living in. . . . He never grasped the true greatness of his own country, or comprehended the nature of the forces with which he was contending, because the values of European civilization seemed to him to be inseparably bound up with the interests of the business community.[49]

The nascent Cold War, which polarized the world into rival ideologies, East and West, began dramatically to influence the appeasement debate in the 1950s. The Munich analogy, however flawed, was employed in Korea, and in the debacle of the Suez crisis of Autumn 1956. In this analogy, Communism played the role of Nazism (in the case of Suez it was Arab nationalism); and it was the responsibility of statesmen to stand against aggression in its early stages, so that it could never evolve into another Munich, with tyrants absorbing smaller nations. The final volume of the Churchill series on the Second World War was entitled *Triumph and Tragedy*, in which the author was anguished that in the wake of the charnel house that was Europe, one wicked tyranny had been replaced by another form of domination, namely Soviet hegemony. All of the grievous sacrifices made to topple the dictators made the Allied victory bittersweet for the figure who had been at the conflict's very center. The influence of the Churchillian genre of historical interpretation cannot be overstated in the appeasement debate, and its sway endured well into the 1960s and beyond.

4

Chamberlain's Support vs. the Foreign Office

As A COUNTERPOISE TO THE ACCOUNTS OF WINSTON CHURCHILL AND his political contemporaries, it is necessary to make a brief digression to consider those viewpoints incorporating support for Neville Chamberlain in the postwar years. Much like Churchill and his intimates, the personal memoirs written in support of Chamberlain and appeasement were from high-ranking political figures, mostly of Cabinet rank. They worked daily with the man, knew him and his policies intimately, and so deserve to have their opinions aired in the historiographical debate. To say that their voices were as compelling in the postwar years as those of the Churchillian genre would be a grievous misstatement, as the "Guilty Men" and their reputations absorbed floggings from all comers during the days of the nascent Cold War in the late 1940s and on through the 1950s. A defense of appeasement after the efforts of Churchill and academics Namier and Wheeler-Bennett, to be covered later, would be problematic at best, but there were indeed those who made the effort, and this section outlines their results.

One of the first attempts to support the Chamberlain legacy was that of Frederick, Viscount Maugham, who wrote *The Truth About the Munich Crisis*, which was published in 1944 in pamphlet form. Maugham was Lord Chancellor in the Chamberlain government from March 1938 to September 1939, and he was a brother of the great British writer and playwright W. Somerset Maugham. Although Viscount Maugham published his work during the war, the points he argued were as defensible then as they would be a decade later, which is why this brief exercise of seventy-odd pages is included in our survey. Maugham, as was his wont as a lawyer, constructed his format with chapter titles such as "The Charge Against Mr. Chamberlain," "The Approach to the Question," and "A Question of Principle for British Statesmen." The "charge," as Maugham saw it:

> It is asserted against Mr. Neville Chamberlain and his Government that Great Britain under his leadership betrayed Czechoslovakia by re-

fusing to go to war against Germany to preserve for Czechoslovakia the Sudeten lands which possessed populations containing more than fifty per cent of Germans. The word "betray" is obviously not very accurately used, for this country had never promised or in any way guaranteed the integrity of the Czechoslovakian boundaries, and had neither directly nor indirectly undertaken any obligations in that matter.[1]

Regarding the criticism that the government, the appeasers, wallowed in craven fear of the great German war machine, the author quoted from a Chamberlain speech of 11 September 1938, in order to debunk that allegation. In the Premier's words: "It is of the utmost importance that Germany should make no mistake about it: she cannot with impunity carry out a rapid and successful military campaign against Czechoslovakia without the fear of intervention by France and even Great Britain."[2] Maugham's commentary:

> That was as far as any British minister could go; and it left little room for doubt as to the first result of a German invasion if France went to war. There would appear to be little ground for criticising the attitude of the British Government at this time on the ground of lack of courage.[3]

Concerning the Munich agreement, Maugham held an opinion that would have been none too popular among enemies of appeasement. On the role assigned to Czechoslovakia in the sobering drama, he remarked:

> It was for France and Britain to decide how far they would go in support of Czechoslovakia, not for the latter to dictate to them. It is really amazing to hear people talk as if the Czechs, after a failure during long years to satisfy or pacify the Sudeten Germans and other Minorities, had a claim on Great Britain to embark on a life and death struggle with Germany in order to preserve the boundaries of Czechoslovakia. . . . It is in my opinion fair to say that the Munich Agreement was one which honourable Czech statesmen could properly accept in view of the circumstances . . . and in particular the fact that allies could not be found who were prepared to go to war with Germany to prevent a peaceful transfer to the Reich of Sudeten territory of preponderantly German character. Their action undoubtedly saved many thousands of Czech lives and many millions of Czech crowns, and a vast quantity of property. It is equally fair to say that France and Great Britain were completely justified, in the circumstances which then existed, in taking the course they did.[4]

Note here that the author spoke movingly of saving Czech lives and property, but nowhere was Czech liberty mentioned. Furthermore, the French behavior was a direct renunciation of their express treaty obligations with Prague, which the French assiduously attempted to evade during the entirety of the crisis. Nevertheless, this is Maugham's account, and here his perceptions must speak for themselves. In regard to Chamberlain's conduct during the fortnight up to and inclusive of Munich, Maugham adamantly objected to those who intimated that the Prime Minister's fortitude had been found wanting in the pressure of those crucial days.

> It is not true that Mr. Chamberlain's actions and conduct in relation to Munich were hesitating, cowardly or confused; nor, I will add, were those of his colleagues. He was a realist and faced the facts like a man. His conduct throughout the affair was that of an able, courageous and honourable Prime Minister.[5]

On the aftermath of Munich, and what positive aspects came out of the eventual total subjugation of the Czechs, Maugham had little hesitation. He concluded by portraying Chamberlain as a hero of sorts, surely a notion that would be regularly disputed.

> This much is clear, that the Munich Crisis gave this country time for a year of preparations of a most urgent kind. Those who know the facts will not doubt that the work then done, based as it was upon the existing plans for complete re-armament, saved the country. When war came . . . there never was a war undertaken with a greater unanimity and a higher resolve on the part of all our people, rich and poor. For over a year after the fall of France they held the fort alone against the German well-trained hordes. That this result was possible must be ascribed in great measure to what was done at Munich, and Mr. Chamberlain beyond a doubt deserves in that matter the thanks of a grateful nation.[6]

Another voice of support for Neville Chamberlain came from his administration's Chancellor of the Exchequer, Sir John Simon, who was also a member of the Prime Minister's notorious "inner circle," that small cadre that formulated much of the policy that emanated from 10 Downing Street. His effort, *Retrospect: The Memoirs of Sir John Simon*, was published in 1952. Like

Maugham, Simon had nothing but admiration for his former chief, and recoiled at what he perceived as the scathing and largely unwarranted criticisms of the era against Chamberlain. To the accusation that the Prime Minister had spinelessly genuflected in the face of acute pressure from the dictator states, Simon bitterly disagreed: "Man of peace as he was, he was no more ready to see the world dominated by force than were the rest of his fellow countrymen. He had never regarded the pursuit of his policy as the same thing as peace at any price."[7] In regard to that policy of appeasement, which would lead to the Four Power meeting at Munich to determine the fate of a supine Czechoslovakia, Simon lauded Chamberlain's courage for making the attempt to save Europe's peace, and he could find no fault with the Prime Minister's conduct during the crisis.

> The Prime Minister's action was justified by the circumstances then existing and the effort he then made should always be remembered in his honour. The fact that his action did not ultimately preserve peace does not, in my judgment, affect the essential rightness of his policy at the time. Even if the effort were to fail, it was still right to attempt it. Moreover, if war was after all to come, what he did secured an invaluable twelve months in which to strengthen our preparations to wage it, and it was his action at Munich, that helped to secure, more than anything else could have done, that Britain went into war against Germany as an absolutely unified nation, with a united Commonwealth at her side.[8]

Simon deflected the criticisms of the antiappeasers, some of whom insisted that Britain should have made a stand in defense of Czechoslovakia in September 1938, when the Czechs possessed a strong and ready army, and the Germans had not yet completed their preparations for an extended war. He hectored Chamberlain's enemies as individuals without a workable plan to use in lieu of appeasement. In his conclusion, Simon stressed that the Prime Minister was just about devoid of options by the time of Munich:

> Then what could Chamberlain do, other than what Chamberlain did? Threaten to declare war forthwith, when the *casus belli* arose out a claim to adjust a boundary which had worked injustice and to rescue people of German race who were suffering under an alien jurisdiction? There is no ground whatever for imagining that this would either have rescued Czechoslovakia or led to a united front. Chamberlain held no cards in his hand in these negotiations, except his conviction that war was an unutterable evil and that if any way of escape from it could be

found which was not even more intolerable, that way must be pursued unflinchingly.[9]

As Simon would surely realize afterward, the attempt to escape war brought it ever closer in the eleven months after Chamberlain's ephemeral triumph at Munich.

Perhaps the most cogent, best written, most persuasive support for Chamberlain in the decade of the 1950s came from Sir Samuel Hoare, Viscount Templewood, who in 1954 wrote *Nine Troubled Years*. Hoare, Foreign Secretary in 1935 at the time of the infamous Hoare-Laval fiasco, served as Neville Chamberlain's Home Secretary and also belonged to his circle of close advisors during the years of Chamberlain's premiership. Hoare commented on the policy of appeasement, and how its meaning had been dramatically modified:

> When Chamberlain became Prime Minister in 1937 . . . appeasement, having been universally applauded, was still a term of faint praise rather than violent abuse. Since the time when Eden first used it with general approval during the debates on the German occupation of the Rhineland in 1936, it had been freely accepted into the reputable currency of political discussion. It was a noble word, and at the time seemed to express a wise and humane policy. What finer achievement could there be for a Minister than to bring about peace between France and Germany, and allay the suspicion and fear that were poisoning the life of Europe? It was only after Munich that a sinister and shady meaning was fastened to a splendid word that expressed an inspiring ideal. . . . Appeasement did not mean surrender, nor was it a policy only to be used towards the dictators. To Chamberlain it meant the methodical removal of the principal causes of friction in the world.[10]

In regard to Chamberlain's leadership and pursuit of European peace, Hoare challenged those who portrayed the Prime Minister as a tyrant, intent upon forcing his personal will on all others, within his Cabinet and in the House of Commons.

> He was not an autocrat who imposed his views upon doubting or hostile colleagues. Appeasement was not his personal policy. Not only was it supported by his colleagues; it expressed the general desire of the British people. This is a fundamental consideration in judging his action. Nothing is further from the truth than the myth that has been invented of his intolerant omnipotence. . . . His colleagues supported

him because they agreed with him, and in agreeing with him, they acted in accordance with the view of the great majority of his supporters in Parliament and a large body of public opinion in this country.[11]

Hoare also responded to the critics of the Munich settlement itself, particularly to those who had condemned the role executed by Chamberlain in the sad drama; he appeared to many as a weak-kneed supplicant, thrice traveling to Germany to plead for peace with a powerful despot. "Chamberlain had no illusions about the possibility of failure. He saw from the first that his efforts would be widely open to misrepresentation. It would inevitably be said that he was either a weakling truckling to a dictator, or a semi-Fascist influenced by a kindred spirit."[12] In the same vein, on the conference, Hoare continued:

Whatever may be said to the contrary, Chamberlain did not agree because of our military unpreparedness. On the contrary, he sincerely believed that it was necessary in the general interests of world peace to let the Sudeten Germans unite with the Germans of the Reich. The fact that we were militarily weak took a secondary place in his mind. Extremely obstinate by nature, he would never have submitted to a threat or surrendered through fear. He was prepared to make an agreement only because he felt that it was definitely wrong to plunge Europe into war to maintain what, even in the negotiations of the Versailles Treaty, was regarded as a precarious and vulnerable compromise.[13]

Hoare referred to the sheet of paper that Chamberlain waved in his tumultuous return to London at the close of the Four Power Conference, and he credited the Prime Minister for his poise under pressure.

From the moment he became Prime Minister, he had set himself the urgent task of exhausting every expedient for preventing the calamity of a European war. If, in spite of his efforts, war came, no one would be able to say that he had failed to take every step to avoid it. The sole fault would be unmistakably on Hitler's shoulders, and the whole Commonwealth would be solidly united in resisting the dictator's undisguised attempt to dominate the world.[14]

Hoare alluded to the Anglo-Soviet negotiations of 1939 in a rather cynical fashion, certain in his belief that the Russians were not sincerely interested in any type of alliance with the West, but also disquieted that Chamberlain's critics had accused him of an ideological bias against the Bolsheviks, which was quite common among certain sections of the Conservative Party.

> If we made a mistake, it was that we continued to believe that there was a chance for an agreement when nothing short of his full demand was in the least likely to satisfy Stalin. Our own good faith and intentions blinded us to the fundamental incompatibility of our objectives. We never fully realised the cynical duplicity that was exploiting our efforts to obtain better terms from the Germans. . . . The long months of fruitless negotiation showed that while even these modest hopes were groundless, we never gave up the attempt to obtain Russian cooperation. It was Russian duplicity and not British prejudice that made these months of baffling discussion end in failure.[15]

The Nazi-Soviet Pact was indeed the prologue to the world's most disastrous war, one that Neville Chamberlain strove mightily to avoid. Hoare concluded by judging his chief in a sympathetic manner, just as for the entirety of his life Chamberlain had empathized with the sufferings of his fellow men.

> For all his efforts, war came. Had, then, the three years of his Premiership been wasted? Worse than wasted, had they brought disaster upon the world? The evidence that I have produced from my many contacts with the problems that faced him, convinces me that the time was neither wasted nor a disaster aggravated by his double policy of peace, if humanly possible, and arms, if war became inevitable. The devastation, political, material and moral, that followed the failure of his crusade for peace does not prove that his policy was wrong, but rather that in face of a world war, it was right and necessary to try out every possible expedient for saving humanity from so terrible a catastrophe.[16]

Nine Troubled Years probably did as well in enunciating the rationale behind the defense of appeasement as any book of its era. Many of Sir Samuel Hoare's arguments are impressive and remain defensible today, forty years after they were first presented.

The final work in our collection of Chamberlain supporters from the immediate postwar period is the memoirs of Lord Halifax, or Edward Frederick Lindley Wood. Halifax, a longtime figure in interwar parliamentary affairs, was the Lord President of the Council in Chamberlain's administration, and he became Foreign Secretary on 1 March 1938, shortly after Eden's resignation. His book, *Fulness of Days*, published in 1957, was widely judged a disappointment from the pen of a man who had been at the very center of power in British politics at such a critical time. The Czech crisis and Munich Conference, which well should have been the centerpiece of any autobiography, were glossed over after barely cursory discussion. The book itself was innocuous in nature, but because of his crucial position at Chamberlain's right hand during the Czech crisis, his opinions must be considered worthy of examination. Halifax commented profusely on the characteristics of Neville Chamberlain, the man and the leader:

> Anyone who worked with him, and I suppose I worked as closely with him as anybody, was bound to be impressed by two things. One was his complete disinterestedness and disregard of any lesser thoughts of self, and the other his unfaltering courage and tenacity, once he had made up his mind that a thing was right. These are qualities of signal value for a democratic leader, and all who have the vision to appreciate how close they lie to the roots of health in a democratic state will feel a debt to Neville Chamberlain for his practical demonstration of them.[17]

Ironically, that same steadfastness Chamberlain would display in his pursuit of European appeasement was to redound to his great misfortune, as his policies disintegrated in the face of Nazi aggression, while he showed precious little desire to change his plans. Halifax continued with his description of his close colleague:

> One of his great qualities indeed was the unflinching honesty of his mind which tended to make him shrink from any economy of unpalatable truth. No one had ever been a more devoted and passionate lover of freedom, but the kind of picture drawn of him by many of his Labour opponents before the war was of a rigid bureaucrat in domestic administration, and in foreign affairs of a man too ready to be half-hearted in his condemnation of totalitarian government.[18]

Chamberlain's lifelong orientation, coming as he did from the business community, allowed him to reason that he could "do business" with European dictators in much the same way he once did with merchants in his hometown of Birmingham. He would be tirelessly supported by Halifax in his quest for appeasement.

Halifax had few things to say about the Czech crisis and the Munich agreement, admitting that even he might well have been a critic, if he had not at the time occupied a position of responsibility.[19] He did, however, mention that he felt some of the criticism of the agreement was misdirected.

> In criticising the settlement of Munich, they were criticising the wrong thing and the wrong date. They ought to have criticised the failure of

successive Governments, and of all parties, to foresee the necessity of re-arming in the light of what was going on in Germany; and the right date on which criticism ought to have fastened was 1936, which had seen the German re-occupation of the Rhineland in defiance of treaty provisions.[20]

Halifax also alluded to mistakes made by supporters of the Chamberlain administration, who clouded the truth by misrepresenting the consequences of the accord.

The unhappy attempt was made by some of those defending Chamberlain's Government to represent what had happened as something which was in the long run going to be of advantage to Czechoslovakia by ridding her of a German population that would never be easy of assimilation and which was therefore bound to give recurring trouble. Such argument sounded in the last degree hypocritical, and the only possible defence of Munich, which was the genuine defence, was that it was a horrible and wretched business, but the lesser of two evils.[21]

Finally, Halifax offered his perspective on the tireless toil of the Prime Minister in the search for peace, an ill-fated quest to be sure, but one that honored Chamberlain's memory a generation after his demise.

But when all has been said, one fact remains dominant and unchallengeable. When war did come a year later it found a country and Commonwealth wholly united within itself, convinced to the foundation of soul and conscience that every conceivable effort had been made to find the way of sparing Europe the ordeal of war, and that no alternative remained. And that was the big thing that Chamberlain did.[22]

As mentioned earlier, there were certainly fewer accounts in support of Chamberlain and appeasement than there were of those etched in acid, reviling the debased "men of Munich." This past segment served to establish the opinions of those who worked closely with Chamberlain and assisted in the formulation of his policies, and thus to stand in contrast to the overwhelming popularity of the Churchillian perspective.

A useful adjunct to the accounts of Chamberlain's Cabinet-rank associates would include the attitudes emanating from the Foreign

Office during the Chamberlain premiership. It is no secret that Neville Chamberlain treated his Foreign Office with a disdain bordering on contempt, repeatedly eschewing the counsel of lifelong professionals to pursue his concept of personal diplomacy. Indeed, in perhaps the most telling example of Chamberlain's attitude toward the Foreign Office, he deemed it unnecessary for his hand-picked Foreign Secretary to accompany him during his three trips to Germany in September 1938. The shadowy if not ubiquitous Horace Wilson would fill that role as Chamberlain's personal emissary. This analysis will include the personal remembrances of several significant Foreign Office members, and will serve as a counterpoise to the perspectives of Chamberlain's confidants.

Upon his accession to executive leadership in May 1937, Neville Chamberlain was determined to end the drift that had characterized British foreign policy under Stanley Baldwin. Unlike his contemporaries who supported the fragile structure of the League of Nations and others who championed the traditional balance of power schemata that had been the major leitmotif of British foreign policy since the time of the Spanish Armada, Chamberlain believed in a highly personalized style of diplomacy in order to remove the principal causes of friction in European affairs. His style curiously lacked ideological content; he felt he could "do business" with dictators, that is, they could be treated as fellow gentlemen. His late-Victorian upbringing would thus in some ways serve to damage his diplomatic efforts. His idealistic Foreign Secretary, Anthony Eden, was rather surprised by Chamberlain's unilateral initiative of July 1937, in which the Premier corresponded with the Italian despot Mussolini in an effort to ameliorate Anglo-Italian relations.[23] Eden, an old League of Nations supporter, had harbored an intense suspicion of Il Duce's motivations ever since the Abyssinian debacle of 1935 and 1936. Indeed, Anglo-Italian conversations and their timing would be the catalyst that would lead to Eden's resignation in early 1938. There were many indications in late 1937, however, that Chamberlain intended to overlook the Foreign Office in his desperate pursuit of European appeasement. One instance involved the prospective visit of the then Lord President of the Council, Viscount Halifax, to Germany in November 1937. At that time, the Permanent Under Secretary in the Foreign Office, Sir Robert Vansittart, was a consistently bitter critic of Nazi ambitions and behavior. Vansittart opposed the visit as a potential embarrassment, but Chamberlain, ever vigilant in his efforts to improve relations with the dictator states, saw the trip as a crucial chance that was not to be missed. The Prime Minister commented on Vansittart's negative attitude regarding the visit in a letter to his sister of 24 October 1937: "When Edward told me all this I was really horrified. I said 'another opportunity to be thrown away.' I can't allow that. . . . But really that F.O.! I am only waiting for my opportunity to stir it up with a long pole."[24] Two weeks later, Chamberlain would comment on a speech given by Eden in the House of Commons, and again in a private letter would offer dramatic evidence of his personally irreconcilable differences with the Foreign Office *mentalite*. The relationship between Chamberlain and his F.O. would continue to be strained until he replaced Eden with the compliant Halifax.

> Anthony's speech in the House of Commons was a great personal triumph for him but it contained some unfortunate passages from my point of view and shows again a characteristic of the F.O. mind which I have frequently noticed before. They never can keep the major objects of foreign policy in mind with the result that they make obstructions for themselves by endeavouring to give smart answers to some provocative foreign statement. . . . Anthony should never have been provoked into an attack which throws Germany and Italy together in self-defence when our policy is so obviously to try and divide them.[25]

Another example of Chamberlain's antipathy toward the Foreign Office was his Machiavellian handling of his chief irritant there. On 1 January 1938, Sir Robert Vansittart, the highest ranking civil servant in the Foreign Office, was sacked from his position as Permanent Under Secretary, and moved into an innocuous sinecure as Chief Diplomatic Advisor. Chamberlain's satisfaction with this turn of events was reflected by a most private communication of his in late December 1937:

> After all the months that S.B. wasted in futile attempts to push Van out of the F.O. it is amusing to record that I have done it in three days. . . . I think the change will make a great difference in the F.O. . . . Van had the effect of multiplying the extent of Anthony's natural vibrations and I am afraid his instincts were all against my policy.[26]

Vansittart's successor as Permanent Under Secretary was Alexander Cadogan, formerly a Senior Deputy Under Secretary. His detailed remembrances from the period, *The Diaries of Sir Alex-*

ander Cadogan, 1938–1945, edited by David Dilks and published in 1971, are the initial portion of our Foreign Office analysis. Cadogan was, logically, less critical of Germany's conduct in Central and Eastern Europe than Vansittart, but was fairly balanced in his perceptions of the Chamberlain administration and the reduced role of the F.O. during the P.M.'s tenure. Dilks noted that Cadogan made many insightful references to the Prime Minister, among them that "he was, in a sense, a man of one track mind. If, after much reflection no doubt, he decided on a certain move or line of policy, nothing would deflect him."[27] On appeasement, Dilks cited a Cadogan letter written well after the war, which alluded to both Chamberlain and Halifax and their ill-fated crusade for peace.

Both were tormented day and night by their search for some peaceful settlement and I could not say that they were wrong in that, provided of course that they did not overstep certain bounds. . . . I am sure that Halifax, like Chamberlain, when he came into the F.O., strongly believed it to be his duty to make every effort to avert a war which we were almost certain to lose (short, of course. of overstepping the limits of what was honourable).[28]

Although Cadogan was critical of Vansittart's ostensible paranoia of the Germans, he was rational enough to sense the danger of Berlin's systematic aggression. In a memorandum to Foreign Secretary Halifax, his newly appointed chief upon Eden's February resignation, Cadogan summarized his perceptions of Nazi motives. "My experience is that German demands, like mushrooms, grow in the dark. They are always higher next week . . . and if they could be got to define their wishes this week, ambitious though they might be, they will fall short of what they will be next."[29] These prescient remarks would, through the late summer of 1938, reflect Cadogan's clear grasp of European affairs. Berlin, working through its stooges in the Sudetenland, would aggravate matters until a casus belli could be justified, and an attack on Czechoslovakia would result. Chamberlain, fearing a war that would envelop all of Europe, sought to remove the tension, and finally determined to solve the crisis on a man-to-man basis in September. The Prime Minister had been totally shocked when, upon arrival at Bad Godesberg for the second meeting with the Germans, Hitler had raised his demands (as Cadogan had surmised in his memo five months earlier) and insisted upon total cession of the Sudeten regions on an immediate basis. The alternative was clearly war, and a distraught Chamberlain then returned to London to meet with his Cabinet. Cadogan reported on that fateful meeting of 24 September, he no less anguished than the Prime Minister:

> Meeting of "Inner Cabinet" at 3:30 and P.M. made his report to us. I was completely horrified—he was quite calmly for total surrender. More horrified still to find that Hitler has evidently hypnotised him to a point. Still more horrified to find P.M. has hypnotised Halifax who capitulates totally. P.M. took nearly an hour to make his report, and there was practically no discussion. . . . I'd rather be beat than dishonoured. How can we hold Egypt, India and all the rest? Above all, if we have to capitulate, let's be honest. Let's say we were caught napping: that we can't fight now, but that we remain true to all our principles, put ourselves straight into war conditions and rearm. Don't—above all—let us pretend we think Hitler's plan is a good one! I've never had such a shattering day, or been so depressed and dispirited. I can only hope for a revolt in the Cabinet & Parliament.[30]

The following day Cadogan was gratified to learn that his advice to Halifax, to reject firmly the Godesberg diktat, had motivated the Foreign Secretary to press the Cabinet to stand against any capitulation to Berlin.[31] Chamberlain had been deeply wounded by Halifax's change of heart, but he acceded to his Cabinet colleagues. The crisis would play out to its sad denouement at Munich on 29–30 September, and the temporary peace would be preserved.

The German seizure of Prague on 15 March 1939 marked the end of "active appeasement" as a policy for the Chamberlain administration. The wreckage of the Munich agreement made clear to the world the worth of Nazi promises. The failure of the P.M.'s strategy did in some ways vindicate those in the Foreign Office who had urged a tough line against German aggression in central Europe, Eden and Vansittart included. Cadogan, like most of the Premier's contemporaries, was stunned by the events of mid-March. His diary entry for 20 March 1939 reflected the determination of most Britons, come what may, finally to stand firm against the Nazi regime. This galvanization of public opinion would act as the catalyst that preceded the British guarantees to Poland and Rumania.

> These are awful days. The crisis is worse, really, than last September, but the public don't know it. It's more critical and more imminent, and more acute. And I'm afraid we have reached the cross-roads. I always said that, as long as Hitler could pretend he was incorporating Germans in the Reich, we could pretend that he had a case. If he proceeded to gobble up other nationalities, that would be the time to call

'Halt!'. That time has come, and I must stick to my principle, because on the whole, I think it right. I don't believe that he can gobble all Europe, or at least I don't believe that, if he does, it will do him much good. But we must have a moral position, and we shall lose it if we don't do some thing now.[32]

Cadogan would continue as the top civil servant in the Foreign Office through the duration of the war, and he would later be reunited with his former chief when Eden returned as Winston Churchill's wartime Foreign Secretary in December 1940.

Another Foreign Office account of the Chamberlain years was compiled from the personal diaries of Oliver Harvey. *The Diplomatic Diaries of Oliver Harvey, 1937–1940*, were edited by his son John and published in 1970. Harvey was the Private Secretary to Anthony Eden from January 1936 to February 1938, and he continued in that capacity with Lord Halifax until December 1939. One of the events that would create the atmosphere that would lead to Eden's resignation from the F.O. in February 1938 was Chamberlain's rejection of an offer from U.S. President Roosevelt for American participation in an effort to ameliorate the causes of European tension. This affair would also serve well to underline the growing split between the Prime Minister and his Foreign Office staff; as Chamberlain actually turned down the American offer without consulting his Foreign Secretary, who had been on an extended holiday in France at the time. Eden was understandably upset, and Harvey commented on the storm that broke between the two men on their initial meeting after Eden's return to Britain.

A.E. said he found (Chamberlain) apparently sincerely believed that our initiatives with Germany and Italy were likely to lead very soon to real settlements! When expostulated with, P.M. could only say that F.O. weren't sincere in their efforts. I'm afraid the P.M. may have committed a colossal blunder which it is too late to retrieve. A.E. will have to consider his position very carefully, for he obviously cannot remain responsible for foreign policy if the P.M. persists in such a line. He cannot accept responsibility for a policy which will antagonise America.[33]

Four days later, on 20 January, Harvey cited a meeting between Chamberlain's *eminence grise* Horace Wilson and J. P. L. "Jim"

Thomas, Eden's Parliamentary Private Secretary, which served to put the F.O. in their proper place, in Wilson's estimation:

> Jim saw Horace Wilson this morning. The latter defended P.M.'s policy of coming to terms with dictators and condemned the F.O. attitude which he represented as obstructing this. He admitted there was a fundamental difference between P.M.'s and A.E.'s policies and seemed prepared for a break: he let it be known that if A.E. did go there would be an onslaught on him and the F.O. for their attitude. . . . He regards U.S. policy as pure bunk and believes the world will greet Roosevelt's scheme with screams of laughter. What ignorance! . . . We know now that P.M. hates American co-operation and wants to make peace with the dictators.[34]

Eden did indeed resign on 20 February 1938, as did his close confidants Lord Robert Cranborne and J. P. L. Thomas. Halifax was appointed Foreign Secretary, and the Foreign Office would then be regularly circumvented by Chamberlain in his pursuit of appeasement, right through the Munich Crisis up to the Nazi seizure of Prague. Oliver Harvey was filled with a sense of dread for the future, evidencing this foreboding in a diary entry from 5 March:

> But what is so dangerous now is the state of mind of Hitler and his determination to have his way in Central Europe. A.E.'s departure has unsettled the whole world and our friends are full of suspicion at what the P.M. may do next: the dictators are encouraged in the belief that we are becoming isolationist and disinterested. A.E. was a symbol for a certain policy which all alike had come to understand. It had steadied our friends and it had kept the dictators guessing; this was the utmost it could do to make our influence felt.[35]

The passage of three eventful months made Harvey no more sanguine about the future of Europe than he had been. If anything, one can perceive a pessimistic, almost fatalistic tone to his thoughts of 5 June 1938.

> We seem to be drifting more and more into the position of allowing Russia to champion the Democracies while we seek to placate the Dictators. An impossible position for this country which is getting visibly restive. . . . We continue to suck up to Mussolini who treats us and our friends to abuse every time he makes a speech. He has not done a single thing to make appeasement easier since we signed our agreement. England cannot afford to be on the side of the Dictators for we shall then soon find we are left alone with them.[36]

Like Cadogan, Harvey gave evidence of a finely tuned insight into international affairs, and a healthy cynicism of Chamberlain's purported "peace for our time." Harvey had been very favorably impressed by Halifax's conduct under extreme stress. In the immediate aftermath of Munich, on 1 October, he wrote:

> Meanwhile the paeans of hysterical praise are almost nauseating. Not a word about poor Benes, at whose expense and by whose consent peace has been achieved. . . . H. [Halifax] told me he thought it was a horrid business and humiliating . . . but yet better than a European war. I do admire the great dignity and restraint which H. has shown over all this. His position has been most difficult, P.M. taking all the limelight and scarcely doing the Foreign Secretary, let alone the other colleagues, the civility of consulting them.[37]

Harvey's perceptions of the Munich settlement were less diplomatically stated, a week later, as he forcefully registered his displeasure with the sordid processes that led to the dismemberment of Czechoslovakia. "Such, then, is the result of all this; Czechoslovakia blotted out as a factor of any independence in Central Europe. . . . Shameful. The Western democracies have bought "peace" by sacrificing a small nation to the dictators because they were afraid or unprepared to fight."[38] Harvey's sense of remorse over the fate of the Czechs was shared by many of his Foreign Office confreres, and was in dramatic contrast to the eternal optimism of the Premier.

A third Foreign Office account was written by a man who accompanied Neville Chamberlain on each of his three trips to Germany in the pursuit of peace, and also took part in the crucial but ill-starred Anglo-Soviet negotiations of 1939. William Strang wrote *Home and Abroad*, his memoirs of the period, in 1956. After having entered the Foreign Office in 1919, Strang became Head of the Central Department in 1937. In regard to Chamberlain's appeasement, Strang thought it worthwhile to ponder the changed meaning of the policy through the recent past.

> My years in the Central Department were the culminating years of "appeasement." This word has become a term of bitter reproach; but it has a respectable earlier history. . . . In the 'thirties, it was chosen to describe their policy by those who thought that it was not beyond the power of diplomacy to improve relations between the democratic Pow-

ers and the dictators. It meant in their minds something like what we nowadays refer to as "relaxation of tension." It acquired its ill repute when too heavy a price began to be paid, a price which not only failed to bring permanent easement, but also carried with it impairment of national credit.[39]

Strang commented on the qualities of the Prime Minister, noting that his "strong will" and "firm confidence in his own judgment" were rare and valuable in a statesman, but that in some ways these same characteristics weighed against Chamberlain in his handling of foreign affairs.[40]

> His mind was dominated by two thoughts. The first was a hatred of war so deep that he would think that heavy sacrifices would be justi- fied in order to avoid it. The second was the belief that the German and Italian dictators were men whose word could be relied on; that it was possible to come to agreements with them which could transform the international situation for the better and give peace to Europe; and that by his personal influence with them he could hope to bring such agreements about. The first was in itself an entirely laudable senti- ment, but it could be a hazardous guide to action in the jungle which Europe had now become. The second was a misjudgment, all the more serious in that it continued to be entertained even in the face of strong evidence to the contrary.[41]

On the popular axiom of the era that appeasement saved Britain from war, Strang answered with a persuasive analysis that was rather critical of Chamberlain's leadership:

> It may be argued that, for all that, his policy was justified in that it did save us from war. True, it saved us from a probable war in 1938, but it did not save us from war. . . . For the present it is sufficient to observe that in 1938, with some loss of honour, we avoided a war which we might not have won, and that in 1939 we had to face a war which we came within an ace of losing but did in the end win.[42]

As mentioned above, Strang was a firsthand witness of the events of September 1938, and as a lifelong Foreign Office man, found the fait accompli presented to the Czechs and their erst- while "allies" at Munich very disquieting. To Chamberlain, who felt the preservation of peace the only imperative, these moral questions were of an ancillary nature.

> To the professional diplomatist accustomed to the decencies of inter- national life, the Munich Conference was a distressing event. . . . What

was disturbing was that, at an international conference, four Powers should have discussed and taken decisions upon the cession to one of them of vital territory belonging to a fifth State, without giving a hearing to the government of that State.[43]

The critical Anglo-Soviet negotiations of summer 1939 were yet yet another concern of Strang, as he assisted Britain's then ambassador to Moscow, William Seeds, in the agonizing effort of building an alliance against Nazi expansionism. As he noted, "The Soviet decision to compound with Germany in 1939 was not a sudden improvisation. As a policy, it had been for months a possible alternative to an agreement with the Western Powers."[44] Strang complained bitterly in a letter of 20 July 1939 to his fellow Foreign Office compatriot Orme Sargent that the Soviets seemed bent on the complete humiliation of the Western powers before any agreement could be reached. The continuous haggling over minor semantic issues and the abstruse, indeed, often opaque reasoning of chief Russian negotiator Molotov would have tested the patience of Job, and Strang's frustration was readily apparent.

It is we, not the Russians, who took the initiative in starting negotiations. Our need for an agreement is more immediate than theirs. . . . The Russians have, in the last resort, at least two alternative policies, namely, the policy of isolation, and the policy of accommodation with Germany. We are being urged by our press and by our public to conclude an agreement quickly: and the Russians have good reason to assume that we shall not dare to face a final breakdown of the negotiations. This is the strength of their negotiating position, and this makes it certain that if we want an agreement with them we shall have to pay their price or something very near it.[45]

Strang understood the game the Russians were playing, and he apportioned part of the blame on the West's diplomatic defeat at Munich. A possible rationale was that no one was sure if appeasement would be successful until after the seizure of Prague, when its failure was evident to even the most sanguine of Britons. Logically, there was no great motivation to woo the aid of the Soviets before March 1939, because the Premier had felt his plan would succeed in maintaining European peace. Strang's thoughts on the Byzantine negotiations:

If the Western Powers did in 1939 think it desirable to try to come to an agreement for common action with the Soviet Union, it may fairly be urged that the grounds for doing so were, objectively considered, no less compelling in 1938; and that though the prospects of reaching such an agreement might not have looked very bright, yet it would have been much better to try, while there was still time. The obstacle was that the Western Powers thought in 1938 that it was a better and more hopeful policy to try to satisfy Germany than to call in the Soviet Union against her.[46]

The failure of the Anglo-Soviet talks would foreshadow the incredible volte-face of 23 August 1939, as the Nazi-Soviet Nonaggression Pact was signed, and the Second World War became inevitable.

Sir Nevile Henderson's *Failure of a Mission* was written in 1940, and forms our final Foreign Office perspective, that of the British Ambassador to Berlin. Henderson became His Majesty's emissary to Nazi Germany in April 1937, just a month before Neville Chamberlain kissed hands and ascended to become Britain's Prime Minister. Anthony Eden criticized the appointment in his memoirs, but Henderson seemed to enjoy the full confidence of his Premier, and he often ignored his nominal superiors at the Foreign Office to report directly to Neville Chamberlain. Henderson discussed the duties and standards incumbent upon any ambassador with a curious analogy:

> An ambassador is not sent abroad to criticize in a country the government which it chooses or to which it submits. It was just as much my duty honorably to try to co-operate with the Nazi Government to the best of my ability as it would be for a foreign ambassador in London to work with a Conservative Government, if it happened to be in power, rather than with the Liberal or Labour opposition, even though his own sympathies might possibly be rather with the policy or ideologies of the latter.[47]

Much like Chamberlain, Henderson displayed a signal lack of ideology in his outlook, seemingly to the point of being able to coexist with any state, no matter how antithetical it was to liberal democracy. This belief in an ability to "do a deal" with the dictators was a theme of appeasement, and Henderson saw his treatment of the Nazis as the only proper conduct.

> The mistake which was too easily made abroad was to condemn everything that was Nazi just because its ideology was contrary to ours and

because some of its principles and many of its practices were utterly
and inexcusably cruel and horrible. Ideological hatreds can be as dangerous to the peace of mankind as the ambitions of a dictator. Both
involve the loss of sanity and judgment and of sense of proportion. The
result at home was too much criticism and too little constructiveness
in respect to Nazi Germany. If Central Europe were to settle down to
peace, something more than criticism was essential.[48]

Upon his appointment as Ambassador to Berlin, Henderson may
well have carried his nonjudgmental philosophy too far, so that he
was playing into the hands of the Nazi propagandists. When he
declared that democracies and dictatorships could coexist, others
could surmise that Britain was weak, unwilling to stand against
German expansionism in Europe. Therefore, Henderson's preju-
dice seemed ironically pro-Nazi in scope. He offered this explanation of his personal orientation:

> I thought that the right policy was to carry conciliation to its utmost
> point before abandoning hope of an agreement. That has always been
> the traditional policy of England; and if Hitler had had better advisers,
> he would have realized that its basis was strength and moral justice
> and not national decadence and weakness. . . . Therefore, I was re-
> solved to err, if anything, on the side of impartiality, to try to see the
> good side of the Nazi regime, if there was one.[49]

His attempts to find that "good side" of a state whose sworn promises were seldom kept and whose foreign policy was well nigh
driven by violence and intimidation, would obligate the Ambassador to assume an overly roseate attitude with regard to Nazi ambitions, to the great disgust of many in the Foreign Office.
    It is logical that one who had such a central role in the events of
September 1938 would later propose to defend the Prime Minister's conduct during that time. Henderson, while present at all
three of the summit meetings, was, with Horace Wilson, a critical
agent in the maintenance of the fragile peace. Many times during
that month he would be charged with the delivery of a Chamberlain communication to the Nazi despot with a world war hanging
in the balance. His conclusions on Munich, then, are far from sur-
prising.

> The humiliation of the Czechs was a tragedy, but it was solely thanks
> to Mr. Chamberlain's courage and pertinacity that a futile and sense-
> less war was averted. As I wrote to him when all was over: "Millions
> of mothers will be blessing your name tonight for having saved their

sons from the horrors of war. Oceans of ink will flow hereafter in criticism of your action." Both statements were correct, but the verdict of history will in any case assuredly be that the course which the Prime Minister took was the only right and sane one in the circumstances as they existed.[50]

To one who was labeled by his rivals as one of the most venal and shameless of appeasers, Henderson's only vindication some fifty years later may be that his "verdict of history" on Chamberlain is still open to debate.

The opinions of those whose perspective emanated from the Foreign Office allow a balance to be struck between a divergence of views; they afford a certain symmetry to those accounts that supported Chamberlain, sometimes almost blindly, out of a sense of past loyalty. The decade of the 1960s would witness great changes in the appeasement debate, as a more sophisticated scholarship would lead to specialization in the various fields, and what had formerly been the voice of condemnation would be replaced by a less judgmental tone. The "Guilty Men" genre, so long supreme, would begin to relinquish its dominance of the historiographical debate.

5
The Sixties—Decade of Change

THE 1960s WERE THE YEARS IN WHICH THE APPEASEMENT DEBATE would be dramatically altered. Fueled by a more sophisticated scholarship that emphasized the empirical rather than the emotional, the "Guilty Men" approach began to be perceived as simplistic, even hypocritical, in nature. Out of this assault on the genre came a call for a more detailed concentration on the rationale behind Chamberlain's policies, his viable options in Britain's particular circumstances, and a more objective attitude that jettisoned the vituperation of those who sought only to condemn. The decade would witness the beginnings of a process in which several specialized fields within the study of appeasement would be investigated in a meticulous fashion. A few examples of those that will be examined in later chapters are the curious relationship of the British media, specifically print, to Chamberlain's appeasement; also, a detailed view of rearmament and defensive planning during his premiership, along with the effect of Britain's economic standing, for better or worse, on those attempts to rearm.

The 1960s, then, were the turning point in appeasement's historiographical debate. Thereafter, various factors that influenced appeasement would be focused upon to a greater extent than would personalities. This would serve to widen the debate and diminish the use of appeasement as a morality play.

An account that evidenced the singular staying power of the "Guilty Men" genre regarding appeasement was A. L. Rowse's *Appeasement: A Study in Political Decline, 1933–1939*, written in 1961. Rowse, an Oxford academic and Labour candidate for Parliament in the 1930s, was very critical of the Chamberlain legacy, and his book was a superb example of a condemnatory leitmotif that served to fuse the Churchillian and "Guilty Men" approaches. As brief as it was (120 pages), it was suffused with a righteous anger and a negative tone. Rowse credited Leo Amery with having been among the most ardent antiappeasers in British politics. He could not be so charitable concerning the roles played by All Souls Fellows such as John Simon, Edward Halifax, and Geoffrey Dawson. His emotional description in regard to the makeup of the appeasers was illustrative.

> That they did not know what they were dealing with is the most charitable explanation of their failure; but they might at least have taken the trouble to inform themselves. . . . They were middle-class men with pacifist backgrounds and no knowledge of Europe, its history or its languages, or of diplomacy, let alone of strategy or war. . . . The plain truth is that their deepest instinct was defeatist, their highest wisdom surrender.[1]

The trio of authors who adopted the pseudonym of "CATO" in 1940 could well have claimed such a statement as their own, which is indicative of the persistence of the "Guilty Men" theme. Rowse contemplated the guilt of Chamberlain during the late 1930s, charging him with "sins of deliberate commission" in yielding to the dictator states, while differentiating his conduct from that of Baldwin's earlier "sins of omission."[2] On one of the gravest of Chamberlain's weaknesses, he opined:

> Chamberlain knew no history . . . indeed, his whole approach was that of a rather simple-minded businessman. . . . Chamberlain had no conception of the elementary necessity of keeping the balance of power on our side; no conception of the Grand Alliance, or of its being the only way to contain Hitler and keep Europe safe.[3]

On the tenor of a foreign policy which allowed the *Anschluss*, Munich, and the German seizure of Prague to take place, Rowse was bitterly critical. On Chamberlain's appeasement, he offered the following sentiments, so very common in the late 1940s, and not surprisingly, embraced by the author in 1961: "It was precisely this spineless concessionism, when faced with blackmailers and murderers, that brought on the war. Every concession made strengthened their position . . . what is difficult to understand was why so many people did not, and would not, see it at the time."[4] Rowse disputed Chamberlain's reasoning against the use of force and the notion of a preventive war. He employed the very "sense of history" that Chamberlain did not possess to bolster his own argument and debunk the Prime Minister's:

> "War wins nothing, cures nothing, ends nothing," had been the burden of his song all along. . . . Unfortunately history has often shown the

contrary to be correct. The Napoleonic war and Trafalgar *won* a century of complete and blissful security for this country; Waterloo *ended* the century-long attempt of France to dominate Europe; as the war we were just about to enter *ended* the similar attempt of Germany.[5]

Rowse concluded his literary rancor with what he perceived a fitting epitaph for the "men of Munich," whose legacy brought to fruition exactly the opposite of what they had intended for the future of Europe. His conclusion:

> The total upshot of their efforts was to aid Nazi Germany to achieve a position of brutal ascendancy, a threat to everybody else's security or even existence, which only a war could end. This had the very result of letting the Russians into the centre of Europe which the appeasers—so far as they had any clear idea of policy—wished to prevent.[6]

This theme had earlier been advanced by the sixth and final volume of Churchill's *History of the Second World War*, in which the final defeat of Fascism became rather bittersweet because it presaged the rise of Soviet communism as a force that would dominate Eastern Europe for nearly a half century after the war. Thus would the promise of worldwide peace and security, which Chamberlain had toiled long and hard for, and which was the driving force behind appeasement, be compromised by the torturous aftermath of the world's most destructive conflict. Rowse's account would not be the last to support the "Guilty Men" perspective, and it demonstrated an example of the emotionalism that had dominated the historiography of appeasement up to 1961, save only a few of the more objective accounts of earlier academic historians. Fortunately, this trend toward a more detailed scholarship would emerge more fully in the decade of the 1960s.

One of the more controversial publications referring to appeasement and the events leading to the second worldwide conflagration within a generation was Oxford historian A. J. P. Taylor's *Origins of the Second World War*, published in 1961. Taylor's rebuke of the orthodox version of the events that ended with the Nazi invasion of Poland of September 1939 sent shock waves through the historical fraternity, and prefaced a firestorm of protest among colleagues, especially in Britain. Taylor's thesis suggested that, far from possessing an overly systematic plan for world conquest, Hitler was simply an opportunistic if not bellicose statesman operating in the realm of a Bismarck or Metternich, always willing to gladly accept what diplomatic triumphs afforded him, and ready at all times to exploit the weaknesses of external adversaries. This notion tended to eliminate the tyrant's demonic side and portray him as a capable head of state akin to many of his European contemporaries. As for Chamberlain, he was thereby obligated to deal on less than favorable terms with this duplicitous, often brutal figure to preserve the European peace he desperately desired.

With regard to Chamberlain's indefatigable efforts to secure a general European appeasement, Taylor broke from the condemnatory school of the "Guilty Men," and strove mightily for an insight, an understanding of what occurred in those fateful years when a delicate peace hung in the balance. His personal analysis of the appeasers, then:

> I want to understand the "appeasers," not to vindicate or to condemn them. Historians do a bad day's work when they write the appeasers off as stupid or as cowards. They were men confronted with real problems, doing their best in the circumstances of their time. They recognised that an independent and powerful Germany had somehow to be fitted into Europe. Later experience suggests that they were right. . . . The "appeasers" feared that the defeat of Germany would be followed by a Russian domination over much of Europe. Later experience suggests that they were right here also. Only those who wanted Soviet Russia to take the place of Germany are entitled to condemn the "appeasers"; and I cannot understand how most of those who condemn them are now equally indignant at the inevitable result of their failure.[7]

Taylor opined at length on the subject of Chamberlain's orientation toward the troubled world situation upon his accession to the premiership in late May 1937. The Prime Minister's core convictions would shape appeasement for the duration of his tenure of office, often in a negative fashion.

> He had no faith in the hesitant idealism associated with the League of Nations. . . . Chamberlain took the lead in pressing for increases in British armaments. At the same time, he resented the waste of money involved, and believed it to be unnecessary. The arms race, he was convinced, sprang from misunderstandings between the Powers, not from deep-seated rivalries or from the sinister design of one Power to dominate the world. He believed, too, that the dissatisfied Powers—and Germany in particular—had legitimate grievances and that these grievances should be met.[8]

This "businessman's outlook," so characteristic of Chamberlain from 1937 to 1940, may well have been efficacious in a Birmingham gathering of rival commercial interests, but would be found to be badly wanting in the sphere of European power politics. To the Prime Minister's great chagrin, such notions as the "gentleman's agreement" and personal honor among fellow statesmen were sadly nonexistent. Taylor stressed that even in the face of grave difficulties, Chamberlain soldiered on with unbroken faith.

> Chamberlain, at any rate, was confident that his programme would work. His motive throughout was the general pacification of Europe. He was driven on by hope, not fear. It did not occur to him that Great Britain and France were unable to oppose German demands; rather he assumed that Germany, and Hitler in particular, would be grateful for concessions willingly made—concessions which, If Hitler failed to respond with equal goodwill, could also be withheld.[9]

This notion of his ability to do business with the dictators would propel the Prime Minister through the fateful summer of 1938, when the Czech crisis seemed inexorably headed toward war.

Taylor utilized the Sudeten German crisis, the rationale for the dismemberment of Czechoslovakia, to contrast the past and present meanings of appeasement for the Western Democracies, and sadly, for the naively faithful President Eduard Benes and his fellow Czechs: " 'Appeasement' had been in origin a high-minded attempt at the impartial redress of grievances. As the controversy between Benes and the Sudetens worked out, it came to be regarded as the craven, though perhaps inevitable, surrender to superior force."[10] Once again, in reference to the paroxysms of relief shared by nearly the entirety of the House of Commons on 28 September 1938 when Chamberlain announced that he would return a third time to Germany in a desperate attempt to obviate an expected European war, Taylor stressed the new meaning of appeasement:

> This was a triumph with bitter fruits. Appeasement had begun as an impartial consideration of rival claims and the remedying of past faults. Then it had been justified by the French fear of war. Now its motive seemed to be fear on the part of the British themselves. Chamberlain went to Munich not to seek justice for the Sudeten Germans nor even to save the French from war; he went, or so it appeared, to save the British themselves from air-attack. Appeasement had lost its moral strength.[11]

With regard to the aftermath of the Munich Conference, Taylor felt anguish that Chamberlain's performance carried the vile smell of surrender, whether deliberately or not. Chamberlain's avoidance of war superseded any ideological notions of the betrayal of allies or yielding to dictators. He had, for the time being, saved the world from war, and for the Premier any other issue was of secondary importance.

> What was meant as appeasement had turned into capitulation, on Chamberlain's own showing. . . . Hitler no longer expected to make gains by parading his grievances against Versailles; he expected to make them by playing on British and French fears. Thus he confirmed the suspicions of those who attacked Munich as a craven surrender. . . . Munich became an emotive word, a symbol of shame, about which men can still not speak dispassionately. What was done at Munich mattered less than the way in which it was done; and what was said about it afterwards on both sides counted for still more.[12]

The seizure of Prague less than six months later stunned Chamberlain and the world. Hitherto roseate in his outlook for the future of European peace, the Prime Minister was obligated to reconsider his policy in the face of Berlin's duplicity. Taylor ruminated on the dramatic events of March 1939:

> Here was the turning-point in British policy. It was not meant as such. Chamberlain saw it as a change of emphasis, not a change of direction. Previously the British government often warned Hitler in private, while pursuing appeasement in public. Now they warned him publicly and went on with appeasement in private—sometimes publicly as well. The British acknowledged the German authorities in Bohemia; the Bank of England handed over to them six million pounds in Czech gold. Hoare thus defined the attitude of the British government in retrospect: "The lesson of Prague was not that further efforts for peace were futile, but rather that, without greater force behind them, negotiations and agreements with Hitler were of no permanent value."[13]

Toward that end, the British sent a small delegation in the summer of 1939 to conclude an alliance with the Soviet Union and thus act as a serious deterrent to Nazi ambitions in Eastern and Central Europe. The talks were erratic and rather byzantine, and little was accomplished. Taylor stressed the actual motivation of the British government at that juncture:

> British "appeasement," too, was mainly improvised, though with this difference: a peaceful settlement with Hitler, at the price of consider-

able concessions, was always the avowed aim of British policy. But the British statesmen waited to pursue this aim until they had improved their bargaining position either by securing alliance with Soviet Russia or by persuading the Poles to compromise over Danzig. . . . There were virtually no official Anglo-German diplomatic dealings between the end of March and the middle of August. . . . "Peaceful revision," to which both sides theoretically aspired, was a contradiction in terms. Revision was put forward as the way of avoiding war; yet it could be achieved only by methods which brought war nearer.[14]

The utter failure of the Anglo-Soviet talks prefaced the signing of the Nazi-Soviet Pact of 23 August 1939, and made the long-feared European war inevitable. Taylor's innovative treatment of the events leading to the Nazi invasion of Poland upset many, but his reluctance to blame those responsible for Britain's sorry state in the late 1930s made his influential work an uncommon one. The insights he offered served to cast a different perspective on the appeasement debate, turning away from wholesale condemnation and toward a greater understanding of the multifarious problems facing Chamberlain and his administration.

An effort that combined a serious attempt to understand the motivations of the Chamberlain administration with the customary condemnation of the "Guilty Men" was *The Appeasers*. It was written in 1963 by Martin Gilbert and Richard Gott, two scholars who had studied under A. J. P. Taylor at Oxford. The work began with an acknowledgment to those who had opposed appeasement during the Chamberlain years, with a rather glib pronouncement that their publication was "a story of British strength in the end; of the defeat of appeasement; of the triumph of honor."[15] The authors stated that to reason that Munich bought a year for Britain to rearm and to unify the Dominions against Germany was futile, since the Germans gained a much greater benefit in the year's time after Munich, both materially and in terms of morale. They cited Chamberlain's motivation during the Czech crisis:

Chamberlain and his advisers did not go to Munich because they needed an extra year before they could fight. They did not use the year to arouse national enthusiasm for a just war. The aim of appeasement was to avoid war, not to enter war united. Appeasement was a looking forward to better times, not to worse. Even after the German occupation of Prague, Chamberlain and those closest to him hoped that better times would come, and that Anglo-German relations would improve. They gave the pledge to Poland, not with enthusiasm, but with embarrassment. They wanted to befriend Germany, not anger her.[16]

Gilbert and Gott stressed that the Versailles Treaty and its arguable injustices against Germany created a palpable feeling of guilt among many Britons, and led the people to support Chamberlain's attempts toward a settlement of grievances.

> It was England who had helped to drive Germany into confusion and anarchy, by agreeing with France to the severe terms of Versailles. By a policy of understanding and conciliation England could remedy her fault. A sense of guilt drove the appeasers into a one-sided relationship with Germany, in which Germany was always to be given the benefit of the doubt.[17]

The notion of a certain "blinders mentality," characteristic of the appeasers, rang true for Gilbert and Gott. The optimism that led Chamberlain to exclaim that "I do believe it is peace for our time" on his return from Munich, now seems Pollyannish at best, but was a sweet relief for those who felt a murderous war imminent in September 1938. The inflexibility of Neville Chamberlain's stance toward the possible use of force, ergo, that every possible option would be exhausted before coercion was utilized, hurt the supporters of appeasement in the long run. As the authors clearly delineated: "Appeasement resulted from mental laziness, not from political immorality . . . the appeasers saw only what they wished to see. They refused to condemn Germany out of hand and tried to adopt as fair an attitude as possible towards a phenomenon about which they knew little."[18] Gilbert and Gott commented on the hypocrisy of the appeasers in regard to the overt wickedness of the Nazi regime, and how after May 1937 appeasement became Britain's foreign policy, for better or worse.

> The appeasers were in earnest. And they knew the caliber of their would-be friends. As a result they began to act behind closed doors, and to scheme in the dark. . . . Originally a mood to be proud of, appeasement became, with the brutalization of German politics, a mood of whispers and cabals. It was the wise, the far-sighted and the sceptical who talked of resisting Germany. . . . Before 1937, appeasement was active at party and hunt, in 1937, it moved with Neville Chamberlain, into Downing Street. The vagaries of a mood became the realities of a policy.[19]

Gilbert and Gott traced the policy that would ultimately lead to the signing of the Munich agreement and the subsequent truncation of the Czech state. After the tension of the summer of 1938, Chamberlain had determined that only his personal presence could assuage the dogs of war that threatened to loose themselves on a luckless Europe. To that end, he made three separate trips to deal with the Nazi tyrant, and try to resolve the Czech crisis peacefully. The authors alluded to high-level meetings between British and French delegations that took place after Chamberlain's initial trip to Germany. In the meeting of 18 September, there were differences between Chamberlain and Eduard Daladier over future guarantees for the rump of the Czech state, and the authors explained the problem.

> The French were prepared to consider the cession of territory. Their greatest concern was to secure a British guarantee for the truncated Czechoslovakia. . . . If France were to lose Czechoslovakia, Britain must share responsibility for the future of those areas beyond. Chamberlain's policy was to allow Germany a free hand in Eastern Europe. By giving a guarantee for the integrity of Czechoslovakia, which had little prospect of remaining a viable state once its frontier areas had been taken away, this policy would receive a severe setback. Chamberlain therefore did his best to avoid the guarantee. Britain was unwilling to defend Czechoslovakia.[20]

The drama of that month, when all Europe and the world were submitted to an emotional roller coaster of hope, despair, and final relief, found Chamberlain lauded as the world's peacemaker, the savior of humanity. Others were to disagree with that analysis, including several in Chamberlain's own Foreign Office. Orme Sargent, an Assistant Under Secretary of State, was quoted by Gilbert and Gott as rather disgusted at the heroic treatment the Prime Minister received after his return to London at the conclusion of the Munich Conference. "For all the fun and cheers," Sargent remarked, "you might think that they were celebrating a major victory over an enemy instead of merely a betrayal of a minor ally."[21] Others were also to dissent with the hero's welcome given Chamberlain, among them the politician and literary figure Harold Nicolson, who was cited by the authors for his ambivalence in a private communication written to a confidant on 30 September 1938:

> I have a nasty feeling that I shall not approve of the results of the Munich conference. People seem unable to differentiate between physical

relief and moral satisfaction. Naturally we were all overjoyed yesterday to have removed from us the actual physical fear which was hanging over us. My moral anxiety remains. The Prime Minister has not really got much understanding of dictatorial mentality, although he seems to have a marked sympathy for it.[22]

That perception of "moral anxiety" would grow among many in Britain, leading up to the seizure of Prague and the loss of the remainder of Czechoslovakia to Nazi subjugation. Gilbert and Gott were utterly correct in their estimation that the Prime Minister never meant to protect the Czech state after Munich. A comprehensive appeasement with Germany was his sine qua non, and other issues were to be discarded, ruthlessly if need be. This blindly consistent approach, even in the face of outrageous treachery, led Chamberlain to hesitate in his criticism of Berlin after the fateful events of 15 March 1939. The authors commented on his reluctant response:

Prague had not been defended by Czechoslovakia's allies. Though guaranteed, it had fallen undefended. Once it had gone, the guarantees given it were forgotten. Chamberlain, Halifax, and Simon made it clear that these guarantees had never been taken seriously. "The condition of affairs," said Chamberlain, "which was always regarded by us as being only of a transitory nature has now ceased to exist, and His Majesty's Government cannot accordingly hold themselves any longer bound by this obligation."[23]

Stiffening domestic resistance to Nazi outrages in Central Europe left Chamberlain obligated to take a harder line with Berlin after Prague's fall, or risk losing the support of his party and parliamentary majority. In consequence, the Prime Minister made a rather stern warning in a speech in Birmingham on 17 March, realizing that deterrence was one possible way to impede Fascist aggression in Europe. Accordingly, a guarantee was concluded with Poland by the end of March that would give the Poles British support in the event of a Nazi attack. Even up to the very outbreak of war, Chamberlain attempted to find a peaceful solution to the causes of tension in Europe, but to no avail. During the Commons debate between the time of the German attack on Poland and the British entry into the war, many were distressed that Chamberlain appeared to be wavering on his guarantee of support to the Poles, and the "national honour" of Britain came into question. Gilbert and Gott stressed the weakness of appeasement when confronted by an imminent war:

The invocation of honor hit at appeasement where it was most weak. The appeasers claimed to have sought a sensible, rational policy. The moral problem had been too much for them. Any accusation that they were acting with dishonor was difficult to answer. It might seem sensible to refuse to go to war for Poland. It could not be honorable.[24]

Chamberlain's long crusade to avoid war was unsuccessful, and the authors cited a hoary Cromwellian allusion to the appeasers as "decayed serving men"; it was then necessary for the appeasers themselves to be swept out of power so that their successors could lead a valiant people to total victory against an implacably evil foe. Gilbert and Gott's account was less simplistic in nature than others of the condemnatory genre only because it sought to find the catalysts and motivations behind the events, and they articulated a keener insight into the workings of that fateful policy.

A publication which, as A. J. P. Taylor did, called for changes in the way the appeasement debate was perceived, was Professor D. C. Watt's watershed journal article, "Appeasement: the Rise of a Revisionist School?" published in *Political Quarterly* (April–June 1965). Watt, at that time Senior Lecturer in International History at the London School of Economics and Political Science, was indignant at the way that the appeasers had been portrayed as weak and conniving individuals, and the fact that the "Guilty Men" school, after a quarter-century of scholarship, still held sway over the appeasement debate. On appeasement, he cited a working definition: "The word has now passed irretrievably into historical usage to cover the period of European politics immediately preceding the outbreak of the second world war. It has taken to itself the status of a myth—loaded with implication, undertones, and overtones."[25] The purpose of his article was to address that mythological condition, and determine how much of it could or should stand in the face of recent scholarship. Watt alluded to Taylor's *Origins of the Second World War* as a direct challenge to the historical orthodoxy in regard to the events of the late 1930s, insisting that "within the academic world one can say with some confidence that the once orthodox view is no longer so easily accepted."[26] That early "orthodox view," Watt continued, was split into two theses, the first being that the war ensued from Hitler's systematic and premeditated drive for world dominion by military aggression; and the second, that Britain's prewar leadership, especially that of

Neville Chamberlain, was desperately intent upon the avoidance of war at almost any price, and pursued the policy of appeasement to that end. British reactions to Nazi perfidy in the eleven months after Munich drove Chamberlain to the war he had so feared and detested.[27] However, Watt stressed, as Alan Taylor had surmised, if there were no deliberate German "blueprint for aggression," then criticism of the appeasers for their conduct was also erroneous. Watt argued:

> If one only argues that Hitler blundered into war with Britain in 1939, one is still left with the need to construct an entirely different picture of the conceptions which underlay British policy, and one is left to wonder uneasily whether past condemnations of Sir Nevile Henderson's view of Hitler's motives and consequent recommendations on policy should not now be revised. There is more to it than that.[28]

That very ambiguity on the question of blame for appeasement was a common theme of Watt's work, as he strove to transcend the simplistic stereotypical notion of the appeasers as stupid and cowardly players on the European stage, and instead would envision the appeasement policy as an intricate and reasoned response to the problems facing Britain in the late 1930s.

Watt divided those who opposed appeasement into two groupings, the right-wing patriotic-chauvinist Germanophobe realists of the Churchill–Amery–Sir Lewis Namier school, and the liberal internationalist and left-wing Popular Frontists who saw the events of the 1930s as a European civil war between populist democracy and oligarchic totalitarianism.[29] This bifurcation would logically also exist in the corresponding scholarship of those historians who had written on the subject of appeasement after 1945. Watt cited some examples of the first group, among them Sir Lewis Namier, John Wheeler-Bennett, and Professor Charles Mowat. Representative of the latter group were A. L. Rowse, Alan Taylor, and Elizabeth Wiskemann. He added that the orthodox right-wing had been substantially bolstered by the initial volume of Sir Winston Churchill's war memoirs, in view of his hallowed reputation as Britain's savior in its darkest hour. In Watt's personal estimation, then, it was not until Taylor detonated his bombshell in 1961 that the orthodox view of the war's origins could be challenged. He also referred to Professor W. N. Medlicott's 1963 work entitled *The Coming of War in 1939*, as a brilliantly defensible alternative to the orthodox version of the history.[30] Watt reviewed the literature on prewar Nazi plans, then cited the infamous Hossbach Protocol of 5 November 1937, in a brief attempt to gain an insight into Hitler's future aggressions. On the British side, Watt ruminated:

> It is in the failure to co-ordinate the evidence on British policy towards the three aggressor nations, that the orthodox view of British policy is most open to attack, and in the degree to which its assertions about the motives of British policy have never been tested by historical research.[31]

A grave weakness in the "orthodox" historical orientation was one which in reality was simplistic to a fault, according to to the author: "It paid much too much attention to the personalities and character defects of the principal actors in the story, Sir Lewis Namier and Sir Charles Webster combining to assure us that their real fault was that they were intellectual mediocrities, timid men, 'lacking guts.' "[32] Watt also bemoaned the lack of studies across the wide sweep of appeasement's ancillary fields, scholastic initiatives that would come in due time with the specialization of the research in the 1970s and 1980s. Among those he called for were studies on the Labour Party opposition; on the principal British advocates of the appeasement of Germany; of the Tory Party's antiappeasers; and of Britain's rearmament efforts, halting though they were.[33] In conclusion, Watt argued very persuasively for a "serious revision" of the orthodox view. This change would, in his eyes, be immediately personified by the accounts of A. J. P. Taylor and Professor Medlicott, who offered, in Watt's rather frank terminology, a "welcome change from the gruff dismissal of all concerned as pusillanimous, stupid, ill-informed and weak-charactered which used to pass as historical criticism amidst the plaudits of the press a decade and a half ago."[34]

The challenge to the orthodox historical view of the policy of appeasement was to change the parameters of the historiographical debate, and for the better. One intriguing barometer of change was a work published by Martin Gilbert in 1966 entitled *The Roots of Appeasement*. Three years before, in collaboration with his Oxford colleague, Richard Gott, Gilbert had savaged "the appeasers" in the book of the same name. In 1966, after admitting he took criticism from A. J. P. Taylor and Lord Strang, he appeared again, "to examine the wide range of the appeasement argument, and to show that appeasement, both as an attitude of mind and as a policy, was not a silly or treacherous idea in the minds of stubborn, gullible men, but a noble idea, rooted in Christianity, courage and common sense."[35] Just as the debate was undergoing changes, so were individual historians evolving their perspectives on appeasement. Gilbert cited his view that the change would be a thoroughly positive one:

> In a subject so clouded by controversy it is at times difficult to separate passion and polemic from reality. . . . The "Guilty Men" tradition in English historical writing has flourished for over a quarter of a century, and ought now to fade away. . . . Historical assessments are best approached in an atmosphere of relative detachment.[36]

One of the main themes in Gilbert's work referred to the differences between the essence of appeasement as practiced before the threat of Nazi Germany, and appeasement as it was embodied during the Chamberlain years. In his estimation, the policy was born on 4 August 1914, at the outbreak of the Great War, when "educated" people from both sides realized that the war was to be a costly, tragic mistake. From that perspective, he commented on the genesis of the policy:

> Appeasement was born in the minds of those who said that the war need never have come, that it was accidental, and that neither Britain nor Germany was more responsible than the other for its onset. It was a determination to prevent by all means a second accidental, "guiltless" war. Appeasement was created by a lack of confidence in the British case, and a resolve never again to drift or fall unwillingly into war.[37]

The critical factor was the relationship of the terrible waste of the First World War to the policies of the interwar years. Those memories, seared into the souls of so many of the "lost generation," would drive political figures like Baldwin and Chamberlain to avoid war at all costs, a policy akin to Eden's assertion of "peace at almost any price." Although excoriated upon its abysmal failure to stop the aggressions of the Nazis, appeasement had its faithful disciples for many years, as Gilbert recapitulated:

> Every Prime Minister between the wars accepted this policy and pursued it. Appeasement was the corner-stone of inter-war foreign policy. For twenty years it dominated all arguments and blessed or bedevilled all policies. Lloyd George cautiously, Ramsay MacDonald enthusiastically, Stanley Baldwin doggedly and Neville Chamberlain defiantly

pursued it throughout their premierships. Their contemporary reputations depended upon its immediate effects; their subsequent stature rested upon its long term success or failure.[38]

The great unknown in the equation of appeasement was the future path of the burgeoning regime in Nazi Germany. After all of their grievances had been redressed, would they indeed labor toward a peaceful, constructive role in Europe, or was a revanchist war against the Western democracies or a course of conquest in Eastern Europe their very raison d'être? This hope of a pacified Europe after the obviation of tension was the desideratum for which Neville Chamberlain was willing to sacrifice so much. Gilbert clarified some of the problems that appeasement faced as Chamberlain assumed the premiership.

> The basis of positive appeasement was the recognition of Germany's legitimate claims for Treaty revision. This had dominated British policy since 1919. It depended for its justification upon the compatibility of British and German civilization; upon the possibility of mutual acceptance of each other's way of life and philosophic tenets. If Englishmen felt that Nazism was incompatible with the British outlook on life, all justification for appeasement fell to the ground.[39]

As Gilbert would explain, the events of the mid- and late 1930s would only serve to portray the genuine nature of the German state, and increase the doubts of many Englishmen as to the efficacy of appeasement.

> Between the end of 1936 and mid-1938 the position of appeasement was severely shaken. It became the focal point of intense and violent argument. Although much of the public and most of the press believed in maintaining peace at almost any price, the perpetuation and strengthening of the Nazi regime was becoming for more and more people too high a price to pay.[40]

Chamberlain was an individual who seemingly never doubted his administration's policy. Throughout the Czech crisis of May–September 1938, he continued to believe that Germany could and should be appeased to avoid a widespread war. In Gilbert's estimation, appeasement died a sudden death on 12 September 1938, when the German dictator demanded the right of the Sudeten Germans in Czechoslovakia to self-determination. After that date, the question of war or peace in Europe lay in Hitler's hands, not Chamberlain's. As Gilbert remarked:

Appeasement could not compete against such whims. Its basis was the reasoned argument, the carefully weighed factors, and the overriding morality of any proposed change. After 12 September 1938 appeasement became increasingly a nervous, jerky, guilt-encumbered affair; not a confident philosophy, but a painful surrender to threats. . . . Chamberlain himself continued to believe most emphatically that war was not inevitable.[41]

Throughout the nearly six months between the Munich Conference and the Nazi seizure of Prague, Chamberlain felt assured that the German megalomaniac had "no more territorial ambitions in Europe," and could be trusted to honor his commitment over the integrity of the Munich agreement. Of course the events of the Ides of March 1939 changed everything, but Gilbert stressed unequivocally that the "abject fear" that had driven the appeasers to betray smaller allies according to the "Guilty Men" analysis was indeed more illusion than reality:

Chamberlain's hopes that war might be avoided were broken. . . . Hitler, who had mistaken appeasement for weakness, tried to convince himself that Britain would not honour her agreement with Poland. But appeasement was never a coward's creed. It never signified retreat or surrender from formal pledges. If, at the last moment, Chamberlain had doubts as to whether war was inevitable, these doubts were not dishonourable, however short-sighted.[42]

The remainder of the summer of 1939 saw the rather ludicrous charade of Britain and France attempting to forge an alliance with the enigmatic Soviets, who at long last accepted the offer of nonaggression from their ideological antagonists in Berlin, and made the world conflagration inevitable.

In his conclusion, Gilbert delineated the differences between the "old" and "new" appeasements, referring to those policies pursued between 1918 and 1937, and those between 1938 through the outbreak of war in September 1939. He, like A. J. P. Taylor and D. C. Watt before him, called for a modern reassessment of appeasement, and Gilbert himself dramatically widened the philosophical nature of the historiographical debate, to his credit.

The old appeasement was rooted in a belief that Britain and Germany had much in common; that their interests often coincided and that their civilizations were in no way incompatible. Neither premise fitted the situation in 1938. From 1919–1937, the public, the Press, and the politicians could all welcome agreements with Germany as leading to peace. The Munich Agreement was welcomed because it averted war.

There was a deep difference between the two attitudes. At bottom, the old appeasement was a mood of hope, Victorian in its optimism, Burkean in its belief that societies evolved from bad to good and that progress could only be for the better. The new appeasement was a mood of fear, Hobbesian in its insistence upon swallowing the bad in order to preserve some remnant of the good, pessimistic in its belief that Nazism was there to stay and, however horrible it might be, should be accepted as a way of life with which Britain ought to deal.[43]

A source that characterized the dramatic metamorphosis of the appeasement debate away from emotional polemics to scholarly analysis was Keith Middlemas' *The Strategy of Appeasement: The British Government and Germany, 1937–1939*, published in 1972. Originally published in Britain under the title *Diplomacy of Illusion*, Middlemas' work was among the first to use the recently opened British archives up to 1939, which had been opened under the newly adopted thirty-year rule as the author began his research. He asserted that the greatest value of the archives was that they revealed the mechanism of policy formation as it was under Baldwin and as it evolved under Chamberlain.[44] As Middlemas explained, his definition of appeasement was "taken to mean the policy of meeting German demands and grievances without asking for firm reciprocal advantages; asking instead only for future 'mutual understanding.' "[45] In essence, it was Chamberlain's notion of "peace at almost any price," a tireless effort in order to save the fragile equilibrium of Europe. Middlemas expounded on Chamberlain's personal orientation to foreign affairs, which was palpably to influence the course of events leading to the outbreak of war.

> His approach to foreign affairs was by no means the myopic view from the Birmingham town hall with which Lloyd George, among many detractors, liked to amuse himself. The horror of war which he shared with most of his contemporaries was based not only on the revulsion against the use of war as an instrument of policy, but on a much deeper belief in rationality as the foundation of all human behaviour. Every aspect of his personality, his religion, as well as his feeling for music, testified to a love of order. About war he wrote with unconcealed hatred and disgust.[46]

Middlemas alluded to one of the central themes of his study of appeasement, which served to portray the Premier as a formidable, even fearsome, adversary in the House of Commons:

The impact of the new Prime Minister's ready-made strategy in 1937 was directly responsible for the policy which the Cabinet followed down to March 1939 and . . . other agencies—Foreign Office civil servants, back-bench MPs, party headquarters and the Press—played subsidiary parts. On their own . . . none of the other "appeasers" could have subordinated the part played in peace-making by the Foreign Office, Chiefs of Staff and the Foreign Secretary himself.[47]

It is ironic that an individual with such an iron-handed grip on his own administration, who admittedly would brook little if any opposition to his wishes, would eventually be perceived by many as a figure of such dire weakness, if not cowardice, on the world stage. Middlemas afforded a corollary assessment of the Prime Minister's hubris in regard to his opposition, whether political or public opinion:

There is no evidence, during Chamberlain's tenure as Prime Minister, of a concerted effort to educate the public to accept his policy, as Baldwin had done several times in his own political life; and Chamberlain's authoritarian attitude to protest, whether from the public or from the Opposition, may be found in a letter of 5 June 1938, in which he referred to Labour back-benchers as "a pack of wild beasts . . . I think what enables me to come through such an ordeal successfully is the fact that I am completely convinced that the course I am taking is right and therefore cannot be influenced by the attacks of my critics."[48]

As a long-time Chancellor of the Exchequer in the years preceding May 1937, Chamberlain contributed much to the 1936 governmental debates over defense spending. Ever the sober businessman, Chamberlain insisted, according to Middlemas, "that he did not wish, as he often emphasised, to choose the cheapest method of defence rather than the best, but he overlaid all argument with the fiat that the Chancellor must emphasise the overall effect of military demands on the domestic economy and social programmes of the Government."[49] If the necessarily rapid defense spending was to have any potentially deleterious effects on Britain's domestic economy, Chamberlain would be there to put a brake on the activity. As he was soon to be Prime Minister, he would have the reins of control over Britain's destiny in a crucial epoch in her history. An alarming lack of intellectual ambiguity characterized the P.M.'s attitude toward his pursuit of appeasement. He would stay the course, unmoved to a large part by the fluidity of events around him. Regarding the defense debates of 1937, in which financial limits on the service budgets served to

slow the pace of British rearmament, Middlemas was rather critical of Chamberlain's economic orientation:

> The principles of rationing and the transfer of the burden to diplomatic
> action were accepted after Christmas 1937. They governed and limited
> British policy in the crises of March and September 1938, just as they
> dictated the isolationist strategy which was to meet the only type of
> war that the Cabinet envisaged. They were imposed largely by Cham-
> berlain's direction and they owed surprisingly little to consideration
> of existing commitments. Seldom have the defences of a nation been
> rearranged with such concentration on economic grounds.[50]

Middlemas developed at some length the rupture between
Chamberlain and his first Foreign Secretary, Anthony Eden, over
the usage of Anglo-Italian conversations to drive a wedge between
Italy and Germany in late 1937 and early 1938. Eden wanted no
part of dealing with Il Duce without tangible proof of good faith;
for example, removal of Italian volunteers from Spain before talks
could be held. Chamberlain perceived this resistance to his desired
ends to be part of a larger battle between himself and an obdurate
Foreign Office, which sought to block his every move to preserve
peace in Europe. The author quoted Chamberlain when the P.M.
referred to the Foreign Office in a less than supportive manner, as
early as 12 September 1937:

> The F.O. persist in seeing Mussolini only as a sort of Machiavelli put-
> ting on a false mask of friendship in order to further nefarious ambi-
> tion. If we treat him like that we shall get nowhere with him and we
> shall have to pay for our mistrust by appallingly costly defences in the
> Mediterranean.[51]

The antagonism between Chamberlain and Eden was to be fueled
to a greater extent by the nebulous January 1938 offer from President Roosevelt for American assistance to lower the level of tension in Europe. Chamberlain dismissed this initiative out of hand,
without even consulting his Foreign Secretary, and the die was
cast. A mere five weeks later, Eden resigned, and Chamberlain's
dominance of the Foreign Office was from that time unquestioned.
Middlemas pondered the resignation and its consequences:

> There had been several different levels of conflict as well as the main
> point of principle . . . between the traditional style of the Foreign Office
> and the hasty private diplomacy of the Prime Minister; between Eden's
> wishful firmness and Chamberlain's wishful realism . . . the distinction

was also one of profoundly different interpretations: between Eden's well documented and fully justified caution in dealing with the dictators and the Prime Minister's awareness—of greater, but not sufficient realism—that time was running out for *any* policy to avert war. In brief, the whole policy of appeasement was at stake.[52]

For that matter, the immediate future of Europe was also at stake. Middlemas would duly cover the entirety of the sad denouement of 1938: the surrender of Czech liberty at Munich; the eventual abrogation of British and French responsibility for the fate of the Czech state. These events would lead to 15 March 1939, when Bohemia and Moravia would be violently thrust into the Nazi orbit. In his conclusions, the author adamantly stated that even though it was to a large extent correct to portray the Chamberlain administration's decision-making from 1937 to 1938 as Chamberlain's "personal province, a rigid satrapy closed against the light of opposition and informed only by the servants of appeasement";[53] yet these circumstances were not all the fault of the Prime Minister. Middlemas asserted, from his own personal perspective, that

> Chamberlain's freedom of action was demarcated by the assent of his colleagues . . . if he was permitted to run the Foreign Office over the Foreign Secretary's head, or to select the advice he wished the Cabinet to hear, or to work with a pliable and sycophantic inner group, the fault was not totally his. The power of the Prime Minister is not so great that his colleagues cannot restrict it: if loyally or weakly they acquiesced, then they abdicated their own responsibility.[54]

In regard to Chamberlain himself, Middlemas was evenhanded in his analysis of the Prime Minister, critical at times but supportive in other circumstances. An illustrative example is a statement the author made in reference to the aftermath of Munich, namely that "the last accusation which should be made against Chamberlain is that of cowardice; but the fact that Munich did not alter his calculations raises a different charge."[55] Perhaps Middlemas's final criticism, sophisticated as it was, can serve as a metaphor to illustrate the dramatic variance between the early polemicism of the "Guilty Men" accounts and the balanced scholarly treatment that he afforded Chamberlain's fateful policies. On the P.M., he concluded:

> His wholly admirable horror of war cannot outweigh the fact that in the last resort Chamberlain avoided the full responsibility of choice by referring to personal standards of morality, which were not universal qualities. Because he believed that it was the ultimate sin to create

war, Chamberlain regarded the sufferings of individuals and minorities as worth while if they served to prevent it. But to exclude as unthinkable the deliberate launching of war creates strategic blindness and led directly to blackmail by leaders who did not acknowledge Chamberlain's standards and used them as weapons against him when they could.[56]

A final account that, like Middlemas', utilized the newly available archival sources was Ian Colvin's *The Chamberlain Cabinet*, published in 1971. Colvin, a member of the press who worked for the *News Chronicle* at the time of Munich, was probably a shade less balanced and more critical of Chamberlain than Middlemas, but he was personally content to allow the documents to speak for themselves. Colvin utilized sources from the Committee for Imperial Defence, Foreign Office papers, various Cabinet minutes and memoranda, and the Prime Minister's papers to buttress his arguments. On the documents and their importance, he remarked:

> The records of 1937 to 1939 are therefore unique, in that they enable us to observe a British Cabinet in action and inaction during crises and immediately before a world war. This book thus becomes rather more than a work of research on Mr. Chamberlain. . . . It is also an examination of the Cabinet in the context of world history.[57]

In regard to Chamberlain's culpability over his failed foreign policy, Colvin noted that there could be no true understanding of the period without a detailed perusal of the official documents:

> No doubt enough is already known to convict Mr. Chamberlain in a general way of having afforded opportunities to both the Dictators at a time when it was still possible to deter or divide them. Why and how his government made these mistakes, and how this serious, upright Englishman came to deserve such an unenviable niche in history, is something that we come closer to understanding when we have read through the Cabinet papers of the time.[58]

One of the more significant Cabinet papers, which really symbolized the theme of Chamberlain's appeasement, was the Chiefs of Staff Memorandum of 12 November 1938, entitled "A Comparison of the Strength of Great Britain With that of Certain Other Nations as at January 1938." The final few sentences were to dovetail neatly with Chamberlain's own perspectives:

> We cannot foresee the time when our defence forces will be strong
> enough to safeguard our territory, trade and vital interests against Ger-
> many, Italy and Japan simultaneously. We cannot, therefore, exagger-
> ate the importance from the point of view of imperial defence, of any
> political or international action that can be taken to reduce the num-
> bers of our potential enemies and to gain the support of potential al-
> lies.[59]

This indeed was the essence of appeasement and, like the Prime
Minister, it was all business, essentially nonideological in nature.
To envision Nazi Germany as a potential ally rather staggers one's
sense of propriety fifty years after the Nazi terror, but ostensibly
was a viable option for Chamberlain and his supporters. Appeasement in many ways seemed, as a policy, to be rather more reactive
than active. Colvin illustrated this proclivity in Chamberlain's own
words at the time of the *Anschluss* in March 1938, when he
quoted the P.M.'s passive reaction to the forceful annexation of
another hitherto democratic state by the Wehrmacht.

> "Here was a typical illustration of power politics," said Chamberlain.
> "This made international appeasement much more difficult." In spite
> of all, however, the Prime Minister felt that this thing had to come.
> Nothing short of an overwhelming display of force would have stopped
> it . . . [Chamberlain continued], "At any rate the question was now out
> of the way. . . . It might be said with justice that we had been too late
> in taking up the conversations with Italy. The next question was how
> we were to prevent an occurrence of similar events in Czechoslo-
> vakia."[60]

Chamberlain and a good number of his Cabinet were to continue
to hold strangely roseate views on German aims in Central and
Eastern Europe. In a meeting on 18 March 1938, ironically Neville
Chamberlain's sixty-ninth birthday, the Foreign Affairs Committee of the Cabinet addressed the German threat vis-à-vis Czechoslovakia. Colvin remarked on Lord Halifax's sanguine attitude
that belied the dire circumstances of the situation.

> "The more closely we associate ourselves with France and Russia,"
> said Halifax, "the more we produce on German minds the impression
> that we are plotting to encircle Germany." He did not accept "the as-
> sumption that when Germany had secured the hegemony of Central
> Europe, she would then pick a quarrel with ourselves. . . . He did not
> credit a lust for conquest on a Napoleonic scale."[61]

Halifax could not know that the Russo-German Eastern front, the
theater of the coming war that would spell the doom of the Third

Reich, would be fought with a savagery that would make the worst excesses of Bonaparte appear to be those of a humanitarian. In a meeting of British and French delegations on 29 April 1938, the Czech situation was discussed at length, and the participants pondered the future, when serious military staff conversations would have to be held. In the event of war over the Sudeten German issue, the responsibilities of both partners in the Anglo-French alliance had to be clearly delineated. Colvin alluded to Chamberlain's absolute horror of war, using a statement from that meeting, when the Prime Minister agonized over the proposition of an open Anglo-French declaration on Czechoslovakia, which would no doubt anger the Germans.

> He considered that this was what the Americans in their card games called bluff. It amounted to advancing a certain declaration in the hope that declaration would prevent the events we did not wish to occur. But it was not a certainty that such action would be successful. It might be true that the chances against war were 100–1, but so long as that one chance existed we must consider carefully what our attitude must be, and how we should be prepared to act in the event of war.[62]

Chamberlain held identical views four months later, when in late August 1938, with the Czech crisis nearing its apex, he refused to call Berlin's bluff by making a definitive statement of Britain's intentions to fight if France were pulled into war by a Nazi invasion of Czechoslovakia. Colvin cited this dramatic episode, using the P.M.'s words:

> The Prime Minister said that he had gone over in his mind very carefully the case for an immediate statement, but he "always came back to the same conclusion as that reached by the Foreign Secretary. No State, certainly no democratic State, ought to make a threat of war unless it was both ready to carry it out and prepared to do so. . . . Although it was possible that such a statement, if made now, might avert war, it was not certain that it would do so."[63]

Chamberlain was internationally revered for his untiring pursuit of peace upon his triumphant return from the Munich Conference. He believed that he had concluded a settlement acceptable to all sides, a businesslike agreement that would be honored by its signatories. Colvin reflected upon Neville Chamberlain's poignant statement to his former air minister Lord Swinton, at the time of the Munich debate in the House of Lords on 3 October. Swinton remarked to the Prime Minister: " 'I will support you, Prime Minister, provided that you are clear that you have been buying time for rearmament.' Producing the fabled scrap of paper from the conference, Chamberlain replied, 'But don't you see, I have brought back peace.' "[64] That peace which the Prime Minister had labored for unceasingly was to be, for him, tragically evanescent. He responded to German criticism of Britain's rearmament efforts, which could, according to Berlin, only be used to wage aggressive war against the Reich. Chamberlain made his line of policy crystal clear to his Cabinet on 31 October, less than a month after the House debate on Munich, and Colvin cited that address:

> Our foreign policy is one of appeasement. We must aim at establishing relations with the Dictator Powers which will lead to a settlement in Europe and a sense of stability. A good deal of false emphasis has been placed . . . in the country and in the Press . . . on rearmament, as though one result of the Munich Agreement has been that it will be necessary to add to our rearmament programmes. (He proposed) to make it clear that our rearmament is directed to securing our own safety and not for purposes of aggression. (He hoped) that it may be possible to take active steps and to follow up the Munich Agreement by other measures.[65]

That overall pacification of European grievances that would lead to a "golden age" of peace was cast upon the shoals when the Nazis seized the rump of Czechoslovakia on 15 March 1939. Chamberlain's fevered obsession of active appeasement would be cut short by the hardening of British public opinion and parliamentary pressure. He did eventually condemn the German spoilage of Munich (so soon after the declaration of "peace in our time"), in his famous Birmingham speech of 17 March, and would conclude alliances with Poland and Rumania as deterrents against Nazi aggression. Colvin alluded rather provocatively, however, to the Prime Minister's initial response to the fall of Prague and the disintegration of the Czech state, before the aforementioned party and public pressure caused him to alter radically his position.

> Mr. Chamberlain in his statement laid blame on the Slovak Diet which had just previously declared Slovakia a separate State and precipitated the crisis. . . . He told the House that the British obligation to Czechoslovakia no longer existed. "It is natural that I should bitterly regret what has now occurred, but do not let us on that account be deflected from our course. Let us remember that the desire of all the peoples of the world still remains concentrated on the hopes of peace."[66]

Perhaps that was true, but the respective governments in Rome, Berlin, and Moscow had other ideas; the world would be at war a mere six months later, with Chamberlain's worst nightmare having come to fruition.

In his conclusions, Colvin stressed the strong-willed nature of the man, his dangerous consistency of outlook that in essence saw what he wanted to see, and his singular vision of appeasement, however myopic. Reflecting on the Premier's makeup, he stated: "When his mind was made up on policy, and that already appears to have been the case early in 1937, Chamberlain could be as hard in pursuit of his aims as any dictator."[67] The businessman's orientation was the consistent theme of Chamberlain's vision for the future of a peaceful and prosperous Europe. When he ran into ideologies or revolutionary movements he would consistently be at a loss to understand what he was facing. Colvin lent an opinion as to the P.M.'s *mentalite*:

> In his family letters, we discover a certain simplicity of thinking, naive at times, as if he had discovered a remedy for international difficulties in a personal diplomacy of his own. . . . His was very much the English approach to foreign politics, one of sustained astonishment that some formula could not be found to suit all parties, as if some deep rooted dispute had never existed.[68]

Accounts such as those of Ian Colvin and Keith Middlemas were characteristic of a new era of scholarship, in their cases fueled by the release of hitherto-classified documents relating to the inner workings of the Chamberlain administration. The polemical condemnations of an earlier age were set aside, to be replaced by more advanced studies that were to evolve into the specific areas of research intrinsic to the understanding of appeasement. The decade of the Sixties, as we have witnessed, brought a new sophistication and critical thought into the parameters of the debate, so much so that a scholar like Martin Gilbert would be motivated to contradict his earlier work and offer an updated synthesis on the genesis and evolution of appeasement. The events of the late 1930s in British history could no longer solely be cast as steps in a Manichean morality play, where one side was despicable in its weakness and shame and the other nearly deified for its collective courage and foresight in the face of an implacable evil. Facts and scholarly analysis would change the nature of the debate, with greater insight and a deeper understanding inevitably the result.

Our next segments of appeasement historiography will indeed deal with specific areas, to wit: the many economic ramifications of the policy and the efforts of rearmament and defensive planning under Chamberlain's overall guidance; and, second, the effect of the print media on appeasement, "for better or for worse." These ancillary fields of study will offer the scholar a depth of insight into the policy that was unavailable to those who wrote in the immediate shadow of the war's end.

6

Economics, Rearmament, and Appeasement

THE 1970S WITNESSED THE BEGINNINGS OF A DRAMATIC TRANSFOR-
mation of the appeasement debate. In 1965 Professor D. C. Watt
had called for intensive scholarship in specified areas in his watershed journal article "Appeasement: the Rise of a Revisionist
School?" Watt's skepticism in regard to the veracity of the "Guilty
Men" genre echoed the earlier doubts of A. J. P. Taylor, whose *Origins of the Second World War*, if nothing else, had fired the volley
that rekindled the debate on a more sophisticated plateau. The ex-
piration of the thirty-year rule regarding official British government documents would serve to contribute mightily to the
advanced research of the early 1970s. The overbearing polemicism
and self-righteous condemnation of an earlier age was to be supplanted by a more carefully analytical and documented scholarship, based on empiricism rather than emotion. The evolution of
the debate to a higher level, then, also required a necessary shift
in methodology. The idea of the domination of the appeasement
historiography by varying "schools" would be altered to one of
acute specification in the 1970s and beyond. The multifarious
problems facing Chamberlain and his intimates prior to the outbreak of the European war would be meticulously examined as factors contributing to the overall substance of appeasement.

Perhaps the most critical example of this trend was the research
that related to British rearmament in the latter half of the 1930s. A
clear comprehension of appeasement as practiced by Chamberlain
would not be imaginable without a thorough investigation of the
detailed particulars of the rearmament efforts, as halting as they
were. Indeed, it was Chamberlain's long-held belief in the idiocy
of diplomatic bluffing unless a nation had the ability to deliver on
its threats, which (in the face of Britain's relative military impo-
tence) caused appeasement to be pursued even to the very brink of
the conflagration. In a greater sense, though, the study of Britain's
economic travail during the interwar years must necessarily be

linked with the story of her rearmament efforts to allow for a proper understanding of both subjects. Economics were, in reality, the key to rearmament, and the fragile constitution of the economy reflected the rather languid pace of those efforts. The twin themes of economics and rearmament, then, were critical elements in the pursuit of foreign policy, which in Chamberlain's case was an overall European appeasement. This section will deal specifically with the correlation between British economics and her spasmodic attempts to rearm for a fateful armageddon, one that remained the ultimate horror for a majority of Britons. A preponderance of the historiography discussed here will be within the purview of 1970 to the present, indicating the modern tendency toward the detailed specialization of those topics critical to the general subject. However, allusion must and will be made to a number of earlier works that served as the standards for their eras, and naturally fueled the later scholarship. An examination of the topics of economics and rearmament, among the most critical of the concerns that Neville Chamberlain faced in his formulation of Britain's policy, is absolutely essential for any insight into the complexities of appeasement.

Any scholar of British interwar economics and rearmament would err gravely by failing to cite one of the most compelling works of the era, *The Economic Consequences of the Peace*, by John Maynard Keynes. This literate and systematic destruction of the Treaty of Versailles, first published in 1920, set the tone for a future policy of appeasement toward Germany. While not solely concerned with Britain's economic travail in the years after the Great War, Keynes' brilliant study became an ideological justification for Chamberlain's tireless toil in the latter half of the 1930s. Keynes critiqued each of the Allied leaders at the Paris Peace Conference, where he had actually been positioned as a economic advisor to the British delegation before resigning because of the harshness of the proposed Treaty. He reserved some of his bitterest criticism for the aging and vengeful French premier, Clemenceau, whose insistence upon a "Carthaginian" peace dictated to Germany would serve to undermine the chances of a lasting settlement. Keynes called for a drastic reduction of the war reparations demanded of the Germans, and for an eventual treaty revision, in the hope that Germany could once again reclaim her role as a great power in a peaceful, prosperous Europe. Nearly half a century after Keynes' book changed the way the world viewed the Versailles Treaty, historian Martin Gilbert would perceive him as "the Isaiah of appeasement,"[1] whose writing became the handbook of reconciliation, and whose warnings became the spur and incentive to all advocates of "peaceful change."[2] Keynes was appalled at the crushing weight of the prospective level of reparations that the Allied leadership sought from the defeated Germans. Just as the visionary George C. Marshall did a quarter century later, Keynes realized that what the German people needed was food, shelter, and hope for a better life, not open-ended revenge. His opinions were compelling:

> I believe that the campaign for securing out of Germany the general costs of the war was one of the most serious acts of political unwisdom for which our statesmen have ever been responsible. To what a different future Europe might have looked forward if either Mr. Lloyd George or Mr. Wilson had apprehended that the most serious of the problems which claimed their attention were not political or territorial but financial and economic, and that the perils of the future lay not in frontiers or sovereign ties but in food, coal, and transport.[3]

He concluded his chapter on reparations with a prescient assertion on the consequence of Allied vengeance:

> The policy of reducing Germany to servitude for a generation, of degrading the lives of millions of human beings, and of depriving a whole nation of happiness should be abhorrent and detestable,—abhorrent and detestable, even if it were possible, even if it enriched ourselves, even if it did not sow the decay of the whole civilized life of Europe.[4]

Keynes' clarion call for humane and rational treatment for an implacable enemy was the essence of enlightened statesmanship, which was tragically a scarce commodity at Versailles. The widespread British guilt of the 1930s for having subjected the Germans to such execrable treatment was one of the many contributory factors to the popularity of Chamberlain's policies during his tenure as Premier. Keynes' vision of a European future under the burden of an unjust settlement was unerring in its clairvoyance, especially regarding the rise of Nazism and Communism. His work remains among the most significant of the interwar years and is crucial to the study of appeasement.

> If we aim deliberately at the impoverishment of Central Europe, vengeance, I dare predict, will not limp. Nothing can then delay for very

long that final civil war between the forces of Reaction and the despairing convulsions of Revolution, before which the horrors of the late German war will fade into nothing, and which will destroy, whoever is victor, the civilization and the progress of our generation. Even though the result disappoint us, must we not base our actions on better expectations, and believe that the prosperity and happiness of one country promotes that of others, that the solidarity of man is not a fiction, and that nations can still afford to treat other nations as fellow-creatures?[5]

An effort that had an influential role in the critical debate over British rearmament was Basil Liddell Hart's 1939 publication of *The Defence of Britain*. A lifelong military pundit who wrote more than thirty books, Liddell Hart was fiercely critical of the inflexible attitudes of the services, especially those of the army, which had at least tacitly accepted the horrific level of casualties during the Great War. He chastised the authorities who had broken with Britain's long-held tradition of a strong naval force and a limited military commitment in most of her past wars, noting the legacy of the Great War: "Rarely have we entered a war in a more favourable situation. None left us so exhausted—as a direct result of our unprecedented effort on land. And, in retrospect, the consequences of the peace that was won hardly increase its value."[6] Liddell Hart championed an idea known as "limited liability," which had been discussed in his earlier work, *The British Way in Warfare*, and had been endorsed by Chamberlain in his plans for Britain's rearmament in the mid 1930s.[7] This concept entailed the possession of a strong navy and the buildup of a formidable air force to protect British interests while keeping a lid on costs and an actual standing army. The themes of defensive warfare and the real inefficacy of aggression were close to the heart of Britain's Prime Minister at the outset of the Second World War. Some of Liddell Hart's more compelling statements seemed to be hauntingly echoed in the personal letters of Chamberlain to his sisters at the very commencement of the conflict.[8] Liddell Hart's opinions on defensive war, then:

> The advantage that rests with the defence in modern war is accentuated by the difference of aim between an aggressor and those he attacks. For him to succeed, he has to conquer. For them to succeed, they have only to convince him that he cannot conquer, and that continued effort will bring more loss than gain. They are thus able to wage a far less exhausting kind of war.[9]

This "exhaustion," according to the author, was the most common cause of defeat in war, and in consequence was the factor that the policy of "limited liability" was created to obviate. The diplomatic setback the Western democracies suffered at Munich, however, would alter the equation that was Liddell Hart's theory, and Britain would be driven to create a huge army at a perilous cost.[10] One of the main fears of Chamberlain in regard to rearmament was the economic dislocation and stress it would cause for the British economy, and Liddell Hart held similar views, which he enumerated in the shadow of the recently concluded Munich Conference:

> The result is that we have now been dragged into the course of building a great land force, combined with the maximum effort in the air and on the sea—a triple strain which, in a prolonged war, or even in a prolonged state of war-in-peace, might bring us dangerously close to breaking point. Such is the consequence of the belated return to collective security—which was an unavoidable necessity for our own defence save in the unlikely event of "appeasement" succeeding.[11]

Basil Liddell Hart, much like Chamberlain, feared the savage butchery that been the legacy of ground warfare in the Great War. His keen sense of the profound waste and squalor of the trenches led him to embrace defensive alternatives that would alleviate the need for a large land force. Only the danger of an impending catastrophe would prompt the British government to prepare an army of thirty-two divisions to aid the French in any defense of Western Europe. His work in the 1930s had a great effect on the course of British rearmament.

Another useful source of information on rearmament was written in 1952 by M. M. Postan, a Cambridge Professor of Economics. Entitled *British War Production*, the volume chronicled British efforts at providing the weapons and ancillary materials of war from the "lean years" of the mid-1920s to the eventual Allied victory in Europe in 1945. Postan perceived one of the main culprits in the weak pace of rearmament to be the "Ten-Year Rule," which had been originally formulated in August 1919 and stipulated that defensive planning would be guided by the assumption that Britain would not be involved in a major war for at least ten years into the future from a given date. He cited the annual average of armament expenditures in the period 1924–1933, inclusive, to be about £23 millions.[12] He then emphasized the salient point that one had to determine the minimum levels of Britain's munitions in order to gauge the true task that faced them in the fateful years of the 1930s, when a nascent Germany bent on revanchist policies was seriously threatening the equilibrium of Europe.

> British rearmament between 1934 and 1939 began and grew with the rising danger of war with Germany, but what set the scale of the problem was not only the magnitude of international danger but also the low level of military equipment in the hands of the Forces in the early thirties. In dealing with the pace of rearmament it is, therefore, important to get the true measure of the deficiency which the rearmament sought to remedy.[13]

From rather modest beginnings in 1934, then, rearmament programs accelerated and decelerated in the face of international events and internal economic fluctuation. Postan insisted that rearmament was not pursued with an imminent war in mind until very late in the decade, which incidentally did little to fortify Britain's diplomatic maneuvering during the interim.

> The diplomatic and strategic assumptions which until the end of 1938 underlay rearmament were not those of an eventual war. Disturbed as the international position had become, war was not yet thought to be probable, still less inevitable. . . . Until 1935 international disarmament was still a popular hope and still the object of British foreign policy. For at least another three years the object of the successive rearmament programmes was not so much preparation for war as the reinforcement of peace. Their purpose was to back up diplomatic efforts with a show of force and thereby to impress the would-be aggressors and to reassure public opinion at home. . . . Indeed, the plans of the Government did not come to be shaped for a land war in Europe until the spring of 1939.[14]

Postan inferred that at a very early date the significance of domestic economic concerns took priority over rearmament for Britain's leadership. This notion of finance as a "fourth arm of defence" for Britain would for years hamper any systematic campaign to rebuild the military capacities of the nation, which remained haunted by the economic collapse of 1931 and would avoid at all costs a recurrence of that horror. Postan's ideas are delineated with clarity.

> The financial dangers of excessive expenditure on rearmament continued to figure in official discussions almost to the eve of the war. As

late as 1938 the Chancellor of the Exchequer [Simon], in resisting further claims of the Services, found it necessary to stress that expenditure could reach a limit beyond which it might defeat the very purpose of rearmament. . . . Britain could not hope to match an aggressor in a lightning war, and her chances of victory rested on her ability to withstand the financial stresses of a long war. To overtax her financial resources and to undermine her financial stability for the sake of military preparedness might jeopardise her very ability to wage war.[15]

After all, the very essence of Chamberlain's appeasement was to satisfy existent grievances and make Europe peaceful again, not to overextend a fragile economy for a cataclysm that might never occur if the policy was successful. Postan's work, published just seven years after the war, is still utilized today as a very relevant source on rearmament.

British historian Brian Bond published his account of *British Military Policy Between the Two World Wars* in 1980. He had earlier edited the diaries of Lieutenant-General Sir Henry Pownall in 1973, and advanced Pownall's negative views regarding "limited liability." They served as a defensible counterpoise to the ideas of Basil Liddell Hart. Pownall, who filled a position as a Military Assistant Secretary on the Committee for Imperial Defence, was diametrically opposed to the scaledown of the land army that Liddell Hart advocated. In a poignant diary entry from 27 January 1936, Bond quoted Pownall's words on the issue of "limited liability":

They cannot or will not realise that if war with Germany comes again (whether by Collective Security, Locarno or any other way) we shall again be fighting for our lives. Our effort must be the maximum, by land, sea and air. We cannot say our contribution is "so and so"—and no more, because we cannot lose the war without extinction of the Empire. The idea of the "half-hearted" war is the most pernicious and dangerous in the world. It will be 100%—and even then we may well lose it. We shall certainly lose it if we don't go 100%. In God's name let us recognise that from the outset—and by that I mean now. The Chancellor's cold hard calculating semi-detached attitude was terrible to listen to.[16]

Of course the Chancellor alluded to by Pownall at that 1936 meeting was the soon-to-be-Premier, Neville Chamberlain. Bond had his own conclusions on the policy of "limited liability," and he asserted them in a compelling fashion. He questioned why a good number of Cabinet ministers in both the governments of Stanley Baldwin, and later, under Chamberlain, desired to block the strengthening of the Regular Army in the period from July 1935 to May 1937, a dangerous policy in the face of Germany's aggressive rearmament and the seizure of the Rhineland. Bond's answers reflect directly on Treasury attitudes that were embraced wholeheartedly by Chamberlain.

> The explanation of this apparent paradox lies in the Government's acceptance of the Treasury argument that finance was the fourth branch of the armed services. In other words economic stability was one of the cornerstones of the nation's defence structure and an integral part of the defensive strategy. . . . By maintaining the stability of the pound and a strong position as regards international credit, Britain could draw upon these assets in the event of war to purchase arms abroad until such times as her industrial capacity could be converted to arms production. In the short term these overriding financial and economic considerations demanded a strategy of restricting Britain's military preparations to measures designed to prevent her succumbing to a sudden knock-out blow, whether from air attack or from the severing of her sea lanes of communication.[17]

In essence, Baldwin and Chamberlain feared the deleterious effects that a full-fledged rearmament effort would have on the domestic economy. One would imagine that the vision of goose-stepping jackboots marching in the shadow of Westminster would have engendered a greater level of fear in the hearts of Britain's leaders, but a future war was perhaps viewed as less probable than economic collapse, at least through 1938.

Bond critiqued Chamberlain's efforts up to and including the Munich Conference within the purview of military matters. He personally gave the Premier low marks for his performance; if not forgivable, this is at least understandable in a self-avowed "man of peace" such as Chamberlain.

> When every allowance is made for Britain's military and political unpreparedness for war, the fact remains that a weak hand was played with crass ineptitude. Defence priorities were excessively influenced by economic considerations with a long war in view, and by the Cabinet's sense of what "public opinion" would tolerate. The professional military advisers dutifully answered the specific questions put to them but there was no fundamental reappraisal of vital national interests. On a more tactical level, Chamberlain not only committed the cardinal error of displaying Britain's military weakness in advance but also made it clear that he planned to pursue foreign policy commensurate

with that weakness. Moreover, and this is truly astonishing, there was no attempt to evaluate Germany's weaknesses, much less to exploit them or to bluff with the not inconsiderable assets in Britain's favour.[18]

Chamberlain's utter horror of another European war colored his defensive priorities, so much so that it may well be argued that rearmament was pursued rather passively, not at all on the "no-holds barred" scale that critics like Churchill had advocated. Bond's insights into the military sphere were valuable for those seeking an understanding of Britain's rearmament dilemma.

A source that took advantage of the thirty-year rule in regard to official government documents was Robert P. Shay's *British Rearmament in the Thirties: Politics and Profits*, published in 1977. Shay's stated purpose was to examine the considerations that shaped Britain's rearmament policy, concentrating especially on those that led the government to decide that rearmament had to be limited.[19] Those considerations were often economic in nature, but at other times they were clearly political. Shay commented on a deep bifurcation in policy between the Treasury and the Foreign Office in 1937:

> In the course of Chamberlain's last year as Chancellor of the Exchequer he and his advisers at the Treasury had come to the conclusion that if the rearmament program continued to expand at the rate it was then expanding, there was a profound possibility that it would undermine and destroy the existing economic and social structures. . . . The Treasury was quick to realize that "ultimately our foreign policy must largely be determined by the limits of our effective strength." Its conclusion was that, where the nation's effective strength was too limited to affect an issue that concerned it, conciliation or, as it quickly came to be called, appeasement, had to be used instead of the threat of force. Appeasement became necessary because the Treasury believed, and the Government concurred, that the British economy could not stand the strain that the marshalling of force sufficient to meet Britain's commitments would entail. The battle between the Foreign Office and the Treasury centered on the question of whether appeasement was an effective substitute for force in the international arena.[20]

Shay cited the efforts of the then-Minister for the Co-Ordination of Defence, Sir Thomas Inskip, and the estimates of defense expenditures he offered to the Chamberlain Cabinet in December 1937 and February 1938. The Treasury had estimated a maximum fixed cost of £1.5 billion for rearmament over the next five years.[21] Inskip found himself looking at a total closer to £2 billion. This was revised down to some £1,650 millions, still a painful figure for Prime Minister Chamberlain. No less a figure than the redoubtable Sir Maurice Hankey, longtime Cabinet Secretary and perhaps the most experienced individual in government service, pressured Inskip to raise the level and pace of rearmament in a private note of 14 January 1938, and Shay quoted from that missive:

> Either we must change our foreign policy or increase the tempo of our rearmament by dropping the principle that trade and industry are not to be interfered with. . . . Unless the number of our potential enemies can be reduced at once I submit that our rearmament policy must be changed. . . . A decision to press forward our armaments without regard to trade considerations might prove a decisive factor in deterring war or, if it came, in averting disaster.[22]

Shay noted that by early 1938 the Prime Minister had duly deliberated over his alternatives and resolved his fateful choice of options for Britain's foreign policy among the ominous war clouds. Ever optimistic amid the eye of that "gathering storm," Chamberlain could only hope for the best in a grievous situation.

> By March the Chamberlain Government had completed the plans by which it hoped to avoid the perils posed to Britain's security and her solvency by the deteriorating international situation. Based on the Treasury's firm belief that a continuance of the existing rate of rearmament would destroy Britain's economy and consequently her ability to defend herself, the Government's program sought to limit the nation's expenditure on armaments while pursuing a foreign policy that would diminish her need for them. The policy by which defence spending was to be limited was known as rationing. The policy by which the nation's enemies were to be conciliated was known as appeasement. Both were rooted in the Government's desire to maintain the economic and social status quo.[23]

Of course, the war scare generated by the Czech crisis would obligate the Chamberlain administration to alter the method by which they pursued their strategy of rearmament. The crushing blow for Chamberlain's appeasement was to fall six months later when the Nazis swallowed up the rump of the Czech state, a shattered entity whose integrity they had guaranteed at Munich. Shay had several intriguing reflections concerning the moralistic opprobrium heaped upon Chamberlain and his "appeasers" by later generations, and these he delineated:

> It should be remembered, however, that the policy by which he *[Chamberlain]* chose to pursue that solution, appeasement, was not devised in the heat of the moment by politicians anxious to save their nation from having to fight a war they lacked the courage to face. Rather it was conceived, as we have seen, in 1937, as a necessary corollary to the Government's decision to ration defence expenditure. Both the defence ration and appeasement were the result of the Government's carefully calculated assessment of the economic, social, political, and strategic realities that Britain faced, and not of any weakness in the character of her leaders. While there is much to criticize in the assumptions that underlay that assessment, assumptions as to the source of Britain's strength and the resilience of both her people and her economy, they are criticisms that speak to questions of political and economic philosophy rather than to those of courage or cowardice.[24]

Shay guardedly avoided the emotional aspects of appeasement as a morality play, and he concentrated instead on the empirical evidence of Treasury and Cabinet documents. This, as was noted earlier, was characteristic of scholarship in the decades of the 1970s and 1980s. In his conclusions, Shay was critical of Stanley Baldwin's feeble attempts at the development of a coherent rearmament program. It would not be until May 1937, upon the accession of Neville Chamberlain to the premiership, that the reorganization of rearmament would be effectively commenced. Shay lauded Chamberlain's talents as an administrator, although allowing that many of the P.M.'s assumptions were on occasion flawed, especially as regards rearmament.

> British rearmament was unquestionably made more efficient and effective by the reorganization. It is a testimony to Chamberlain's abilities as an administrator that, despite the restraints he continued to impose on rearmament, Britain was better prepared for war when it came than she would have been had defence planning been allowed to continue as it had under Baldwin . . . however . . . the whole reorganization of the defence program was embarked upon not out of concern for the adequacy of Britain's military preparations, but out of concern about the effect that the increasing cost of those preparations would have on the economy. . . . In the Government's view the stability of the prevailing social and economic order was the ultimate source of Britain's strength.[25]

Shay then took the Conservative Party to task for their lack of vision in regard to the rapidly worsening international scene. This emphasis on turning inward and being concerned with domestic economic matters in the face of a volatile world situation was symptomatic of Britain's quandary, formulated by Shay:

> While the Government's arguments about the importance of Britain's economic stability were no doubt valid, the risks that it was willing to take with her military preparedness in order to safeguard that stability make it apparent that the Government was as concerned about the social and economic order per se as about Britain's defences. There was almost an implicit assumption that Britain and her social and economic order were identical, and that if that order were upset, not only could Britain no longer defend herself, but there would no longer be a Britain worth defending.[26]

In conclusion, Shay established a salient connection between the languid pace of British rearmament and the political and economic interests of the ruling Conservative Party. In regard to the preservation of the extant social and economic order, which would have become well nigh anachronistic in the event of a transfer of political power to Labour, he mused:

> It is not likely incidental that the Conservative Party, which dominated the Government, represented the interests of the class that derived the greatest benefit from that order, or that the members of the Government were themselves of that class. Nor is it incidental that the specific restraints placed on rearmament benefitted the elements of the business community that formed the backbone of that class.[27]

Shay's detailed research into British rearmament epitomized the empirical scholarship of the recent past. His balanced treatment was far from uncritical, but the criticisms served to illuminate the issues in a serious and valuable analysis.

A study complementary to Shay's was written in 1979 by Dr. George Peden, an economic historian from the University of Bristol, entitled *British Rearmament and the Treasury, 1932–1939*. Peden, in relation to Shay's work, tended to be more supportive of the Treasury viewpoints and policies.[28] This was fairly uncommon, as a majority of the accounts concerned with the Treasury between the wars usually employed a less than complimentary tone, as if it were solely to blame for Britain's military unpreparedness. Peden stressed that because no Ministry of Defence existed before the Second World War, the allocation of funds came to be negotiated "directly between the Treasury and three independent defence departments. This gave the Treasury a co-ordinating function in interdepartmental policy-making, and even in individual departments' execution of policy."[29] Because there was so much interdepartmental wrangling among the services over which would be granted top priority in the rearmament planning, the Treasury held the formidable high ground as the ultimate arbiter of funding. Peden explained precisely the particulars of the monetary allocations to the various services, and the the Treasury's role in the same:

> Each defence department was supposed to prepare its annual sketch Estimates in the light of the general policy approved by the Cabinet, and forward them, early in the autumn, to the Chancellor of the Exchequer for review in the light of the overall financial position. In fact decisions on high policy had often still to be made when the different departmental claims were forwarded to the Treasury, and the coat of policy might well have to be cut according to the cloth of finance. . . . Defence expenditure always required Cabinet approval in principle, and Treasury approval in detail.[30]

Peden expounded in greater detail on the Treasury's determined efforts to regulate defense spending in the years leading up to Munich, years in which rearmament was viewed as secondary to domestic fiscal solvency.

> The Treasury's attempts to limit defence expenditure were not motivated solely by careful calculations of what the country could afford, for, especially when such calculations were made four or five years in advance, as they had to be in connection with the rearmament programme, no exact figure could be arrived at. The Treasury wanted fixed limits to each defence department's expenditure because even in normal times this was the Chancellor of the Exchequer's only really effective weapon in controlling defence expenditure.[31]

Peden alluded to the widespread fear of domestic economic dislocation among Britain's governing elites if the rearmament campaigns pressed forward without any further delay, concerns about the haunting prospect of an overall economic collapse in the fashion of the events of 1931. The Treasury were singularly wary of those circumstances, a palpable factor in the erratic pace of rearming Britain. Forecasts of gloom and doom were the rule from the Treasury, and the author crystallized the sense of anxiety:

> When from the end of 1936 Treasury officials began to talk of Britain's economic strength "slipping away," essentially what they were talking about was the adverse current balance of payments, and its effects on the country's international purchasing power represented by its gold and foreign exchange reserves, overseas investments, and ability to raise international credit.[32]

Peden delineated the Treasury's heartfelt insistence on fiscally orthodox behavior in the difficult times they were experiencing. He employed the significance of Inskip's December 1937 *Interim Report on Defence Expenditures* as a background to shed light upon the Treasury's conception of limits to rearmament at that time.

> The basic Treasury assumptions were that the maintenance of peace between the British Empire on the one hand, and Germany, Japan, and Italy on the other, was possible; that this objective required deterrence of aggression through rearmament as well as diplomacy, but that Britain's armed forces should not be enlarged beyond a level at which her economy could maintain them. The underlying fear was that rearmament might precipitate a balance of trade crisis followed by a financial crash on the scale of 1931, weakening Britain's position in the world just when an appearance of strength was necessary to deter the dictators, and it was only by degrees that fears arising from the experience of 1931 were overborne by fears of impending German aggression.[33]

A salient variable in the Treasury situation in late 1937 was that the newly installed Prime Minister had also been the driving force behind Treasury policy through the 1930s, and Chamberlain's formidable influence continued to dominate Treasury affairs without rebuke from his somnolent Chancellor Simon. In the summary of his chapter on the Treasury's "Influence on Financial Limits," Peden recapitulated the basic theories behind limitations on rearmament that were embraced by the Treasury, at least until the Czech crisis of 1938.

> Underlying financial problems there were economic, social and political problems. Treasury officials had to take society—and prevailing economic beliefs—as they found them, and give advice accordingly. . . . British defence had to be planned on the basis, at least down to 1939, of long-term deterrence. There can be no doubt of the importance of the Treasury's view as to economic and financial limits, at least down to about February 1939. As Chamberlain told the Cabinet after Mu-

nich, he had been "oppressed with the sense that the burden of armaments might break our backs" ever since he had become Chancellor.[34]

As mentioned above, the individual services competed for priorities and defensive allocations from the Treasury before the outbreak of war. One of the more prevailing doctrines of the interwar
years was that of an Italian who wrote on the future efficacy of air
power in warfare. According to Giulio Douhet's estimation, "the
bomber would always get through." This rather pessimistic axiom
was, however, accepted as gospel by several political heavyweights
in interwar Britain, among them the then-estimable Prime Minister Stanley Baldwin. The perceived need for both bomber and
fighter aircraft for both offensive and defensive warfare was judged
a top priority by the Treasury, and was reflected in the monetary
amounts budgeted for the Royal Air Force in the years 1936–
1939.[35] The Royal Navy, too, was not ignored, as the ability of the
nation to protect its commercial interests was an imperative. As
for the army, the notion of "limited liability" which was espoused
by strategists such as Basil Liddell Hart held sway for much of the
decade, and dovetailed well with the hopeful policy of appeasement that the government pursued, leaving for the Regular Army
the figurative status of "weak sister" among the three. Peden summarized the Treasury's positive influence on manufacturing a
modicum of order out of the chaos that existed in the rivalries between the services:

> The Treasury's influence on the execution of defence policy, as on the
> formation of that policy, was strongest at the level of broad priorities
> between departments. Selective application, and relaxation, of the
> brake of Treasury control enabled the Air Ministry to become the big-
> gest spender of the three defence departments. . . . Frustrating though
> Treasury control must have been seen from within any one defence
> department, the Treasury seems to deserve credit for ensuring that
> Britain's minimum requirements for air and trade defence were met
> first.[36]

Finally, to those critics who had all along believed that the miserly
policy of the Treasury had retarded or emasculated Britain's ability to rearm, Peden was adamant in his opinion. "Far from being
paralysing, the Treasury's use of the power of the purse forced
ministers and military men to come to decisions about priorities,
and thereby ensured that essential elements in Britain's defences
were completed first."[37] Historian Brian Bond reviewed Peden's
work and called it by far the "most cogent and persuasive study

that has yet appeared of the Treasury's role in British rearmament in the 1930s."[38] Armed with a pro-Treasury slant rare in the historiography, it is indeed a valuable and contemporary source on the critical fields of economics and rearmament.

One of the most exhaustive treatises on the fields of British economics and rearmament and the manner in which they affected appeasement was first published in English by a West German Professor of International Politics, Gustav Schmidt, in 1986. Entitled *The Politics and Economics of Appeasement: British Foreign Policy in the 1930s*, it was initially written as *England in der Krise: Grundzüge und Grundlagen der britischen Appeasement-Politik (1930–1937)*, in 1981. Very early in his analysis, Schmidt clearly enunciated what he called the "guiding idea" of his study on appeasement.

> Appeasement as British foreign policy in the 1930s was propelled by a paradoxical attempt to solve, or at least to regulate, conflicts by means of diplomacy and political strength at a time which was marked rather by the end of diplomacy. British policy was faced with a crisis, with the negative effects of an accumulation of changes, none of which seemed to bear promise of relief either at home or abroad. The crisis arose out of the failure of diplomacy to paper over the long-term cracks which split the global reach of Britain's objectives, her commitments and the resources at her disposal, from traditional means and methods of resolution. It arose out of the distrust of Britain's allies, as well as her opponents, in British diplomacy.[39]

Schmidt buttressed his arguments by linking British and German foreign policies of the 1930s in an intriguingly symmetrical analogy.

> If it is possible to define German foreign policy as an unsuccessful attempt to preserve the domestic status quo (and to destroy the international status quo) by means of rearmament, following only too soon by the realisation that [rearmament] jeopardised the domestic status quo, then British policy in the fields of security, armaments and foreign affairs in the 1930s may be seen by contrast as motivated by a fear of destabilisation of the domestic status quo, which led—at least temporarily and within certain limits—to a greater willingness to accept changes in the international status quo.[40]

As Shay and Peden had done earlier, Schmidt advanced the idea that to many in the ruling Conservative Party, the fear of domestic economic disruption and possible collapse as a result of profligate spending on rearmament was of higher priority than was anxiety over foreign aggression, at least to the end of 1937. Schmidt stressed that economic vitality was due to the vigilance of those who controlled the nation's purse:

> Rearmament (until March 1938) was limited by the precept that the future of the economy must not be impaired by directing resources (capital and workforce) to sectors where concentration would only lead to accumulating "overcapacities" instead of restoring growth in leading sectors; this was the meaning of the formula "business as usual."[41]

In the same vein, the consequences of forced rearmament on a "liberal" nation like Great Britain would be bleak at best with the accompanying high levels of inflation and economic dislocation. Schmidt continued with his discourse on this troubling dilemma for Britain's leaders:

> Enforced rearmament was seen to be potentially synonymous with a self-inflicted blockade of the British socio-political system. The gain it was hoped rearmament would bring—namely, the re-establishment of British freedom to develop a more assertive foreign policy—was thought to be likely to be cancelled out by the effects of a "war-like economy" on domestic politics. The basic view in Britain that foreign policy risks were preferable to a domestic political conflict with labour, since the latter placed greater restrictions on Britain's room to manoeuvre, continued to hold sway.[42]

In his conclusion, Schmidt offered a rather sophisticated insight into the essence of Chamberlain's appeasement as he characterized the policy:

> British appeasement policy in the 1930s cannot simply be seen as a reaction to problems caused by Hitler's Germany but must also be seen in the context of British attempts to regain the initiative in attempts to achieve a general European settlement and thus to influence the future course of events in ways which would serve Britain's vital interests. . . . London's policy was directed at maintaining Britain's freedom of action in order to be able—in contrast to 1914—to continue right up to the last moment to explore the possibility of a settlement, and thus to avoid another round of blood-letting. It was considered necessary to "appease" Germany (even against the better

judgment of many concerned), firstly because France was going through a period of weakness and, secondly and more importantly, because it was assumed that Britain, as in the First World War, would have to bear the main burden of responsibility for countering Germany's *Griff nach der Weltmacht* (bid for world power).[43]

Schmidt's magnum opus, while at times verbose, is a major contribution to the field for the impressive thoroughness of the research and the cold logic of his conclusions.

A brief but significant commentary on the role of the army during Britain's rearmament efforts was written by Michael Howard in 1972, entitled *The Continental Commitment: the Dilemma of British Defence Policy in the Era of the Two World Wars*. Howard, a fellow of All Souls College, Oxford, stated that Chamberlain, initially as Chancellor and later as Prime Minister, discouraged all possibilities of a British army on European soil. No doubt inspired by the ideas of the military strategist Basil Liddell Hart, Chamberlain advocated the strategy that came to be known as "limited liability."

> Chamberlain remained implacably hostile to all idea of involvement on the Continent. When in December 1936 the War Office pointed out the illogicality of providing a Field Force but no reserves to back it up with, he sent a powerful memorandum from the Treasury. This argued, first, that national resources were simply not adequate to provide for the Royal Navy, a powerful Air Force, the air defence of Great Britain, Imperial commitments, and an Army on a continental scale as well.[44]

The furious pace of international events, however, would obligate the notion of "limited liability" to be supplanted by a boom in defense spending, as German aggression in Central Europe manifested by diplomatic triumphs such as the *Anschluss* and Munich signalled danger to the British nation. It was the Nazi annexation of Bohemia and Moravia in March 1939 that shocked Chamberlain's administration into planning toward an expanded army for continental use, something that the Prime Minister dreaded for many reasons, among them the wholesale savagery and mindless devastation of the Great War. Howard commented on the events after 15 March 1939:

> In exactly the same way as in the years before the First World War, political and military logic had forced reluctant British Ministers to the

conclusion which they had for so long tried to evade: that the British Isles could only be defended on the Continent of Europe, and that in consequence a firm commitment to continental allies was inescapable. But this time the Government did not far outrun public opinion. As the German invasion of Belgium in August 1914 had resolved the differences between those who considered international affairs in terms of law and morality and those who saw them in terms of *Realpolitik*, so did Hitler's annexation of the non-German territories of Czechoslovakia on 15 March 1939. For the British people as a whole this day may be said to have marked the effective beginning of the Second World War: when, where and how hostilities would begin was a matter of tactical detail.[45]

By the time of the Nazi seizure of Prague, only six months' time would remain before the outbreak of the cataclysm that Chamberlain had so feared. Britain attempted to put the time to some good use by shoring up her Regular Army for the much-feared battle in Western Europe. Howard outlined some of the details of that transformation:

It is certainly doubtful whether the Army had faced the implications of . . . transforming itself from a small professional force concerned primarily with Imperial Policing into a cadre to train and command a conscript force over a million strong to take part in large-scale continental warfare . . . the Field Force, which at the beginning of 1939 still consisted of 5 Regular divisions only, was by a stroke of the pen converted to 32 divisions. . . . During the course of the war the target rose yet higher, to 23 armoured and 73 infantry divisions.[46]

Howard pondered a critical question that surely must have bedeviled Chamberlain and his colleagues at the time of the army's explosive growth, namely, how much of these costs could be paid for? Logically, he looked to the Treasury for answers.

In the whole story of British rearmament, the Treasury had played a vital, indeed the dominant role. Since no pre-war Prime Minister was likely to overrule its advice—certainly not when so formidable a figure as Neville Chamberlain inhabited No. 11 Downing Street—it was with the Treasury that responsibility really lay for reconciling the apparently contradictory responsibilities: nursing Britain's convalescent economy back to health, and equipping her with the military resources she needed to play her part as a major actor in the international system.[47]

Howard concluded that Britain faced difficult options in its rearmament efforts: it would be impossible, working within the narrow financial parameters, to be "all things to all people," and still remain solvent.

> Britain's resources were limited, and in her rearmament programme she faced a genuine problem of resource allocation which compelled a choice between a force-structure capable of sustaining the burden of Imperial Defence and one which would carry effective political weight on the Continent. Chamberlain's aversion to a continental commitment grew out of his six-year struggle, as Chancellor of the Exchequer, to tailor the defence programme to what the Treasury believed the capacity of the national economy to be.[48]

Howard's account is useful in recapitulating the series of events that led to the expansion of the army and the decision to contribute that army to the defense of Western Europe. Although the Treasury ofttimes appeared parsimonious, it is critical to remember that financial solvency was perceived as one of the great weapons to be husbanded in the event of a long war, and Howard's monograph added to the collective pool of knowledge on rearmament.

We now turn to the actual mechanism of budget preparation and how budgets were formulated during the critical interwar period. This was the main theme of B. E. V. Sabine's 1970 study, *British Budgets in Peace and War: 1932–1945*. The author broke down the annual expenditures for each of the fourteen years in question, the first six budgets being most relevant because they were generated by the then-Chancellor Neville Chamberlain. The steady growth of the rearmament costs reflected the deterioration of the international political situation brought on in large part by Germany's aggressive behavior in the latter half of the decade. In regard to the discussions over the proposed budget of 1936, which was presented to Parliament in April of that year, Sabine framed Chamberlain's changing perceptions of the eventual costs of rearmament, (they may well have been modified by the Rhineland crisis of 7 March 1936).

> There was in any case a certain unreality in the arguments since the cost of rearming was still an unknown: as late as 1935 Chamberlain himself was thinking in terms of £120 millions over the next five years; and only in the course of the current debate had he acknowledged its

magnitude and evolved the idea of funding it partly by taxation and partly by loans.[49]

That proposed total of £120 million over the next five years is set in dramatic contrast to the early 1938 Inskip estimate of £1.65 billion for the quinquennium of 1937–1941. Small wonder that Chamberlain and his supporters in the Treasury felt that events were spinning out of control, that economic collapse on the scale of 1931 might well nigh be imminent. Out of this context came Chamberlain's notion of a revenue-producing plan that was to be known euphemistically as the National Defence Contribution. Created in April 1937, the NDC was a vehicle by which the government could garner something positive out of an overly negative situation. Sabine explained the particulars, here referring to Chamberlain:

> He felt he should tax those profits which were not part of the current general expansion of trade but, in so far as they were consequent upon orders placed by the Goverment, arose directly from the expenditure of the State, and to underline this purpose he proposed to call the tax the National Defence Contribution.[50]

Ideally, in Chamberlain's estimation, the NDC would serve a dual purpose of being a check on profiteering and a brake on the expected boom.[51] To his chagrin, the negative response from the City and a good portion of British industry caused him to pull in his horns on the idea after a limited trial run. Sabine effectively crystallized Chamberlain's motivations in that chaotic time by quoting from the peroration of his budget statement of April 1937, which clearly manifested the dire fiscal position of the nation. In the Chancellor's words:

> I have endeavoured to avoid, on the one hand, the tremendous increase in taxation which would have been required if we had attempted to defray without borrowing the full cost of rearmament because I was convinced that the shock of such a sudden and tremendous increase of our burden would have checked, perhaps even have reversed, the process of convalescence. On the other hand, I have increased taxation with a careful choice of method to exercise a decided check upon any development of speculation without impairing the present upward trend of national welfare.[52]

In short, it required a delicate balancing act by Chamberlain to pursue a burgeoning rearmament effort while simultaneously acting as a vigilant watchdog over the nation's economic solvency. In the final analysis, this concern with the relative health of the economy would be one of the chief spurs to the government's future foreign policy of appeasement. Sabine's account reflected the domestic crisis and its ramifications and allows the scholar to gain a workable understanding of those critical years for the Treasury.

A monograph that concerned itself with one of the most horrific fears of the interwar period was written in 1980 by Uri Bialer. Entitled *The Shadow of the Bomber: The Fear of Air Attack and British Politics, 1932–1939*, it went to the heart of the rearmament issue, mirroring the widespread fear of many Britons that the next war would bring death and devastation out of the sky to the crowded cities of Britain on an almost biblical level. Bialer referred to the very raison d'être of his work when he stressed:

> The purpose is to show that the fear of a knock-out blow by air attack played a crucial part in the early debates on rearmament and resulted, in 1934 and 1935, in decisions to base rearmament largely on the air arm. It was also of significant importance to the understanding of Britain's decision late in 1937 to enfeeble her ability to intervene by land in a continental war. This decision, known as the "limited liability" formula, prevented any military preparations made in peacetime with a view to large scale military operations in Europe. These decisions were important stages in the long debate on priorities in British rearmament.[53]

Bialer perceived the danger of air attack as the paramount concern of most military planners in Britain, due to the overestimation of the strength and capability of the German Air Force and the accepted axioms of the period in regard to the unlimited potential for destruction from the air. These fears had an estimable effect on Britain's rearmament effort, as the author would clearly outline:

> British anxiety concerning the air menace increased in proportion to the degree to which the Nazi regime entrenched itself within Germany and cast a lengthening shadow over Europe. . . . The period 1935–1937 was decisive for the consolidation of the knock-out blow concept. During these years, the Government finally accepted the theory that, in a future war, Germany might try to achieve a quick and decisive victory by means of a large-scale and devastating air attack.[54]

Accordingly, the defense allocations spent on the Royal Air Force in 1938 and 1939 were dramatically higher than they had been earlier in the decade, with the Regular Army suffering the most from the concept of "limited liability." Bialer noted that the debate on British strategy over rearmament priorities in regard to the separate services was over by early 1938. He commented on the eventual denouement of that debate:

> The unmistakable consensus of opinion within the Government was that Britain had to concentrate on air rearmament and on the construction of defences designed to counter the danger of air attack—even if doing so implied forsaking the ability to intervene by land in a European war. . . . In that year, the "limited liability" formula won general acceptance; priority was given to anti-aircraft defences within the Army's budget; and the concentration on air rearmament was unmistakable . . . on the evidence now available it seems reasonable to suggest that the Government's deep sensitivity to the air threat contributed towards a particular perception of British strategy. The decision to prefer air rearmament, and to oppose the maintenance and deployment of a large army on the continent, ultimately implied an essentially defensive and anti-European strategy.[55]

The widespread fear of sudden destruction from aerial bombing underlay the feelings of utter relief when Britain, which had been at the brink of war during the Czech crisis of September 1938, was saved from that conflict through the efforts of Prime Minister Chamberlain's personal diplomacy at Munich. Uri Bialer lent a period flavor to his research when he quoted from the memoirs of Harold Macmillan at the time of Munich. Macmillan's deep concern was evident in the following passage, written in 1966:

> Among other deterrents of war in 1938, expert advice had indicated that bombing of London and the great cities would lead to casualties of the order of hundreds of thousands or even millions within a few weeks. *We thought of air warfare in 1938 rather as people think of nuclear warfare today.*[56]

These eloquent words give testimony to one of the most grave concerns of the interwar years, that of sudden and systematic destruction of civil populations from the air. Sadly, all too soon, both the Axis and the Allies would hone their respective skills in the field of terror bombing during the war. Bialer's brief but important book touched the core of one of the great catalysts of rearmament and appeasement, the fear of attack from the air.

A volume that would become a valued reference source on rearmament was Norman Gibbs' *Grand Strategy, Rearmament Policy*, published in 1976. The first of six volumes of the *United Kingdom Military Series: History of the Second World War*, Gibbs' effort represented an "official" history that employed many of the voluminous government documents relating to the interwar years and Britain's vacillation over rearmament and economic health. It was reviewed in 1978 by a British historian who offered that, "if it had been published in the 1950s . . . it would have been regarded as the standard work on inter-war defence policy."[57] Massive in scope, it covered the strategic assessments, economic considerations, military planning, and rearmament programs of all three of the services, and the ways in which these variables were influenced by the frantic pace of global events in the 1930s. Gibbs utilized Cabinet conclusions and various official documents to analyze the crucial ramifications of rearmament on the British economy and the course of foreign policy. In regard to the significance of Thomas Inskip's *Interim Report on Defence Expenditures*, which was presented to the Cabinet in December 1937, Gibbs quoted at length from what had been a watershed document in the formulation of rearmament policy:

> We must therefore confront our potential enemies with the risks of a long war, which they cannot face. . . . It is true that the extent of our resources imposes limitations upon the size of the defence programmes which we are able to undertake, this is only one aspect of the matter. Seen in its true perspective, the maintenance of our economic stability would more accurately be described as an essential element in our defensive strength: one which can properly be regarded as a fourth arm in defence, alongside the three defence Services, without which purely military effort would be of no avail.[58]

Inskip's theme of economic stability was embraced and promoted wholeheartedly by the Prime Minister, and this "fourth arm of defence" metaphor was a major leitmotif of the government's strategy during the Chamberlain years. Gibbs amplified this theme when he alluded to a Cabinet meeting of 16 February 1938 in which Chancellor of the Exchequer John Simon made a statement to his assembled colleagues that served to typify the administration stance on economics and rearmament, and at the same time revealed some of the growing impetus behind appeasement as a viable policy:

Simon denied that the Treasury was acting in any narrow Departmental sense in its fight to limit expenditure on defence. He reminded his colleagues once again of the great and rapid increase in defence expenditure in recent years and warned them that, in his view and that of his advisers, the expenditure of £1.65 billion on defence . . . not only placed a terrible strain on the national finances, but that it could not be increased without financial disorganisation to an extent that would weaken the resistance of the country. . . . No Minister openly disagreed with the Prime Minister that the alternatives which faced the country were either expense on a scale which carried its own dangers, or an improvement of relations with potential enemies how ever difficult it might be to find the proper compromise.[59]

The government's attitude of "business as usual" for industry (that is, rearmament efforts would proceed without hampering the peaceful commerce of private industry) would continue through 1937, at least until the *Anschluss* of 11 March 1938, when Nazi intentions to dominate Central and Eastern Europe became evident.

The *Anschluss* caused a good share of frayed nerves and hand-wringing in the Chamberlain Cabinet, and at a Cabinet meeting on 22 March, eleven days after the invasion, the Prime Minister was urging that the speed of Britain's pace of rearmament had to be quickened. Gibbs noted also that the Cabinet had determined that the idea that the course of normal trade was not to be interfered with should now be canceled.[60] More dramatically, in a House of Commons statement of 24 March 1938, Neville Chamberlain announced the acceleration of the rearmament programs, with most of the weight concentrated on the Royal Air Force and the air defence of Great Britain. Gibbs related that the Prime Minister made it clear that from that point on, it would no longer be "business as usual." However, Chamberlain was of the mind that his appeasement policy combined with a steady rearmament could deter any aggressive behavior from the dictator states, and perhaps make unnecessary any tremendous military buildup and wastage of Britain's precious but limited wealth. The Treasury would continue to slavishly husband the nation's resources and so protect its fragile economic constitution from overextension.

Much of this agonizing over tight financial control was altered radically after the war scare brought on by the Czech crisis of the summer and autumn of 1938. Gibbs commented on the Treasury's modified perceptions in the wake of Munich:

The impact of the Munich crisis broke down not so much all forms of control as control exercised on the assumption of long-term planning on a fixed financial basis. . . . What is interesting about this particular post-Munich development, and what also remained, broadly speaking, true of the increasing tempo of rearmament programmes throughout the remaining months of peace, was that there was no longer a continual effort on the part of the Treasury to set a ceiling for defence expenditure, nor were Departments asked to tailor their plans to strict overall financial limitations.[61]

In short, after Munich, the gloves were off. Six months later, Germany annexed the rump of the Czech state and effectively discredited Chamberlain's plans for a European appeasement. By the beginning of 1939, the government had also begun its planning for the expansion of the Regular Army, and "limited liability" had seen its day in the sun. In his conclusions, Gibbs credited Chamberlain for having assumed an activist role in the formulation of Britain's defense policy throughout the decade of the 1930s. He was, in Gibbs' estimation, "more responsible than any other person for Britain's grand strategy as it developed . . . to the outbreak of war."[62] If that seems like a case of damning with faint praise, it is perhaps prudent to remember the circumstances that the Prime Minister was in. Gibbs, to his credit, does that with a fair minded and rather nonjudgmental analysis of Chamberlain's efforts, which even though they were ill-starred, were far from inconsequential in nature.

An ancillary factor that weighed heavily upon British rearmament efforts was that of accurate military intelligence (or rather the dearth of it!), regarding Nazi Germany during Neville Chamberlain's tenure as Prime Minister. Realistic perceptions of the levels of German military potential relative to Britain's defensive capabilities were critical to the pace of British rearmament. In a negative sense, too often getting the true picture of Nazi capacity for conquest was much like peering into a funhouse mirror for the British, who repeatedly and badly misestimated the Reich's aggressive potential in the six years leading to the outbreak of war. A very relevant source on this crucial topic was the 1985 publication of *The Ultimate Enemy: British Intelligence and Nazi Germany, 1932–1939*, by Wesley Wark. The author stated that it was the egregious misjudgments of German striking power, in one direction or another, that hampered any clear-sighted view from Whitehall on the proper policy for these perilous times. At the outset of the Nazi regime in 1933, according to Wark, Britain's perceptions of German capabilities were of necessity much different than they would be at the time of Munich, and he pondered the less than accurate estimations on both counts:

> The reception of intelligence is shaped above all by expectations on the part of policy makers and military strategists about what should happen. Faulty expectations are at the heart of intelligence failures. The preconceptions the British authorities did bring to the earliest phases of their study of the Third Reich were usually a compound of parochial British thinking about how rearmament should be managed, applied to the German case, and of rosy-tinted misconceptions about the nature of the Nazi regime.[63]

The underestimations of the early 1930s would be contrasted, as the decade advanced, with what Wark repeatedly cited as "worst case scenarios" of German capabilities to annihilate the major cities of Britain with overwhelmingly destructive aerial power. With the benefits of hindsight we now realize that even at the time of Munich, with the Channel ports still in French hands, the Germans had nowhere near the death-dealing capability in the skies that many Britons had feared they possessed. The drama of trenches under construction in St. James' Park in late September 1938 belied the actual truth of the matter, namely, that the danger of German air attack, if it existed, was very minimal.[64] This tendency to "fear the worst" from the Germans actually strengthened Chamberlain in his tireless pursuit of a European appeasement, leading the government to avoid analysis of Nazi Germany's weak points. According to the author:

> At the time of the Munich crisis, a highly cohesive military intelligence picture of Nazi Germany had been put together. This picture, while suggesting that Germany was now in a very good position to use force to destroy Czechoslovakia and to manipulate the balance of power in Europe, excluded, significantly, all those pieces of information that pointed to German unreadiness for a long war or uneasiness about its prospect.[65]

Wark commented cogently on the consequences of Britain's less-than-prescient intelligence gathering at the time of Munich:

> It is possible to speculate that better intelligence on the German army, in terms of an earlier understanding of the menace posed by German rearmament, might well have improved the British reading of the bal-

ance of power in the crucial months of the spring and summer of 1938 and might even have altered the timetable of the British decision to oppose Hitler by force. What is less likely is that better intelligence alone, without a radical change of strategic and financial priorities as they affected the three British services, would have improved the readiness of the British army for war in Europe.[66]

Wark chronicled the establishment of the IIC or Industrial Intelligence Centre, the organization most intimately concerned with monitoring German economic preparations. He stressed that the IIC was founded on the recognition of the interlocking nature of economics and military power in industrial states; it shared and propagated the conviction that Germany had been planning for total war, especially in the latter half of the 1930s.[67] In 1937 the Foreign Office requested of Desmond Morton, the IIC director, a research paper outlining reasons why Germany seemed able to follow a massive rearmament program and export arms as well.[68] Morton's reply to the F.O., quoted by Wark, proved illuminating in the differences it raised between the German and British forms of government:

> Morton found the root of Britain's rearmament problems in her *laissez-faire* attitude to defense economics. [In Morton's words], "I think that we must be wasting a great deal of money as a result of our lack of planning, lack of method, lack of decision and perhaps, above all, lack of recognition, in deed as well as words, that Industry and Economics must be regarded in modern war as a fourth arm of Defence and must therefore be allowed to play a larger part in Defence councils."[69]

This in contrast to the systematic and all-encompassing rearmament sanctioned by Chamberlain's antagonists in Berlin. Up through the time of the Munich conference and the five months leading to the Nazi sack of Prague, Chamberlain was reluctant to gear the economy totally toward rearmament. Wark cited a May 1938 Cabinet meeting as illustrative of the Premier's motivation to avoid state control of the British economy:

> Chamberlain rejected the idea that the British state could intervene in the economy in the way that the Nazi state had done. There could be no imitation of the "tremendous measures" for control over labor, of the "elaborate measures" for control of raw materials, or of the "drastic technical devices and stratagems in the region of finance." . . . Britain was significantly behind Germany in rearmament, could not imitate the Nazi system, and therefore could not hope to rival the Ger-

man rearmament effort. Totalitarianism, in an economic perspective, was seen as an efficient means to an end—the end being industrial mobilization for total war. Democratic regimes, by contrast, possessed no comparable means to this end.[70]

This notion of economics as a "fourth arm of defence" made it ultimately impossible for Chamberlain to commit his economy totally toward rearmament for a war he desperately hoped would never occur.

In regard to Chamberlain's Chiefs of Staff and their views of international relations in Europe, Wark stressed their dark foreboding in the months preceding the apogee of the Czech crisis in the summer and autumn of 1938. On the Chief of Staff, he stated:

> They feared war in 1938, having schooled themselves in pessimism since 1936; they used a bleak picture of the military balance to urge the government toward greater defence spending; and they pressed for diplomatic solutions. The political risks of taking such a stand were slight; such warnings were entirely compatible with the Chamberlain administration's policy of appeasement.[71]

Wark cited his conclusions on British intelligence in the period immediately preceding Munich and he charged that the overweening sense of impending disaster in the sanctums of Whitehall soured any chance for a sober, clear-eyed analysis of Nazi strengths and weaknesses, playing into the hands of the Prime Minister's policy. Alluding to the two years between the autumn of 1936 and late 1938, Wark stressed:

> British appeasement policy, under a new prime minister, Neville Chamberlain, reached its high point. Undeniably, this policy was influenced by the pessimism that flowed from intelligence circles. The near and medium-term military balance was presumed to be perilous, a perception that was instrumental in convincing the cabinet to avoid the dangers of any attempt at deterrence, above all during the Munich crisis. An Anglo-German confrontation was thereby postponed, yet the German armed forces of September 1938 in terms of war readiness and overall mobilized strength, were a much inferior foe compared to the military machine that performed so impressively in the campaigns of 1940.[72]

Chamberlain's near obsession with a balanced budget and stable domestic economy meant that no matter the international danger, the "fourth arm of defence" would remain a dominant theme of British strategy at least until the war scare of September 1938. The dreary, often flawed assessments of Britain's intelligence community regarding German capabilities did little to galvanize British spirits for a war that no one wanted. Wark's contribution to the understanding of appeasement detailed the crucial nature of credible and accurate intelligence and the use of the same in the formulation of a state's foreign policy, in this case a policy as risk-laden as was Chamberlain's appeasement.

A useful correlation to the outstanding group of sources on economics and rearmament that have been cited here are a few relevant journal articles, too brief to be published in book form, but whose ideas nevertheless deserve a precise examination in order to garner their insights for our use. This can only serve to add to the collective comprehension in regard to these critical entities that influenced the Prime Minister's appeasement policy. The first of these was written in 1972 by F. Coghlan of the University of New Brunswick, in the journal *History*, and was entitled "Armaments, Economic Policy and Appeasement: Background to British Foreign Policy, 1931–1937." These were incidentally the years that Neville Chamberlain served as the Chancellor of the Exchequer, and his influence there was as dominant as any has been in this century. Coghlan took exception with those who believed that the economic complexities of the time drove Britain's leaders into a fearful shell of inactivity. "It would be too strong to conclude that Britain's will to rearm was paralysed by economic arguments but the latter were powerful and were advanced by persuasive parties on all sides."[73]

Coghlan clearly outlined the perspective of then Chancellor Chamberlain, whose strong personality and work ethic placed him in a position while at the Treasury as the indisputable heir apparent to the ailing Prime Minister Stanley Baldwin.

> To the mind of Neville Chamberlain . . . this national consensus of opinion, supporting the restriction of expenditure on arms, confirmed views which he had held for years. Social expenditure was much more congenial to him than arms expenses, and he was deeply aware of the country's great need for more education, better housing and social welfare.[74]

The irony is that this self-avowed man of peace, due to external events on the continent of Europe over which he in reality had little or no control, would be obliged to head the nation during the fateful years of Britain's rearmament efforts. Coghlan sought to mete out a justifiable blame for the charge that the government was dilatory in its rearmament efforts of the middle and late 1930s, in the face of a systematic German rearmament campaign that threatened the equilibrium of Europe. Coghlan's assessments on that theme:

> The British Cabinet's reluctance to commit itself to full rearmament in the years from 1931 to 1937, owed much to sympathy with disarmament ideals as well as to economic fears and the determination of a democratic government to have the cheapest possible defence system. . . . Yet in assessing the degree of responsibility among the "appeasers" in successive Cabinets, it should be noted that no man enjoyed more authority than Neville Chamberlain and played a greater role in establishing policies which made the ultimate appeasement policy seem the only logical line to all save the few outside Government circles. . . . In 1937, Chamberlain used his assumption of the Premiership to gain control of foreign affairs, and his replacement of Eden by Halifax and Vansittart by Cadogan can be seen as evidence of his determination to complete his economic plans through the appeasing of European tensions, a programme which he believed threatened by those who wished to take a strong line towards Italy and Germany.[75]

To a man who intensely condemned war as an instrument of policy, Chamberlain seemed, according to Coghlan, ill-fitted for a time in which all Europe hung on the edge of the abyss. Coghlan alluded to a Chamberlain statement from 1937 that revealed his anxieties with the necessarily increased spending on the weapons of war. "I cannot dismiss the hope that we and the other nations of Europe will presently find some less suicidal way of ending our fears and suspicions of one another before we are all ruined by our efforts to defend ourselves."[76]

To that end, Chamberlain resolved to embrace the dual policies of limited rearmament with a foreign policy that sought to remove the bona fide grievances that threatened the security of Europe and necessarily the world. As Coghlan would perceptively note, however, in the face of the dictator states on the march, Chamberlain could find few adversaries as rational and responsible as himself. The absence of a conventional field force of any weight could only serve to underawe the Nazi and Fascist leaderships, ever ready to subjugate a lesser neighbor if an opportunity arose. Coghlan stated his conclusions on appeasement and Chamberlain's legacy, utilizing the cautious pace of rearmament in the mid 1930s to illustrate a forceful analogy:

> Limited expenditures implied limited commitments, as Harold Nicolson pointed out in a letter to the *New Statesman*, 15 February 1936, when he wrote that Britain must either face up to vastly increased expenditures on armaments or desist from making threats to the aggressors. With the success of his domestic economic policies in mind, Chamberlain was content to follow the latter part of this advice. Appeasement was the result not of the decisions of 1938 but of the economic currents and fiscal policies of the post-1919 period, which severely circumscribed the options available to the British governments of the 'thirties.[77]

One other source that bears mention in our rearmament survey is Dr. George Peden's 1984 article from the Birmingham-based journal *History*, entitled "A Matter of Timing: The Economic Background to British Foreign Policy, 1937–1939." Peden credited British historians in the recent past for making an independent contribution to an understanding of "appeasement" by drawing attention to the economic factors limiting British rearmament and the resulting weakening of British diplomacy.[78] Peden, who had written a masterful book on the Treasury five years earlier, commented on the rationale behind the Treasury stances on Britain's rearmament, whether tight control or an explosion of expenditures:

> The pace of British rearmament was restricted by the Treasury so long as it was Cabinet policy to give economic stability priority over armed defence. Once the Cabinet decided to reverse that priority in 1939, Britain went on to devote a higher proportion of her gross national product to military expenditure than Germany.[79]

This overriding concern with the economic health of the nation would prove to be a double-edged sword for Chamberlain and his intimate circle. In what seems close to an actual catch-22 scenario, a nation like Britain had to be well-armed in the event of war, but there was a palpable chance, in the eyes of the government, that the rearming itself might destroy the nation's ability to defend itself because of the consequent economic collapse. Peden addressed this apparently insoluble dilemma that bedeviled the Prime Minister.

The balance struck between defensive strength and economic stability in 1937–1939 at least allowed Britain to survive the initial Nazi onslaught, and to have the financial credit to draw upon the considerable resources of the Empire and Commonwealth during the war. On the other hand, the attempt to preserve economic stability before the war, by not placing the economy on a war footing comparable to Germany's before 1939, had undoubtedly, as Halifax had remarked in December 1937, thrown "a heavy burden on diplomacy."[80]

That diplomacy, as we well know, had little if any chance of success when confronted with the aggressive lust for conquest of the "thousand-year Reich." Peden made a compelling point when he proposed that the heavy rearmament program pursued by Britain beginning in the weeks and months after Munich might well have been a contributory reason for the war itself. He concluded with a cogent analysis of those last few months:

If adequate forces for deterrence cannot be maintained indefinitely, then agreement must be sought with the potential aggressor, to remove the causes of war and to agree on a mutual reduction of armed forces. In such circumstances, if no satisfactory agreement is forthcoming, one must prepare for war. This seems to have been what happened in British policy towards Germany between 1937 and 1939. Hopes of avoiding war persisted in the summer of 1939, but the scale of defence plans from the spring of that year implied preparation for war, whereas earlier plans had been on the basis of long-term deterrence. "Appeasement" was the attempt to remove the causes of war before the economic burden of armaments made war inevitable.[81]

This chapter has attempted to make comprehensible the byzantine relationship between interwar British economics and an erratic series of rearmament efforts, and how these critical entities influenced the Prime Minister's untiring crusade to create a peaceful Europe by means of a thoroughgoing appeasement of grievances. To Chamberlain's credit, arguably no one of his age worked harder or applied himself with a greater pertinacity toward the solution of a country's problems, both in the foreign and domestic spheres. When one relates his workaholic tendencies and innate sense of responsibility to the burdens of his office with comparable political figures of the present, many modern-day politicians would appear to be on perennial vacations. When one views the total spectrum of arguably insoluble problems facing his administration, then ponders specifically the economic and military realities, one must wonder if there indeed were viable answers. Could Neville Chamberlain, if he had been more successful, have driven the events of the day rather than always being forced to react to an enemy's fait accompli, been a proactive leader rather than a reactive one? In the final analysis, the study of the economic and military considerations is imperative for a true comprehension of appeasement.

7

Appeasement and the British Print Media

THE TROUBLED RELATIONSHIP BETWEEN THE CHAMBERLAIN ADMINIS-tration and the British print media during the appeasement years could not have occurred without impacting both entities dramatically. Chamberlain has often been accused of muzzling the press to protect his foreign policy initiatives. The "quality" press, especially *The Times*, have been charged with having been so willing an agent of the Premier's wishes that to characterize them as supine might be an understatement.[1] This chapter will chronicle the print media's influence on the policy of appeasement, and perhaps more importantly and conversely, the effect of Chamberlain's appeasement on the British press. Seemingly apocryphal outrages such as the rumor that *Times* editor Geoffrey Dawson had regular communications with the German Embassy before printing anything he perceived as anti-German will be probed for their veracity, and a number of sources will be utilized. Surely the print media played a pivotal role in Chamberlain's disquieting slide from the dizzying heights of "peace for our time" on 30 September 1938 to the agony of early May 1940 and his fall from power. This curious and uncomfortable reciprocity between the government and the press will be examined closely for its ramifications upon Neville Chamberlain's policies.

A valuable source on Britain's press and appeasement was *The History of The Times: The 150th Anniversary and Beyond, 1912–1948*, edited by Stanley Morison, et al., in 1952. This exacting effort, covering nearly two eventful generations of the history of Britain's flagship newspaper, justifiably allocated a seventy-page chapter to "Appeasement, 1933–1938." A reference to the sentiment of *The Times* in June 1933, just five months after the Nazis came to power, alluded to the possibility of future British concessions to the Germans to assuage them for their unfair treatment in the immediate aftermath of the Great War and the flawed Versailles Treaty, which had bedeviled Anglo-German relations for nearly fifteen years. The article from 28 June 1933 stated: "Europe in fact is placed in the dilemma of having to refuse to force what reason suggests should at least in part be conceded, or else of yielding to extremism what earlier was refused to moderation."[2] Morison pondered the significance of the above statement:

> This was a position from which the paper did not recede until the spring of 1939. For six years the paper saw no reason why an action that was justified by ethics and politics before January, 1933, should be held to be falsified by the events of the 30th of that month. A political concession made to a possible friend was not distinguished from one made to a probable enemy, because Britain could not imagine that Germany would ever again be her probable enemy.[3]

This almost baffling sense of a lack of ideology among the authorities at *The Times* was an attitude they shared with Neville Chamberlain, who as a lifelong Victorian businessman felt sure that he could "do business" with anyone in order to secure the peace of the world. The longtime editor of *The Times*, Geoffrey Dawson, had likewise a signal lack of ideology with regard to European politics, and strongly supported Prime Minister Chamberlain in every way possible. In an ironic twist, Dawson wrote a letter to his one-time Geneva correspondent for *The Times*, H. G. Daniels, which complained about the virulent attacks in Germany upon the British press on 23 May 1937, just days before Chamberlain accepted the seals of office and became Prime Minister on the twenty-eighth of that month. Morison cited Dawson's letter to Daniels, which reflected the long-term view of *The Times* toward appeasement:

> It would really interest me to know precisely what it is in *The Times* that has produced this antagonism in Germany. I did my utmost, night after night, to keep out of the paper anything that might hurt their susceptibilities. I can really think of nothing that has been printed now for many months past which they could possibly take exception as unfair comment. . . . I should be more grateful than I can say for any explanation and guidance, for I have always been convinced that the peace of the world depends more than anything else on our getting into reasonable relations with Germany.[4]

To Dawson as well as to Chamberlain, a European war was an obscenity to be avoided at all costs, and the Sudeten German controversy of the spring and summer of 1938 was to be settled accordingly. Many in positions of authority in Britain were rather more sympathetic to German claims of self-determination for the Sudeten Germans than they were for Czechoslovakia as a nation. Among the most crucial opinions were those of editor Geoffrey Dawson and his right-hand man, assistant editor Robin (actually Robert) McGowan Barrington-Ward. One or the other of these men would edit *The Times* through the interwar years, then through the most destructive war in human history, and on to 1948.[5] In early September 1938, Dawson would cause quite a stir by creating a *Times* leader that suggested that the Sudetenland should be ceded to the Reich. Within a month's time it would be, and Morison commented on examples of the outright vapidity of both *The Times* and the government, whose lack of vision was appalling in the circumstances.

> The makers of the Munich policy were convinced that they were rendering a service to Czechoslovakia and to civilization. It was not understood after 1936 that the question was not whether the West should fight for Czechoslovakia, but that the West should at least refrain from placing the Republic in a situation where she could fight neither for herself nor the West; it was not perceived that, after the *Anschluss*, Czechoslovakia, shorn of the frontiers of the Kingdom of Bohemia which had been unchanged since 1198, would be powerless. It was not seen that, with or without an international guarantee to Czechoslovakia, Germany would gain an increase of population and the release of the troops which had hitherto been set aside to deal with the 35–40 Czech divisions. On the contrary, it was firmly believed in Printing House Square that the Republic would be "stronger" for these losses and the reduction of risks; it was only necessary to compass an ethical solution by an agreed acceptance of German demands. The consequences to Europe would be what they would be. The rectitude of British policy must be vindicated; nor was it seen that German claims did not repose upon a sound ethical basis.[6]

The editor of *The History of the Times* concisely summarized the denouement of the Munich Conference, when the heart of the Czech state was eviscerated to prevent a wider European war, with the relieved imprimatur of London and Paris. Chamberlain's hysterical popularity in Britain and the world in the immediate aftermath of Munich was a testament to the critical importance of a supportive mass media, especially a trusted "mouthpiece" like *The Times*, whose support for the Chamberlain administration was unquestioned until the sack of Prague in March 1939. Morison's parting shot on Munich:

In the spring of 1936 and in the autumn of 1938 *The Times* failed to assess correctly the importance of a close understanding with France, and to recognize that the liberation of Germany from the restrictions of Versailles could be a safe policy only if conducted in agreement with France. . . . Britain sought to rely instead, with the eager support of *The Times*, on a policy of revision by "negotiation" and "agreed settlement"; in effect it amounted to a surrender to agitation and pressure short of the use of armed force. Dawson and Barrington-Ward failed to see that Munich was not an agreed settlement; that the Czechoslovak republic had not freely negotiated; that the conditions essential to a stable Europe were not present; that Germany had accomplished her will against the consciences of Britain and France; and that she had done so by the possession of superior striking power and the will, behind the threat, to use it—not merely against Czechoslovakia but against Britain and France.[7]

One of the dangers of any analysis of appeasement's effect on the British print media is that one might surmise that *The History of the Times* is indeed the history of all British print news of that period, because of the intimidating international reputation of *The Times* as a spokesman for Chamberlain's views. This was certainly not the case, and although Britain's print media were far from unanimous in their views, *The Times*, because of its storied reputation and the volume of news and analysis it printed, was indeed one of the most dominant voices. *The History of the Times* is a necessary background source for any research into those critical issues.

One cannot complete a study of appeasement's effect on the British media without consulting a biography of one of the dedicated "archpriests" of appeasement, *Times* editor Geoffrey Dawson. John Evelyn Wrench wrote the earliest and most renowned, *Geoffrey Dawson and Our Times*, which was published in 1955. Wrench noted correctly that either Dawson or his close aide, assistant editor Robin Barrington-Ward, personally were responsible for the majority of leader articles on the front pages of *The Times* in the critical days of the late 1930s. Wrench cited a *Times* article from 28 October 1937 entitled "The Claim to Colonies," in which Dawson decried the popular assumption that Germany should be treated as an outlaw nation in violation of the Treaty of Versailles. Dawson's words were illustrative:

Every article of statesmanship suggests that a halt should be called to a process which must otherwise lead to war and to the downfall of civilization in the West. Let us at least be clear at what point a stand should be made, and let us make a supreme effort, so far as Great Britain is concerned, to do what is possible for appeasement before that point is reached.[8]

On this point, Wrench offered a digression on the differing meanings of the term "appeasement," specifying how the secondary definition had evolved:

It is proposed here to note that the word "appeasement" is used in the primary sense, of "bringing about a peaceful settlement." Bitter critics of this country's foreign policy on the eve of the Second World War have since made it a mere term of abuse, signifying "the propitiation (at all costs) of him who is angry." It is a healthy corrective to refer to this sober statement of an unchallengeable aim by *The Times* in 1937.[9]

Neville Chamberlain would discover a true soulmate in Geoffrey Dawson as far as support for an overall European appeasement in the late 1930s was concerned. Dawson, who had first served as editor-in-chief of *The Times* as early as 1912, resumed that role in 1922 after *The Times* had suffered a rather disastrous interlude under the leadership of Alfred Northcliffe. Dawson, fully and securely ensconced in the editorship by 1923, would serve uninterrupted in that capacity until late 1941, when his hand-picked successor Barrington-Ward would assume the post. He, like Chamberlain, wanted desperately to avoid a European war that could possibly rival the carnage of 1914–1918. Wrench articulated the relationship of these two powerful figures in the eye of the "gathering storm":

Geoffrey remained in close contact with Neville Chamberlain during the latter's premiership, lasting three years, and was in entire agreement with the policy of appeasement, and despite the stupendous difficulties he too was steadfastly seeking a way of escape from the catastrophe of another world war. A study of the records available certainly gives the impression that Chamberlain valued the Editor's opinion and was strengthened in his own views by the knowledge that Geoffrey agreed with his policy and would support it in *The Times*. ... There is no doubt that both Geoffrey and the Prime Minister felt that almost any sacrifice should be made to prevent Armageddon. They knew full well that the First World War had not, in fact, been the "war to end war," and they also were agreed that if a second World war were to begin it was impossible to foresee when or where it would end.[10]

Wrench credited the Prime Minister and Geoffrey Dawson for the realization that Britain was in no position to defy the Nazis in 1938 over the Czech crisis, and he argued that Chamberlain's good sense in playing for time at Munich allowed the rearmament that saved the country during the Battle of Britain.[11] This was a popular argument in defense of Chamberlain back in the 1950s, in the years before it was widely realized that the Germans profited more from their own rearmament efforts during this period than did the British. Wrench cited the public reaction immediately after Munich in regard to letters sent to Dawson:

> If there were some critics of the European policy of *The Times*, which there undoubtedly were, the great majority of the readers endorsed the paper's attitude. Geoffrey received very large numbers of letters congratulating the paper on its leadership in the autumn of 1938. Many writers considered the plight of Europe was in part due to the terms of the Versailles Treaty of 1919. Many correspondents rejoiced that the paper refused to stir up hatred and suspicion between the European Powers.[12]

Of course, the hopes of Chamberlain's administration for a comprehensive European appeasement were dashed by the events of March 1939, when the duplicitous Germans seized the remainder of the Czech state that they had successfully emasculated at Munich. Dawson was similarly crestfallen by the failure of appeasement, but he remained amenable to any sort of agreement that would obviate a widespread war, even in the perilous days of late August 1939, after the shocking Nazi-Soviet Nonaggression Pact had been signed. In a *Times* article of 28 August 1939, Dawson dealt with the political situation on the very brink of war, and Wrench quoted his words:

> Public attention must needs be concentrated, at this eleventh hour of the gathering storm, on the communications with the German Government which have been in progress during the last two days. . . . In the meantime, however, the mere news of the Ambassador's mission provides a basis for examining the British attitude towards negotiation. . . . There is nothing in fact that might not be settled by the civilized method of negotiation if only there were confidence that negotiation would not be paralysed by threats of violence and that any resulting settlement would be honoured. It was not "Munich" that destroyed confidence in German good faith but the fact that the Munich Settlement was followed five months later by the brutal invasion of the very peoples which it was designed to preserve.[13]

Four days later the Wehrmacht invaded Poland, and over that weekend Britain went to war, the war that Chamberlain and Dawson had striven so mightily to avoid. The final insight into Geoffrey Dawson's motivation as editor-in-chief for well nigh the entirety of the interwar period came from a sentimental letter he wrote to former Prime Minister Neville Chamberlain on 9 October 1940, upon the announcement that the illness that would soon take Chamberlain's life had forced him to retire from politics. Wrench quoted that poignant communication:

> The Conservative meeting this afternoon seems to set the seal on your decision to retire from active public life, and I, for one, am profoundly saddened by it. As I told you you the other day, I am an impenitent supporter of "Munich"—whatever that may mean to the people who use it as a term of reproach. No one could have sat in this place, as I did during the autumn of '38, without realizing that a war at that time and on that issue would have bewildered and antagonized all the British Dominions and found even this country deeply divided. I have never admired anything more than your courage in averting it then— unless it be your courage in recognizing that, in spite of all your efforts, it was inevitable when it eventually came. I have no doubt at all that history will take this view.[14]

In spite of Dawson's confidence, the historiographical debate on the efficacy of Chamberlain's actions is still very much alive today. John Wrench's biography of the leading supporter of the policy of appeasement in the British media is a source of critical importance.

A source that added to the existing documentation on *The Times* and its interwar support of appeasement was a work on Robin Barrington-Ward, the assistant editor of *The Times* from 1927 to 1941, and then editor-in-chief from late 1941 until his death in 1948. Written by Donald McLachlan, *In the Chair: Barrington-Ward of the Times, 1927–1948* was published in 1971. Barrington-Ward had worked shoulder to shoulder with Geoffrey Dawson in the formulation of *The Times'* editorials and leader articles that did so much to mold public opinion in the years leading to the September 1939 war. McLachlan duly credited his subject's dedication in the illusory pursuit of a European appeasement:

> Barrington-Ward wrote most of the leading articles which argued obstinately, through crisis and calm, for understanding with Nazi Ger-

many, and it was he who decided for the most part what articles of a descriptive or argumentative kind should appear on the right-hand side of the leader page.[15]

On the question of whether Barrington-Ward and Dawson ever truncated news reports to prevent hurt feelings among the Germans, McLachlan offered that the practice was simply part of the business of printing a newspaper. He alluded to the famous Dawson letter of 23 May 1937 to H. G. Daniels (which became an symbol of appeasement over its obviously deferential tone toward Berlin) in order to shed light upon the practices of the elite in Printing House Square:

> Whatever may be said generally of the restrained editorial attitude towards Germany, neither Dawson or Barrington-Ward was taking pains to suppress news offensive to Berlin for some time before and after the date of the letter to Daniels. . . . Whoever was in the chair had a right to suppress or limit publication of emotional, sarcastic and sometimes violent letters about the Nazis and German internal conditions (of which there were plenty) so long as he believed a general settlement to be possible.[16]

The fact that both Barrington-Ward and Dawson were, whether deliberately or inadvertently, acting as censors for Neville Chamberlain rather cuts across the grain of the notion of a "free press," but offers clear evidence as to the high level of public support the Prime Minister's policy had in the eighteen months before the Munich Conference. The upshot was that *The Times* was recognized as a virtual "mouthpiece" for policies emanating from Whitehall.

A sorrowful letter written by Barrington-Ward to George Ferguson of the *Winnipeg Free Press* on 27 April 1939 defended the Chamberlain administration's pursuit of appeasement, even as the March 1939 destruction of the Czech state had rendered the policy obsolete. The Canadian paper, of which Ferguson was assistant editor, had been critical of British policy toward Germany. McLachlan quoted Barrington-Ward's letter as the latter leveled some withering criticism at a Chamberlain critic:

> What would you have put in the place of "appeasement" in the then existing circumstances? Unconditional encirclement? Would you have fought, and would Canada have fought, to prevent the re-occupation of the Rhineland, the *Anschluss*, or the union of the Sudetenland with the Reich? Did we give the Germans at any time the hope and opportunity of accomplishing their aims peacefully?[17]

McLachlan continued by delineating what Chamberlain's policy of appeasement meant explicitly to Barrington-Ward in the exercise of his duties with *The Times*, at least up through 15 March 1939:

> Appeasement to him meant exhausting every possibility of negotiation before accepting the inevitability of war as the basis of national policy. Even if he had admitted to himself that the Nazis were greater villains then he had believed, there would have remained the question of what precisely was to be done against each act of aggression. He did not believe in bluff. . . . "Resistance to aggression" meant in fact readiness for war; and readiness for war meant the ability to defend Britain against German air attack and a public opinion convinced that there was no alternative.[18]

To Barrington-Ward, Dawson, and Chamberlain, the desire to go the extra mile (in Chamberlain's case in September 1938 several hundred extra miles) to find a peaceful settlement to the "gathering storm" hovering over Europe was their absolute priority. The avoidance of the abattoir that was the legacy of the Great War drove the editor and assistant editor of *The Times* to great lengths in their desperation to obviate a conflict that might mean the end of the tightly structured society they, along with their Prime Minister, loved so well. McLachlan's book added to the collective insight on the internal affairs of *The Times* during a supremely critical period.

A key source that examined the varying opinions of British newspapers in the years leading up to the outbreak of war was *The British Press and Germany, 1936–1939*, by Franklin R. Gannon, published in 1971. In his introductory chapter, aptly entitled "The Anatomy of Appeasement," Gannon stressed that the popular papers, in light of the furious competition for readership, had to give the people what they wanted, which was entertainment rather than information. To that end, in regard to their reportage on the rise of Nazi Germany, it only made sense (and cents!) to avoid critical or analytical broadsides that might heighten the temperature in the already feverish capitals of Western Europe.

> None of the popular papers, except the *Daily Mail*, actually supported or condoned Nazi Germany, but they were similarly reluctant to exacerbate international affairs by adopting a hard line towards it. Both financially and intellectually it was unwise or impossible for the British

Press to adopt a strongly critical line towards Nazi Germany: the readers did not want to read it, and the intellectuals did not want to write it.[19]

Gannon pondered the ideological makeup of the men who controlled Britain's newspapers; he contended that the gulf between outright "appeasers" and those critical of Chamberlain's policy was much wider after the war than it ever had been between March 1936 and September 1939.

> With one or two minor exceptions, the journalists and editors of the British Press between the wars were men who thought of themselves as liberals in the broadest sense of the term: the paradox is that they were all right, or very nearly right, in so thinking. Understanding of this seeming paradox is fundamental to any proper understanding of the policy and psychology of appeasement of Germany. . . . It was the seeming vindication of one side with the coming of war in 1939 which gave easy rise to the forgetting—and, in some cases, the deliberate obfuscation—of the common ground shared by appeasers and anti-appeasers of Germany. The war seemed to prove beyond doubt or cavil that appeasement had been a short-sighted policy from the outset.[20]

The claim that appeasement as a policy was roundly vilified as a result of its failure and the resulting outbreak of war is hardly to be challenged; the crucial question is, just where were these stout legions of antiappeasers on 30 September 1938, when Neville Chamberlain basked in the afterglow of his triumph, hailed as the peacemaker of the world?

Gannon's major achievement was to analyze the views of most of the important dailies, and to consider their positions for or against Chamberlain's appeasement policy. In reference to the *Daily Mail*, it was the only one that openly condoned the policies and unashamedly claimed admiration for Nazi Germany. Dominated by Lord Rothermere, it envisioned the robust Nazi state as a strong bulwark against the much more dangerous Asiatic Bolshevism emanating from the Soviet Union. As for Lord Beaverbrook's *Daily Express*, its own raison d'être was nothing more than what it perceived as splendid isolation from the world and cultivation of the Empire and ties with the United States.[21] According to Gannon, the *News Chronicle* was in the top five in circulation; its ideology was that of the old Liberal Party. The author made the interesting assertion that the *News Chronicle* was the paper that most annoyed the Nazis with its reportage back to Britain of events inside Germany. An enlightening sidebar to the role

of the *News Chronicle* occurred in the first few days of 1939, when
H. G. Wells published editorial articles in the *Chronicle* that contained predictions for 1939. His criticism of the Nazi regime was
evidently intolerable for the German ambassador, Herbert von
Dirksen, who complained to the Foreign Secretary forthwith.
Gannon quoted Halifax as receiving the complaint that Wells had
described Hitler as a certifiable lunatic who should be put away;
the Ambassador wanted to register the strongest objection to it.[22]
The ironic consequence of this incident, reported Gannon, was
that von Dirksen later would complain in person to Chamberlain
at a social event. The Prime Minister would manifest clearly that
he himself flatly deplored these attacks and admitted that the
News Chronicle was in fact "the most dangerous British newspaper and that it had even attacked the King, the Queen, and the
British Government in an irresponsible way."[23]

Other important papers considered by Gannon were the *Daily
Herald*, the Labour Party newspaper, which had a very widespread
circulation, and the *Daily Telegraph*, which although Conservative and very much supportive of the Chamberlain government,
was closer to the Eden-Churchill line in regard to the policy
toward Nazi Germany.[24] The *Daily Telegraph* was to merge with
and swallow up another publication in late 1937, namely the
Morning Post, which was right-wing Tory and virulently anti-
Communist. Gannon alluded to Chamberlain's response when informed by Lord Lloyd in late 1937 that the *Morning Post* would
have to be sold to avoid bankruptcy: "Chamberlain reportedly told
him that he had no use for independent conservative criticism, and
that accommodation with Germany was of the utmost importance
and would only be hindered by the *Morning Post* continuing as in
the past."[25] A concise verdict by Gannon upon these two newspapers revealed some of the grave difficulties faced by those who harbored any misgivings vis-à-vis appeasement as pursued by
Whitehall:

> Both the *Daily Telegraph* and the *Morning Post* represented British
> conservative opposition to Nazism. Their reservations about the pol-
> icy of appeasement could not be implemented because they supported
> the Government on other seemingly equally important issues, and also
> because they realized that there was no possible acceptable alternative
> to Chamberlain.[26]

Among the newspapers that published only on Sundays, *The
Observer* was one of the most renowned, and certainly the oldest,

having been founded in 1791. It was led by its editor-in-chief, J. L. Garvin, a figure Gannon referred to as the British press's most outspoken Czechophobe.[27] A virulent critic of the Treaty of Versailles, Garvin perceived that Chamberlain was totally justified in coming to the end he did at the Munich Conference, even if it meant the betrayal of a weaker ally. As Gannon would relate, however, after the mask was removed by the Nazi sack of Prague in March 1939, there would be no more ardent anti-Nazi in the British press than Garvin.[28] A very insightful vignette cited by Gannon would corroborate Garvin's change of heart. In a June 1939 meeting with the brilliant German Rhodes scholar Adam von Trott zu Solz, who would ironically perish later in the anti-Nazi resistance, Garvin made a statement closer to the later Churchillian genre than anything a good appeaser would have dared to offer: "Garvin . . . was deeply depressed and pessimistic, and let it be understood that it was better to end an honourable history of 800 years with a desperate struggle, rather than allow oneself to be kicked around like a fool and a coward."[29] The other well-known Sunday paper was the *Sunday Times*. Its stance was pro-Chamberlain, favoring an Anglo-German settlement to avoid any cause for war, and its major foreign voice on foreign affairs from the 1920s until 1940 was Herbert Sidebotham, better known by his nom de plume of "Scrutator." Gannon pointed out that Scrutator was praised in his era for his "brilliant maturity and often uncanny insight"; a colleague insisted of his articles that "no others . . . then written were more widely and attentively read by influential people."[30] However, the author took Scrutator to task for his slavish obeisance to one of the more repelling regimes of recent human history.

> In the light of events . . . the Scrutator articles on Germany and Anglo-German relations seem examples of the most extreme kind of appeasement, ignoring not only the menacing external actions of the Nazi regime, but also the internal policies and barbarisms which even most of the ardent appeasers found repugnant.[31]

In essence, this lack of an ideological judgment of the Nazis was analogous to Neville Chamberlain's attitude, the notorious "blinders mentality," that would haunt the Prime Minister after the failure of his efforts for peace.

Among other notable daily papers, Gannon credited *The Times* as a worthy source of accuracy and more importantly, consistency, in its editorials and leaders referring to international affairs. An allusion to the events of September 1938 concerned Geoffrey

Dawson's irritation at a possible libel committed against *The Times*'s esteemed reputation, and Gannon cited the situation:

It is very likely that the threat of severe legal action was used against Claud Cockburn whose newsletter *The Week* had claimed in a special number of 8 September 1938 that that *The Times*'s famous leader of 7 September had been sent to the German Embassy in Carlton House Terrace for approval before publication, and on 14 September that it was in fact a long-standing rule at Printing House Square that all editorial items relating to Germany be sent there for vetting.[32]

However, Gannon dispelled this notion with a categorical denial of any deliberate or systematic censorship of unpalatable news by either Dawson or his chief deputy, Assistant Editor Robin Barrington-Ward, during their respective tenures "in the Chair." The close relationship between the top two men at *The Times* and the Premier served to fuel rumors of pro-German censorship on Fleet Street, but Gannon strongly denied any such behavior:

To think that Dawson would intervene to censor news he found disagreeable from his own or the paper's point of view is to understand neither the paper nor the man. It also neglects to take into account the journalistic integrity of the people whose work would thus be censored for policy, and, especially in domestic affairs, a well-informed readership which would be immediately aware of any such tendentiousness.[33]

Gannon credited *The Times* with having especial relevance for the modern scholar, when he noted that it remained "the best and most complete source of reliable contemporary information about, and assessments of, events in Germany."[34]

Lastly, Gannon credited the *Manchester Guardian* with having long been committed to an attitude that held that the Versailles Treaty was flawed and unjustified, along with what Gannon perceived as "the overriding determination that war must never again be the arbiter of man's affairs."[35] Its outstanding political reporter Frederick Voigt, named as the greatest British political journalist of the 1930s by Gannon, was a clear-eyed veteran of international intrigue who saw the Nazis as the revolutionary threat they were well before the war was forced upon the West by the signing of the Nazi-Soviet Pact in August 1939. Indeed, as Gannon argued, Voigt was prescient enough to predict the eventual alliance of Berlin and Moscow: "It was his philosopher's foresight which enabled Voigt to see that both Communism and Nazism were threats to the West. . . . He understood that Russia and Germany were not unlikely partners on the basis of their common interests."[36] Gannon concluded his analysis of the *Manchester Guardian* with a clearly evident insight into the treacherous waters that would have to be navigated by many of the British dailies in those dangerous days of the impending cataclysm.

> From 1933 to 1939 the *Manchester Guardian* had a clear conception of what Nazi Germany was and what it meant. Because of other commitments and ideals, however, it was unable to draw the logical conclusions of this insight and was forced, each time it was confronted with the continual German heinousness it had always predicted, suddenly to urge tolerance and moderation either because war was unthinkable, or because no one's conscience was wholly clear, or for whatever reason.[37]

This impressive synthesis of the editorial stances of at least ten major British papers, in regard to Britain's difficult relationship with Nazi Germany in the three years leading to war, is a valuable research tool for any thorough study of Chamberlain and the print media. It clearly evidences the great popularity that Neville Chamberlain would enjoy while there was a possibility his efforts on the international stage would succeed.

A far more critical source that charged the Prime Minister with deliberate and systematic manipulation of the British Press is found in *The Abuse of Power: The War Between Downing Street and the Media from Lloyd George to Callaghan*, by James Margach, published in 1978. Margach, a news correspondent for some forty-four years, wrote individual chapters on the experiences of most of the twentieth-century Prime Ministers with the media, and his work on Neville Chamberlain is very relevant to this study. His personal acquaintance with all of the Premiers beginning with Baldwin added to the plausibility of his commentary, which was none too supportive of Chamberlain.

> Neville Chamberlain was the first Prime Minister to employ news management on a grand scale. His aim had nothing remotely to do with open Government, access to information and the strengthening of the democratic process; it had everything to do with the exploitation of the press to espouse and defend Government thinking. From the moment he entered No. 10 in 1937 he sought to manipulate the Press into supporting his policy of appeasing the dictators. As he became increasingly passionate over appeasement and the more it came under attack from the media, the more he abandoned persuasion, turning instead to the use of threats and suppression to coerce the Press into co-

operation. . . . Finally, in order to cling to power Chamberlain was prepared to abuse truth itself. He made the most misleading and inaccu-
rate statements which he was determined to see published so as to
make his policies appear credible and successful. Quite simply, he told
lies.[38]

Margach's vitriol was aimed also at Geoffrey Dawson, editor.
Here the author clashed with Franklin Gannon's analysis that
there was no deliberate news censorship of articles critical to the
dictators:

The conduct of Dawson and *The Times* is a reflection of events across
Fleet Street, but in magnified form. Not only did Dawson excise vital
pieces from foreign correspondents' despatches, especially from Berlin, lest they give offence . . . he even slipped in comments of his own,
completely distorting the balance of the reports in the hope of comforting and currying favour with the Nazi leaders. Dawson's actions con-
stitute a frightful warning to everybody, at whatever level, in the
media: the integrity and independence of journalism is in grave jeopardy when the media become active participants in the affairs of Government and Whitehall.[39]

In Margach's estimation the overweening hubris of Neville Chamberlain made him dead certain that his policy was the only one
possible in the circumstances, which made him less than charitable when subjected to media criticism. Margach made a strong
statement on the Premier's bullying behavior: "I am in no doubt
that Chamberlain's dictatorial personal influence on newspaper
proprietors, editors and writers made his Premiership, in my experience, the most inglorious period in the history of the British
Press."[40] Ironically, the same single-minded sense of purpose that
drove Chamberlain to move mountains to avoid war would condemn him as a target of obloquy when the foundation of his appeasement policy collapsed like a house of cards in March 1939.
Margach commented on the peacemaker's tragic fall:

Despite, or because of, his ruthless Press manipulation over at least six
years, he experienced a disastrously bad Press when his appeasement
policies collapsed in ruins on the outbreak of war. Newspapers started
campaigning for him to go because they could not understand how the
Man of Munich could become the Man of Victory.[41]

It is interesting to note that Margach ascribed a greater influence
than usual to Chamberlain at the Exchequer, when he alluded to
the "six years" of press manipulation, though the premiership

lasted barely thirty-six months. His criticisms of Neville Chamberlain's abuses of the British Press reflected the tenor of a more sophisticated and multifaceted scholarship characteristic of the last fifteen years, and he lent some added controversy to the appeasement debate.

Any chapter on the British press and its relationship with Chamberlain's policy of appeasement would be seriously vitiated without mention of the exhaustive two-volume work by historian Stephen Koss, *The Rise and Fall of the Political Press in Britain*. Volume Two, which covers the twentieth century, was published in 1984. Koss devoted two chapters, essentially sixty pages, out of a weighty 700-page tome to the immediate prewar years and the fulminations of many of the renowned daily newspapers in regard to the war clouds over Europe. He cited an unspoken "gentlemen's agreement" among news editors and proprietors to consistently downplay the war scare so that the bad news would not become a self-fulfilling prophecy, and actually bring the nation closer to a conflict. On the relative consensus among news editors, he remarked: "Resolved to avoid—or, at least, not to hasten—the inevitable, they took it upon themselves to calm prevailing fears. In this way, they variously qualified as appeasers or the *de facto* accomplices of the statesmen who practised appeasement."[42] In the specific case of one of the more well-known figures of the era, *Times* editor Geoffrey Dawson, Koss balked at the fact that Dawson had been labeled as one of the archpriests of appeasement. He offered that a majority of Dawson's contemporaries managed the content of the news, to whatever degree, and that the *Times* editor's actions were no more invidious than the rest of Fleet Street. On Dawson, Koss remarked:

> Despite the ignominy he has suffered as a key member of the so-called Cliveden Set, depicted by Low in the *Evening Standard* (3 January 1938) as performing "the Shiver Sisters Ballet" under the direction of Goebbels, he was representative of a far wider phenomenon. If *The Times* under his editorship deliberately—and, as it proved, foolishly—minced words, it was merely doing what each of its rivals did to a greater or lesser extent. . . . In any case, *The Times* can be condemned no more for trading on its inflated reputation than for following standard editorial procedures.[43]

The controversy over Whitehall's alleged pressure on Britain's press barons to treat appeasement in a positive light was also addressed by Koss. Unlike James Margach, Koss doubted the efficacy of any strong-arming of the press, and he alluded to a fiercely independent nature among news editors and proprietors: "Whatever tutelage they may have received from whatever minatory power would have been superfluous, for they were resolved to commit their own mistakes."[44] On a even more sanguine note, Koss denied the possibility that Chamberlain's influence was a crucial factor in the eventual editorial stances of the British press, and he characterized governmental attempts to manipulate coverage as potentially counterproductive to Whitehall's interests: "There was no harm in trying, but also no guarantee that the effort would not serve to stiffen a paper's resistance."[45] The popularity of Neville Chamberlain at the time of Munich and the palpable fear of war among the British people led most papers to support appeasement while it seemed successful. Koss' work lent insight to the debate over appeasement and the print media.

A source rather critical of Chamberlain's handling of the media was published by Richard Cockett in 1989, entitled *Twilight of Truth: Chamberlain, Appeasement and the Manipulation of the Press*. A revised Ph.D. thesis at the University of London, Cockett utilized *Twilight of Truth* to search for an answer in regard to Chamberlain's phenomenal popularity in the British press in the years before and in the immediate aftermath of the Munich Conference. In the author's own words:

> It is the contention of this study that due to the incestuous relationship between Whitehall and the press that had developed during the 1930s, the press in fact could do nothing but help Chamberlain pursue appeasement. . . . It is a sad fact that the press was just as much responsible for surrendering its freedom during the years of appeasement as the government was responsible for consciously trying to subvert editorial independence.[46]

Cockett stressed the notion that as the Chamberlain administration fully consolidated its power after 28 May 1937, the Prime Minister became increasingly more adamant in regard to what he perceived as loyalty from both political colleagues and journalists. Any criticism of governmental policy, whether justified or in the realm of partisan politics, was to the Prime Minister analogous to treachery and treason, and he would not readily brook opposition to his policies.

As Chamberlain's premiership progressed, he became increasingly aggressive towards the journalists and openly manipulative, refusing, for example, to answer off-the-cuff questions and insisting that any question should be submitted four hours in advance if the journalist were to expect a reply. . . . This revealed Chamberlain's ambivalent attitude towards the press: he was happy to court it in order to win its support for his policies, yet he treated individual journalists with utter disdain.[47]

Cockett pondered the loss of independence for a newspaper when its relationship with governmental authorities had become overly intimate. He cited the example of the close friendship between Viscount Halifax, Chamberlain's Foreign Secretary from March 1938 on, and Geoffrey Dawson. It was inevitable that Dawson and Chamberlain would become intimates, with dire consequences for *The Times*'s subsequent journalistic integrity. As Cockett stated:

Throughout the 1930s it can be said that Dawson was privy to more Cabinet thinking and secrets than most members of the government, whether the Prime Minister was MacDonald, Baldwin or Chamberlain. Dawson's role during appeasement was to bear this out all too well. It was not for nothing that *The Times* was thus taken to be the semi-official conduit of the British government's thinking abroad, and every nuance of its long and elegant leaders was scrupulously scrutinized in the chancelleries and embassies of the world. It was a charge that was always strenuously denied by both *The Times* and the government, but it was one which was, nonetheless, fundamentally true—as the actions of Dawson during the appeasement years were to demonstrate.[48]

A press leak during November 1937 that alluded to a planned hunting trip/diplomatic initiative by Lord Halifax to Germany convinced Chamberlain of the need to limit the flow of information swirling through his administration. The News Department of the Foreign Office was blamed, according to Cockett, and Chamberlain vowed to limit its access to news in the future. In addition, he was soon to remove not only Lord Vansittart from actual influence in the Foreign Office, but was to force out his own Foreign Secretary over ostensible policy differences in late February 1938, to be replaced by the ever malleable Lord Halifax. Cockett detailed the governmental paranoia toward a few newspapers during September 1938, when Britain and Germany rushed to the brink of war, only to be saved through Chamberlain's intervention at Munich. During the Prime Minister's second trip to Germany, to Bad Godesberg, he had been faced with an ultimatum of German annexation of the Czech Sudetenland by 1 October 1938 or war. Cockett stressed that Chamberlain had actually wanted to submit to the diktat, but was foiled by resistance in the press, specifically the criticism of the *Daily Telegraph*. As usual, the Foreign Office was again to be blamed for blocking the path of appeasement, to the great chagrin of the Prime Minister.

> It was the inner Cabinet's belief that opposition to the capitulation . . . now rested entirely in the Foreign Office News Department, and it was only that department's influence that was making the press "revolt." The fact that the Chamberlainites could attribute opposition to their plan solely to the machinations of an emasculated Foreign Office News Department demonstrates how entranced they had become by the Whitehall games of news control. They could no longer even entertain the idea that there might be real public opposition to their plans; they were trapped in a twilight world of self-delusion that was largely of their own creation. Increasingly, Chamberlain and the inner Cabinet were becoming victims of their own tight control of news; any criticism was now freely attributed not to genuine conviction but to bureaucratic in-fighting.[49]

Cockett asserted that many newspapers were, in the wake of Munich, cajoled or intimidated by the government into undiluted support for the fatuous agreement that delivered the Sudetens into the arms of the Reich. He named Sir Samuel Hoare as one of the administration's contacts who communicated repeatedly with various newspaper proprietors and editors. Perhaps the most egregious example of "muzzling" was what occurred in the offices of the *News Chronicle* on 30 September 1938. The paper, which had to its credit been very critical of the probable scuttle if the government had acceded to the Godesberg diktat, was stopped in its tracks in its attempt to publish a true account of the ramifications of the Munich settlement. Sir Walter Layton, who as editor-in-chief had been repeatedly visited by Samuel Hoare before Munich, refused to allow any critical coverage in the flush of the Prime Minister's diplomatic triumph. The *News Chronicle* correspondent in Prague, Vernon Bartlett, had issued his account, which stated that "the Munich agreement was an almost complete capitulation."[50] Layton refused to allow its use, and replaced the critical tone with something akin to "profound thankfulness . . . the agreement had saved great numbers of innocent Czechs from war."[51] Cockett concluded his analysis of Munich's consequences with an assertion on the rather bogus unanimity of the British press, which was in many cases a matter of the owners and editors fashioning their accounts against the collective will of their own newspaper staffs. In his words:

> This has, indeed, always been one of the major justifications for the Munich agreement in the eyes of the Chamberlainites, that it had the overwhelming support of the British public, as demonstrated by the press. But what Chamberlain, through his consistent and secret cultivation of the personal touch with the press, managed to achieve was to mask the real divisions that lay at the heart of government and society. Through the government's insistent courting of the proprietors, editors and political journalists, it managed to achieve an appearance of national unity—whereas in fact on most papers this appearance was achieved against the wishes and views of most of the staff.[52]

As Cockett related, only one newspaper immediately after Munich attempted to give an accurate indication of the feeling of the country, and that was the *Yorkshire Post*.[53] The *Post*'s editor, Arthur Mann, although a member of the Conservative Party, characterized the Prime Minister as a "commonplace politician," at a time when the country needed leadership. Although he received some censure for his criticism of Chamberlain, Mann was courageous enough to offer his resignation if the paper's owner could prove Mann's judgment of the Prime Minister to be in error. Cockett cited a Mann leader from 8 December 1938, which was significant for its rare courage in the face of Chamberlain's overwhelming popularity after Munich. The leader stressed that by

> repeatedly surrendering to force, he has repeatedly encouraged aggression. . . . Our central contention, therefore, is that Mr. Chamberlain's policy has throughout been based on a fatal misunderstanding of the psychology of dictatorship and that a P.M. who is by nature unfitted to deal with dictators has habitually disregarded the advice of those most expertly qualified to correct his private judgement. . . . It is because we believe that Mr. Chamberlain's policy is even now threatening the safety of the realm, and is likely in the near future to threaten it with danger still graver, that we are stating in detail our case against it.[54]

Not surprisingly, Mann would later be characterized as somewhat unsound of mind and body by Rupert Beckett, the chairman of the *Yorkshire Post*. This, according to Mann's critics, no doubt altered his judgment in a negative fashion toward the Prime Minister.[55]

In conclusion, Cockett commented on the dangers of a supine press, especially during a crucial period like that of Chamberlain's tenure as Premier. However morally or ethically wrong it was to

manipulate the press, the government's efforts would prove counterproductive to Chamberlain's desire of an overall European appeasement. Cockett's judgment of the Prime Minister was
persuasive.

> He had successfully demonstrated how a government in a democracy
> could influence and control the press to a remarkable degree. The dan-
> ger in this for Chamberlain was that he preferred to forget that he exer-
> cised such influence, and so increasingly mistook his pliant press for
> real public opinion. . . . Chamberlain's mistake was in believing that
> by controlling the press he was capturing public opinion—of course,
> the truth of the matter was that by controlling the press he was merely
> ensuring that the press was unable to reflect public opinion.[56]

And, finally, his last word: "If a democracy can be defined as a
healthy, continuing clash of opinion, then the Chamberlain government, through its close control of the press, certainly succeeded in subverting democracy during the years 1937 to 1940."[57]
Richard Cockett's work, asserting that governmental pressure was
levied on the British press to tailor their articles to a proappease-
ment stance, is an example of the detailed sophistication of very
recent scholarship, and a source that debunks much of the earlier
work on the controversial relationship between the print media
and the champions of appeasement in the interwar years. Franklin
Gannon, for example, had sincerely stated twenty years earlier
that the high degree of professionalism among newspapermen as a
group would have obviated any chance of deliberate truncation or
censorship of suspected anti-German themes from foreign correspondents. Conversely, Cockett took that selfsame censorship as
standard operating procedure for most of the media, especially
faced with as formidable an authoritarian figure as Neville Chamberlain.

A final source on the reciprocal effects of appeasement and the
British print media was a 1991 publication by Benny Morris, entitled *The Roots of Appeasement: The British Weekly Press and
Nazi Germany During the 1930s*. Morris concentrated on weekly
publications that were necessarily read habitually by the intellectual and political elites, whose opinions would oftentimes propel
public opinion and debate. He stressed that the weeklies created a
consensus that favored the support of appeasement as early as
1935, and continued in that vein until September 1938 and the

watershed event of the Chamberlain tenure as Prime Minister.[58] If the majority of the weekly journals and periodicals were not soured on appeasement immediately after Munich, the events of March 1939 lifted the mask, and German duplicity was evident to even the most conciliatory of Britons.

The *Spectator* was one of the weeklies that followed the fateful path of appeasement in support of Neville Chamberlain's view of a pacified Europe. Morris opined that the weekly, with Henry Wilson Harris as editor from 1932 to 1953, embodied the nonconformist conscience of Britain, with its faith squarely behind the League of Nations as the sole hope and guarantor of world peace until 1935–1936.[59] It would continue to press for appeasement between Great Britain and Germany until March 1939, although one of the proprietors, J. Angus Wilson, was ardently against all forms of totalitarian government. Morris cited Wilson's words from 1937: "The *Spectator* is at once opposed to the Fascist form of politics as operating in Germany and Italy to-day and to the Communist ideal dominating Russia, seeing in both policies the same goal of a totalitarian state."[60] This posture of equanimity in the face of the dictator states hid the *Spectator*'s virulent loathing for Communism and all its works;[61] such sentiments were quite common, according to the author, among British conservatives who foresaw the Nazi menace as a bulwark against a tide of Bolshevism emanating out of Moscow.

Another significant weekly that Morris cited was *The Economist*, edited by Sir Walter Layton from 1922 until September 1938. Morris noted that by the late 1930s Layton had his hands full with the management of the *News Chronicle*, and rarely wrote any of the journal's leaders after 1933. However, Layton's philosophy was reflected in *The Economist*'s content, week after week. As Morris stressed: "Layton's thinking in the 1930s was governed by a pervasive vision of British strategic and economic weakness and by an overriding concern for the safety of the mother country, the colonies and the Dominions."[62] Until at least 1935 Layton was a staunch supporter of the League of Nations, as was Harris of the *Spectator*. With the widespread perception after the Rhineland crisis that the League was no longer efficacious, Layton later turned to the notion of the Grand Alliance of Britain, France, and Russia, an idea supported also by Winston Churchill. Morris noted *The Economist*'s view of the enigmatic Russians, the personal bête noire of many British Conservatives.

> *The Economist* found Communist theory and Bolshevist practice repellent. But it never ascribed aggressive intentions to Stalinist Russia.

And, confronted by the choice of evil ideologies on the Continent, the journal never evinced uncertainty as to which was worse: "If I had to choose between Communism and Fascism—which God forbid—I should choose Communism," declared Sir Walter Layton. However, like the *Spectator*, *The Economist* often predicted that an inevitable outcome of a new world war would be the subversion of social structures, paving the way for revolution.[63]

In the final analysis Morris credited *The Economist* with being consistently unflagging and unreserved in its condemnation of Nazi Germany through the years 1933–1939.[64] If so, it was truly one of the very few that had the temerity to cross Chamberlain's administration with negative reportage on the increasing fluidity of the European scene.

The "leading Conservative weekly review during the 1930s" was *Truth*,[65] whose editor, Joseph Ball, was to become a very intimate companion to Prime Minister Neville Chamberlain later in the 1930s. *Truth*, like many of the weekly journals, wavered between treaty revision for the Germans one week and a hard line in defense of treaty obligations the next. This barometer usually changed according to the perceived threat from the Germans, which incidentally increased as the decade passed. Morris noted that the journal's embrace of appeasement was necessary from a prudent military view:

> The safety and interests of Britain and its Empire, in its view, demanded the abandonment of friends and former allies. . . . *Truth*'s *glissement* towards appeasement in 1934 was prompted by an appreciation of Britain's physical weakness and infirmity of purpose, and comparative German strength.[66]

Ball would later defend Chamberlain to the bitter end after the Premier's fall from power in May 1940,[67] with the journal's philosophies nearly the same as the Prime Minister's, in that bluff or threats without the ability to back them up were useless. According to Morris, probably "the most important of the serious weeklies of the 1930s, certainly the most widely read and the most widely quoted,"[68] was the *New Statesman*. It had a wide appeal to members of the Labour Party, and to those left of center in British politics. He added that the policies of the journal are only understandable in the light of the character as well as the mind-set of the editor from 1931–1960, Basil Kingsley Martin. Morris quoted Labour M.P. Hugh Dalton, who described Kingsley Martin as "a most emotional, unstable person with little judgement."[69] As for the leadership of the *New Statesman*, Morris commented on the confused vacillations of the editor, which could be perceived as a metaphor for those chaotic times:

> With rare lapses, Kingsley Martin alone determined and formulated *New Statesman* policy between 1931 and 1939. In all that concerned the Dictator States, that policy was meticulously inconsistent and confused. At the core of the confusion, aptly mirroring the soul of the editor, lay an almost ineffable abhorrence and fear of war. A single issue of the *New Statesman* carried articles variously and clamorously espousing British isolationism, pacifism, positive appeasement and military resistance to the aggressor states.[70]

Out of this numbing uncertainty one can begin to understand the serenity that Neville Chamberlain must have possessed once he made up his mind that appeasement of the dictator states was the way to avoid war and pacify Europe. Perhaps the fabled "blinders mentality" was the only way to preserve his sangfroid in the midst of frightfully volatile events. No such confidence was included in the makeup of Kingsley Martin, however, and Morris alluded to Martin's abject fear of another cataclysm to rival the Great War in its devastation. "Through the thirties he remained unable to face the prospect of a new world war, even if—as he often recognised—that were the only means of stemming aggression and destroying the dictators."[71] As for the *New Statesman*, Morris concluded, it was not any concern with treaty revision, but rather "a fear of war which prompted the frequently appeasing stance towards Nazi Germany."[72]

Finally, the *Sunday Times* was among the most flagrant in its appeasement of the Nazis, and proprietors, editors, and writers seemed to support the policy. After 1936, Lord Kemsley, an ardent appeaser, was owner; William W. Hadley was editor; and the infamous Herbert Sidebotham was still pumping out prose under his alias, Scrutator. Hadley, according to Morris, was convinced of "the virtues of appeasement and was a friend and supporter of Neville Chamberlain."[73] Of Scrutator Morris remarked, "The *Sunday Times* rarely made a pretence of basing its foreign policy on anything save what it regarded as British self-interest. Certainly morality, as commonly understood, had no place in Sidebotham's perceptions and advocacy of foreign policy."[74] To carry that a bit further, Morris quoted from a Scrutator column from 1936, which clearly manifested the appalling lack of ideological foundation that many of the ardent appeasers suffered from; it was that same failing that convinced Neville Chamberlain that he could and should "do business" with the dictators to save the peace of Europe. Morris's salient quote, culled from a 1936 Scrutator article: "Perhaps the first and most welcome change of mind is to disabuse ourselves of the idea that we and our friends are better morally than other nations [for] in the domain of political morals all nations of western Europe [that is, including Germany and Italy] are on much the same level."[75] Morris' immediate response to that quote was, "Moral relativism of this order, in pursuit of appeasement, would have made Chamberlain blush."[76] Indeed, it may well have, but as Morris so thoroughly revealed in the course of his work, it seemed like the Prime Minister really did not need the support of many of those periodicals that freely rendered theirs; it was only when his policy had clearly failed, after Prague, that Chamberlain had to pay the price of his prestige and political support.

In the course of his ill-starred but unflagging campaign to pacify the grievances of the dictator states, Neville Chamberlain's impatience with opposing viewpoints simply brought out the worst aspects of his personality and leadership. The attribution of "treachery or treason" to those who had legitimate differences with his pursuit of appeasement led to an eventual near-blackout of truth in the daily and weekly presses, and his administration's use of strong-arm tactics to suppress any negative reality smacked more of the modus operandi of Dr. Goebbels than of Europe's leading democracy. James Margach may well have been right when he remarked that when appeasement at long last had shown itself to be a failure, Chamberlain, who used the levers of power to manipulate freely, was then cruelly cast out, tainted by his policy's disastrous downfall. Lord Acton's axiom of the corrupting characteristics of power rang true once again in Chamberlain's case, and Margach has the final word in his chapter on appeasement and the British print media:

Neville Chamberlain vividly demonstrated what power can really do to a man, transforming his character and temperament. When I knew him first, long before he became Prime Minister, he was the most shy, kindly, generous-minded and warm-hearted of men, always friendly and understanding although by nature cold, indrawn and lonely. But when he became Prime Minister and his appeasement policy first overwhelmed and finally destroyed him he became the most authoritarian, intolerant and arrogant of all the Premiers I have known.[77]

It is important to remember that other P.M.s have attempted censorship of the press, especially wartime P.M.s Lloyd George and Churchill; the latter became so infuriated at the *Daily Mirror* during the war that an attempt was made to shut it down permanently. However, wartime inevitably dictates special circumstances where the aegis of "national security" can be utilized to muzzle criticism of the government, and Churchill's eternal glory as the savior of 1940 outshines every negative aspect of his legacy. Chamberlain's sad fate becomes more poignant because his systematic and rather successful censorship of Britain's fourth estate prefaced his admission on 3 September 1939 that "everything I have worked for . . . has crashed into ruins." The hoary admonition that "only the victors write history" is doubly true in the twin failures of Neville Chamberlain and appeasement.

8
Munich: An Overview

THIS EXTENDED HISTORIOGRAPHICAL REVIEW OF BRITAIN'S APPEASE-
ment policies during Chamberlain's tenure as Premier has touched
upon a multitude of the most significant sources. These were initially introduced in a strictly chronological fashion; later, through
the decade of the 1960s and beyond, the analysis of appeasement
evolved into a more sophisticated methodology that was much
more specialized in nature. The study of appeasement became less
emotional and more clinical, with an emphasis on the many factors
that compelled Neville Chamberlain and his supporters to pursue
the elusive dove of peace in the eye of the gathering storm. Nonetheless, such specialization, as Professor Paul Kennedy commented over a decade ago, had

> ignored the moral issue and stressed the strategic, economic and politi-
> cal motives behind the British Government's external policies . . . in
> seeking to explain appeasement, they have also tended to justify it . . .
> but without much consideration for the moral and ethical aspects.[1]

He concluded that only someone who combines the mentality of
the appeasers with military and economic rationales can explain
the phenomenon.[2] In Kennedy's concise eloquence we find the *raison d'etre* of the present effort.

One cannot, however, complete a detailed analysis of appeasement historiography without a thorough evaluation of those works
dealing with Munich itself and the consequences of the events of
September 1938. From Neville Chamberlain's personal assessments of his own diplomatic handiwork in the days and weeks following the conference to accounts published in the late 1980s, our
extended analysis will offer a sense of perspective on the scenario
that constituted the very apogee of appeasement, of Chamberlain's
all too brief shining moment as the world's peacemaker.

※

175

Upon his undeniably triumphant return to England on 30 September 1938, Prime Minister Neville Chamberlain was lauded on an international scale as the "angel of peace," a fearless statesman whose unflagging determination alone in the pursuit of a peaceful Europe obviated the deadliest of conflagrations. Scores of congratulatory telegrams and missives celebrated his courage and foresight, among them an enigmatic response from the putative leader of the free world, President Franklin D. Roosevelt, whose simple message, "Good Man," has been subject to much historical interpretation since it was written. Having had the fortunate opportunity personally to sift through these documents in the Chamberlain collection at the University of Birmingham, I cannot repudiate the irresistible yearning for peace that existed on a worldwide scale, and particularly among the British people in the autumn of 1938. So very much has been written on Munich and the "betrayal" of the Czechs that the mention of the city itself has long been synonymous with the misbegotten policy of appeasement of vengeful and insatiable dictators, quite willing to seize by diplomacy what they had threatened by conquest. It is only proper, therefore, that Chamberlain's own words should be allowed to justify his historical stance from September 1938, for it is the legacy of this much misunderstood and vilified man that active appeasement became the British credo in the three years of his administration. A collection of many of Neville Chamberlain's most significant speeches was published in 1939 under the heading of *In Search of Peace*. In a Birmingham Town Hall address on 8 April 1938 the Prime Minister alluded to the dual nature of his appeasement policy:

> Our policy is based upon two conceptions. The first is this: That, if you want to secure a peace which can be relied upon to last, you have got to find out what are the causes of war and remove them. You cannot do that by sitting still and waiting for something to turn up. You have got to set about it. . . . The second conception is this: In any armed world you must be armed yourself. You must see to it that your preparations, or defensive and offensive forces, are so organised and built up that nobody will be tempted to attack you, but that, on the contrary, when your voice is raised for peace, it will be listened to with respect. These, then, are the two pillars of our foreign policy—to seek peace by friendly discussion and negotiation, and to build up our armed forces to a level which is proportionate to our responsibilities and to the part we desire to play in preserving peace.[3]

One of the critical flaws in Chamberlain's worldview related to his late Victorian era businessman's orientation toward foreign powers, which would cause him considerable grief when he dealt with that most duplicitous of regimes, Nazi Germany. The Prime Minister sincerely believed that he could deal with the gangsters from Berlin just as he would rival interests in the Birmingham business community. Like Franklin Roosevelt years later, Neville Chamberlain had an unerring faith in the efficacy of personal diplomacy. He would utilize this medium in a desperate effort to avoid another European bloodbath on the scale of the Great War.

In mid-September 1938, then, Chamberlain would thrice travel to Germany to negotiate a peaceful end to the Sudeten Czech crisis. His personal letters to his sisters during the period offer valuable insight into his *mentalite* in those desperate days. In regard to his initial visit of 15 September 1938, Chamberlain unwittingly utilized the weather conditions while on the plane as a telling metaphor for the entirety of his diplomatic efforts. As he later related to his sister Ida: "As we neared Munich we entered a storm and for a time flew blind through the clouds while the aeroplane rocked and bumped like a ship in a sea."[4] His naivete and lack of coherent vision, with an unwarranted optimism in the face of very dire circumstances, would clearly be evidenced in his assessments after his first meeting with the German dictator. Again, the Prime Minister was ever so ebullient about the chances for peace, in the belief that no rational statesman would desire to use war as an instrument of foreign policy when all grievances could be settled among peaceable rival states. Chamberlain's thoughts on the first of his three meetings with Hitler: "In short I had established a certain confidence which was my aim and on my side in spite of the hardness and ruthlessness I thought I saw in his face I got the impression that here was a man who could be relied upon when he had given his word."[5] The events of the next six months would not bear out the truth of the Prime Minister's perceptions, and he would soon despair for ever having trusted the German dictator. The frantic preparations of late September, in which gas masks were widely distributed and trenches dug in the London parks, were stilled only by an eleventh-hour reprieve from Berlin, as the Four-Power Conference to cede the Sudetenland to the Reich was announced on 28 September during a session of the House of Commons. This dramatic scenario of spontaneous joy and relief was alluded to in another Chamberlain letter to his sister Hilda on 2 October 1938: "That the news of the deliverance should come to me in the very act of closing my speech in the House was a piece of drama that no work of fiction ever surpassed."[6] Chamberlain left for Munich and his rendezvous with destiny the following day, and the Sudetenland was in German hands within a fortnight. The aftermath remained to be debated, whether this action constituted a shameful betrayal of a vulnerable but gallant ally, or, as the Prime Minister wished to believe, that the truncation of the Czech state would somehow make it stronger and more secure.

In the post-Munich House of Commons debate, Chamberlain was obliged to defend his policies and answer the claims of having sacrificed a smaller power to Nazi aggression to avoid war. Chamberlain's speech of 3 October, included in the text of *In Search of Peace*, was crucial for an understanding of his motivation during that nerve-wracking time. In his words:

> When we were convinced, as we became convinced, that nothing any longer would keep the Sudetenland within the Czechoslovakian state, we urged the Czech Government as strongly as we could to agree to the cession of territory, and to agree promptly. . . .It was a hard decision for anyone who loved his country to take, but to accuse us of having by that advice betrayed the Czechoslovakian State is simply preposterous. What we did was to save her from annihilation and give her a chance of new life as a new State, which involves the loss of territory and fortifications, but may perhaps enable her to enjoy in the future and develop a national existence under a neutrality and security comparable to that which we see in Switzerland to-day.[7]

This dream of "Swiss" neutrality and security for the rump of the Czech state was to be cruelly illusory in the months after Munich. The emasculated remnants of that sorrowful country would be snatched up by the Wehrmacht and the Gestapo in less than six months, despite the fact that its remaining integrity had been so solemnly guaranteed by the British and French. The Prime Minister, as was his wont, continued to perceive the totalitarian states of Europe with an alarming lack of moral or ideological insight, as if the dictator nations were equal partners with the Western democracies. In a Guildhall speech of 9 November 1938, two years to the day before his untimely death, Chamberlain responded to critics of the Munich accord:

> First of all I should like to get rid of the idea that at Munich there was a clash between different systems of government and that the result was a victory for one side or the other. . . . At any rate I, who happened to be there, can tell you that at Munich there was no clash—there was no question of a victory or defeat for either side. And I think if we are wise we shall find that one of the most gratifying features about Munich was that four Great Powers, owning different systems of govern-

ment, were able to sit down together to agree without quarrelling upon the main outlines of a settlement of one of the most thorny and dangerous international problems of our time.[8]

From that very same address, Chamberlain defended his conduct at Munich, and he would go to his grave convinced that he had done the right thing in September 1938: the alternative would been another European civil war. His assessment of the consequences of the Munich conference, which, in a bitterly ironic twist, had meant to preserve peace but would accelerate war:

> Now that the crisis is over, it is very easy to find fault with the solution, but the fact is that in the situation with which we had to deal, it was not possible to present the ideal solution as the alternative to force. We were dealing with a situation which had arisen from forces which had been set in motion nearly twenty years before, and the surgeon who has to deal with long-neglected wounds or disease must cut more swiftly and more deeply than he who is dealing with the first symptoms. If the settlement at Munich imposed upon Czechoslovakia a fate which arouses our natural sympathy for a small state and for a proud and brave people, yet we cannot dismiss in silence the thought of what the alternative would have meant to the peoples not only of Czechoslovakia, but of all the nations that would have been involved. I have no shadow of doubt in my mind that what we did was right. In doing it we have earned the gratitude of the vast majority in Europe and even in the world.[9]

Modern scholarship has also made it fairly well evident that Chamberlain meant for the Munich settlement not only to be a "breathing space" in which to rearm the British nation, but also the first step of an overall pacification of Europe, one in which he had hoped the Germans would work in concert to build a strong and peaceful continent.[10] That is why the eventual sack of Prague was so terribly disheartening to the Prime Minister, and would quickly lead to his dramatic address of 3 September 1939, where he admitted that his life's work was in ruins. His legacy continues to be central to the appeasement debate, more than half a century after both his political and physical demise.

A poignant account of the events that led to the breakup of Czechoslovakia was offered by the then Czech President Dr. Eduard Benes, published posthumously in 1954 under the title *Mem-*

oirs of Dr. Eduard Benes: From Munich to New War and New Victory. Benes had been one of the founding fathers of the Czechoslovak state that had been carved out of the ruins of the old Hapsburg empire at the Versailles Peace Conference. Benes had been an intimate of Tomas Masaryk, the father of the new Czechoslovakia, served as Czechoslovak Foreign Minister from 1918 to 1935, and was President of Czechoslovakia from 1935 until his country's dismemberment in September 1938. On that subject, he was understandably bitter regarding his erstwhile Western allies as he recounted some of the folly of those eventful years. Benes portrayed his country as one of the few that remained morally correct in the face of military terror, in this case the many threats emanating from Berlin.

> Such was the moral and political catastrophe which overwhelmed everyone who deserted the path of right and began to come to terms with Hitler in this threatening European maelstrom. In excusing themselves for having done so, some might argue that even we who remained faithful to our principles were nevertheless not saved from Nazi occupation by our fidelity. Yes, but what an enormous moral difference lies between us! Our official policy had been warning the world for years, and right to the last moment it had stood firm in desperate opposition against capitulation to fascism and finally it was forsaken by nearly the whole world. . . . I only wish to make it clear that in the years 1936–38 Czechoslovak policy rightly diagnosed what was the matter in Europe. It did everything, really everything, to retrieve the situation of Czechoslovakia, of its friends and of all Europe in the face of Fascist gangsterism and pan-German Nazism and of war itself.[11]

In regard to the actual Munich settlement, at which incidentally no Czech representative was allowed to be present—shades of Versailles—Benes revealed the widespread shock among most of the Czech leadership, who felt sure that their Western allies would protect Czech interests. He referred to the tentative Anglo-German agreement to cede the Sudetenland to the Reich (under the aegis of self-determination!) of 15 September 1938 and its immediate aftermath:

> When we refused, there arrived from France and Great Britain on September 21st an ultimatum accompanied by emphatic personal interventions in Prague during the night on the part of the Ministers of both countries. . . . We were informed that if we did not accept their plan for the cession of the so-called Sudeten regions, they would leave us to our fate, which, they said, we had brought upon ourselves. They explained that they certainly would not go to war with Germany just "to

keep the Sudeten Germans in Czechoslovakia." I felt very keenly the fact that there were at that time so few in France and Great Britain who understood that something much more serious was at stake for Europe than the retention of the so-called Sudeten Germans in Czechoslovakia.[12]

The long view was one that was rarely taken in those heated days of virtually endless anxiety over impending war. To be sure, Chamberlain and his "inner circle" could not have had the luxury of looking six months to a year down the road, when fabricated stories of Czech excesses against innocent Sudeten Germans were emanating hourly out of Dr. Goebbels' offices in Berlin.

As for the aftermath of Munich, Benes utilized the tragedy of 15 March 1939 as a backdrop for a powerful condemnation of his Western allies, which in his lamentable circumstances was arguably justified. Benes' criticisms brought back to mind the utterances at Geneva in 1936 of Haile Selassie, who warned the League of Nations that if small nations could fall to aggression, larger ones would most assuredly follow. Benes' conclusions:

> The guarantee given us by the Western Powers during the Munich crisis to compensate us for our temporary submission to force proved to be politically worthless on March 14th and 15th. This was the second failure to honour a pledge and international obligation. . . . The whole outside world, including Paris and London, had no doubt that the Anglo-French undertaking to Czechoslovakia given when she accepted the Munich treaty, had again been broken. . . . So the Munich "dictate" had been destroyed by its own authors, through the non-observance of the solemn obligations which all four Great Powers had voluntarily undertaken, had forced on us by irresistible pressure and then had themselves ignored. In the whole history of mankind it is hard to find such a complete political fiasco—the fiasco of the whole Munich policy and "appeasement" which collapsed when the truncated Czechoslovak republic was forcibly occupied. But also in the whole history of Europe there is scarcely a precedent for such unprincipled behaviour by the Great Powers against a small friendly Nation which had done its utmost to fulfil its own obligations.[13]

It is a sad but arguable irony that Benes and his fellow Czechs had more to fear from London and Paris than from Berlin; at least the Germans made no secret of their antipathy toward Prague, while the Western democracies posed as allies, but were willing to abandon the Czechs for what to them seemed the far more crucial imperative of a possible European appeasement.

Another collection of primary source material on Munich and its aftermath is entitled *Documents and Materials Relating to the Eve of the Second World War*, initially published by the Ministry of Foreign Affairs of the Soviet Union in an English-language edition in 1948. This two-volume collection included documents seized from the Nazi archives by the victorious Red Army during their sack of Berlin in the spring of 1945. The initial volume contained material relating to the period from November 1937 and Halifax's visit to Germany, through the end of 1938, the aftermath of Munich. The second half of the material contained the private papers of Herbert von Dirksen, onetime German ambassador to Moscow, Tokyo, and London. Although much of this material was rather politically charged in the immediate postwar period and utilized accordingly to justify many of the positions taken by the Soviet Union before the outbreak of war, it remains of a crucial primary source nature, and therefore is included in our review. The initial reference is from the Munich Conference itself, from Document 34, a "Communication of the German Delegation in Munich to the German Foreign Office on the Course of the Munich Conference." According to the document, early on in the proceedings Neville Chamberlain had thanked both of the dictators for inviting him to Munich, and he stressed that:

> This conference gave Europe a new respite, whereas yesterday catastrophe seemed imminent. He quite agreed that swift action must be taken, and he especially welcomed the Fuhrer's statement that he did not want to resort to force, but to establish order. If the problem were approached in this spirit, he was certain that results would be achieved.[14]

This statement from the Prime Minister corroborated his long-held belief that the Germans seemingly could have their way in central and eastern Europe, so long as the takeover was peaceful and nonviolent. Chamberlain would only bridle if force or the threat of imminent force were employed by Berlin with impunity. A bit later, according to the document, while alluding to alleged Czech excesses against the Sudeten Germans, Mussolini solemnly inveighed that

> The Great Powers must assume a moral guarantee for the evacuation and for the prevention of destruction. They must tell Prague that the Czech Government must accept the demands, otherwise it must bear

the military consequences. What was needed was a request by the Great Powers, whose moral duty it was that this territory shall not be a wilderness when it is turned over.[15]

The thought of being lectured on moral duty by a brigand like Il Duce must well have been an added humiliation to Edouard Daladier, if not Chamberlain, who in his obsession to avoid war may not have perceived the rather odious irony of the situation.

A second document, very relevant to these efforts, was Document 37, "A Czechoslovak Foreign Ministry Record of the Czechoslovak Delegation's Visit to Munich." This was written by Dr. Hubert Masarik on the morning of 30 September 1938, in the immediate hours and minutes after the Munich agreement was drawn up. Masarik alluded to the fact that it was not until 1:30 A.M. on the thirtieth that the Czech delegation was led into the conference hall to meet with Messrs. Chamberlain, Daladier, and their respective British and French diplomatic underlings. After a very brief consultation concerning the affected areas to be ceded to Germany, Masarik bluntly asked Daladier and French Foreign Minister Alexis Leger whether they expected an answer to the completed agreement from the Czech government. Masarik recorded the Frenchman's answer, so painful for a majority of the Czech nation:

> M. Leger replied that the four statesmen had not much time. He added positively that they no longer expected an answer from us; they regarded the plan as accepted and that our Government had that very day, at latest by 5 P.M. to send its representative to Berlin to the meeting of the International Commission and finally that the Czechoslovak official whom we sent would have to be in Berlin on Saturday, in order to fix the details of the evacuation of the first zone.[16]

On a personal note, Masarik continued, "it had been explained to us in a sufficiently brutal manner, and that by a Frenchman, that this was a sentence without right of appeal and without possibility of modification."[17] In other words, a fait accompli.

A final document dealing with the immediate consequences of the Munich conference was Document 39, the "Transmission of the Munich Demands by the German Charge D'Affaires in Prague Hencke to Czechoslovak Foreign Minister Krofta." After those demands were delivered, Czech Foreign Minister Kamil Krofta received the French, British, and Italian Ministers (Messrs. de Lacroix, Newton, and Franzoni respectively) in Prague, and announced the Czech response to the gathering. Krofta's words, from 30 September 1938, were plaintive yet eloquently prescient in light of events of the near future:

> On behalf of the President of the Republic and of the Government, I declare that we submit to the decisions adopted in Munich without us and against us. . . . I do not want to criticize but for us this is a catastrophe which we have not deserved. We submit, and will try to secure a tranquil life for our people. I do not know whether your countries will benefit from this decision taken at Munich, but certainly we shall not be the last. After us, others will meet with the same fate.[18]

Less than two years later his words would haunt France, who had so readily abandoned an ally, only later to surrender the military struggle with Germany in the same spirit of defeatism.

Before the historiographical review of Munich is moved into more recent years, it is necessary to credit one of the most authoritative sources on Munich and its aftermath ever written, still essential after fifty years. This was John Wheeler-Bennett's *Munich: Prologue to Tragedy*. Because Wheeler-Bennett's analysis of Chamberlain's Munich "victory" was so compelling, I felt it worthy of inclusion here. Due to the fact that it was written in 1948, the Churchillian flavor of the piece is still quite evident, and arguable today:

> Had Mr. Chamberlain returned to London, not with garlands but in sackcloth, and urged Britain to embark upon a policy of "blood, sweat, toil and tears," our national record would have been cleaner and we should have been the better prepared, both morally and materially, for the ultimate conflict. Had the British people been made aware that what Mr. Chamberlain had, in effect, brought back from Munich was not peace but a breathing-space before war, the lamentable state of unpreparedness in 1939 and 1940 might have been repaired.[19]

As for the Prime Minister, a self-styled "man of peace," the logic and lucidity of Wheeler-Bennett's prose would not have altered his unshakable faith in the efficacy of appeasement, or alerted him to the perilous fragility of his "peace for our time," in his golden days of worldwide adulation in October 1938. Only in March 1939, to paraphrase Duff Cooper, would the "mailed fist" shatter Chamberlain's hopes of a genuine European peace.

An account that strove for a greater level of sophistication than earlier volumes was *Munich*, written in 1963 by Keith Eubank. Published twenty-five years after the Munich Conference, Eubank's text sought to unravel the mythology and facile simplification that clouded the reality of September 1938. Very early in his work he set forth his perceptions on the Prime Minister, appeasement, and the reason for its failure:

> Although Chamberlain called his policy "appeasement," he did not mean peace at any price. Appeasement was the study and peaceful solution of problems that could cause war. By removing these causes, he hoped to avoid the war. Another world conflict with millions dead and wounded was, to him, an unspeakable horror, and he was willing to do everything in his power to prevent such a catastrophe. . . . The great weakness of Chamberlain was his failure to comprehend that a head of government would deliberately plan a world war. . . . Chamberlain's appeasement policy was useless because Hitler was determined to dominate Europe. Too much precious time was lost before Chamberlain grasped this fact.[20]

Indeed, it was difficult for the old Birmingham businessman to conduct foreign affairs much differently from the manner in which he administered his family's business interests at the turn of the twentieth century. Straight talk between men and a signal lack of ideology or intermediaries were characteristics of Chamberlain's style. To him, a man's word was his bond. His dealings with Nazi Germany would eventually disabuse the Prime Minister of any notion of Victorian propriety when Berlin's duplicity became evident in the five months following Munich.

In regard to the agreement itself, Eubank saw similarities with the excesses of 1919:

> The terms of the Agreement were not as vicious as the spirit. By threats of force and marching troops, Britain and France had been brought to the conference table to divide up the territory of an independent nation, undefeated in battle. Czechoslovakia had not been given any chance to state her case; it was worse than the "Diktat" of Versailles. Then Germany had at least been able to object in writing; this course was denied Czechoslovakia in 1938. . . . Worst of all, there was no real guarantee in the Agreement, only a statement of intentions.[21]

Eubank saw much significance in the little scrap of paper that was to wave from the Prime Minister's hand at Heston Airport upon his triumphant return from Munich. He described it, in Chamberlain's perspective, as "a holy instrument, not to be taken lightly."[22] He credited Chamberlain for his successful effort to pressure the Nazi tyrant into that short statement that stressed that in future, consultation would be the method by which the respective countries would deal with international problems. Eubank's view on Chamberlain at Munich was rather unorthodox, not hitherto embraced by his contemporaries:

> Unwittingly Chamberlain had trapped Hitler; the peaceful old gentleman had fooled the cunning dictator, bestowing upon him one of his worst defeats. Hitler had pledged himself to consult first with Chamberlain before he seized any more territory; this was never his intention. Properly applied, their bilateral agreement would mean that Hitler could not make any move without first consulting Chamberlain. Chamberlain did not realize how cunning his trap was; he had led Hitler to make an error—a fatal one.[23]

However, once the remains of the Czech state had been seized by the Nazis, all the agreements from Munich, personal as well as international, became worthless. With the sack of Prague, the Nazis had included, against their long-stated propaganda, non-Germans in the Reich for the first time. So much for the ideal of self-determination. There was, according to Eubank, some level of hypocrisy in Chamberlain's response of 17 March 1939, his famous Birmingham speech. Referring undoubtedly to British liberty rather than Czech, the Prime Minister would "sacrifice almost anything for peace save the liberty that we have enjoyed for hundreds of years, and which we shall never surrender."[24] These sentiments, which belie Chamberlain's sober equanimity and seem more Churchillian in nature, would ironically lead the Prime Minister, the "man of peace," to formulate a fatuous guarantee to Poland that would result in Britain's being dragged into war not even six months after the fall of Prague.

In his conclusion, Eubank articulated several persuasive factors that led to the British and French conduct at Munich. Again, he refused to accept the simplistic, one-dimensional analysis of weak and fearful politicians happily duped by Nazi promises into betraying the last democracy east of the Rhine. His reasoned analysis:

> To denounce the Munich Agreement as cowardly surrender is simple, but there is more to the tale. Other forces sent Chamberlain and Dala-

dier to Munich. They did not go there out of sheer folly. They made the journey because it seemed the only alternative to a war no one wanted. . . . None has been more condemned for the Munich Agreement than Chamberlain. He did not accept the Munich Agreement out of cowardice but because he was unwilling to drag the nation into a world war over an issue that did not seem worth the loss of countless lives. He doubted that the nation would have followed him into a war to coerce a minority who wanted to exercise the right of self-determination.[25]

Referring to the lack of will in London or Paris for world war in September 1938, Eubank offered his rationale for the Anglo-French "capitulation" at Munich:

When the four powers met at Munich, only Germany was prepared to pay the cost of victory—war. The governments of Britain and France wanted to avoid war over the Sudetens because such a cause was unworthy of the cost. Appeasement of Hitler through the Munich Agreement seemed worthwhile if it avoided a world war which Britain and France never wanted and for which they were unprepared in armaments and in spirit. Here is the answer to the riddle of the Munich Agreement: to wage war required sufficient cause, a will to war, and the men and armaments. Because these were lacking in 1938, Chamberlain and Daladier had no other choice than to sign the Munich Agreement.[26]

The argument that Chamberlain did what he had to do under the perilous circumstances Britain faced at Munich is one quite defensible, and is an illustrative example of the course taken by many of the Prime Minister's supporters in the historiographical debate of the last half-century.

One of the more intriguing efforts published on the thirtieth anniversary of Munich was that of Keith Robbins, *Munich 1938*. Robbins insisted, much like Keith Eubank before him, that the "Guilty Men" interpretation of Munich was overly simplistic and had led to the growth of a historical mythology that obscured the true consequences of September 1938. The purpose of his book, he stressed:

It is, . . . to look at the development of the Munich crisis without the hindering concept of "appeasement," and certainly without "the appeasers." In the immediate post-war years, it was convenient to suppose that Munich was the result of the "Policy of Appeasement"—a policy clearly definable, and associated with Neville Chamberlain. There is some substance to this contention. But it is not the whole story. . . . Munich must be considered in the light of fifty years of European history, not merely three or four years of British foreign policy.[27]

To that end, Robbins deigned to take his readers, through the diplomatic thickets of a quarter of a century, from before the Great War to the Nazi seizure of Prague. Included in his introduction were a few compelling paragraphs in regard to appeasement historiography that are valid some twenty-five years after they were written. He alluded to the conventional portrait of the Thirties, with its supporters and critics of appeasement, as far too simplistic.

> Some writers believe that on one side ambled the "Men of Munich," flabby and unprincipled, stupid yet guileful, cunning but ignorant, ruthless and at the same time irresponsible; whereas on the other, strode with firm purpose and iron step the "anti-appeasers," men of resolution and insight, determination and bravery, men with a sure grasp of principle and historical precedent who were mild with the firmness of wisdom. The division of opinion is not so clear-cut. Few men are consistent in their political beliefs; even fewer are as consistent as they think. In addition, the ramifications of the crisis were deeper and broader than both sides supposed. Many men straddled uneasily across what were supposedly great divides; their emotions tugging one way, their intellects another.[28]

This analysis of ambiguity served properly to dovetail with many of the challenged historical assumptions of the 1960s; the old consensus was breaking down, and empirical studies were beginning to replace the high moral tone of the postwar years.

In his assessment of the consequences of Munich, Robbins advised a policy of caution against a rush to judgment, one way or the other. He included his perception of Chamberlain's motivations in the joyous aftermath of the crisis:

> The cluster of moral and political issues surrounding "Munich" cannot be resolved to universal satisfaction. Each historian, each individual, must draw together his impression of Munich from the conflicting elements of cowardice and miscalculation, bravery and bewilderment, insight and blindness displayed by the statesmen and nations concerned. The Prime Minister seems to have been genuinely proud of his achievement. He had succeeded in preventing the outbreak of local war with the risk that it would spread. He was determined in his pur-

suit of this policy, but hardly ruthless. Chamberlain was not a sentimental man; he was sorry for the Czechs but felt no need for tears. . . . He did not believe that the Sudetens would ever settle down happily in Czechoslovakia; their grievances would prove a perpetual irritant in Central Europe. The Munich settlement might not bring perpetual peace but it stood a slightly better chance then attempting to keep the Sudetens inside Czechoslovakia against their will.[29]

Robbins took to task the popular (among Chamberlain supporters) perception that the Prime Minister's Munich "victory" earned a crucial year of time to rearm before the eventual war in September 1939. He expressed his conviction, as had A. J. P. Taylor in 1961, that Chamberlain had definite hopes for a lasting peace in the aftermath of Munich; thus the Munich agreement itself could be utilized as insurance against Nazi terror. If Berlin misbehaved and abrogated the pact, the world would witness her duplicity.

The concept of the "breathing-space" is usually taken to involve a comparison between the armed forces of Britain and France and those of Germany in September 1938 and then in September 1939. It is a spurious use of hindsight, giving the impression that all parties knew in September 1938 that another year had been gained. But the precise date of future war remained a mystery—it could have been months or years. . . . In any case, Chamberlain never shifted from his basic conviction that Britain would only ever fight a war of defence. . . . Because of this widely shared conviction, Britain did not go to war in September 1938, nor in March 1939, nor could she give the slightest assistance to Poland in September 1939.[30]

Keith Robbins' conclusion, much like many accounts that had been sympathetic to Chamberlain in the 1950s, perceived Munich as a necessary trial that Britain needed to endure to enable her to stand bravely for freedom during a horrific world war.

Munich was the necessary purgatory through which Englishmen had to pass before the nation could emerge united in 1939. When war came, it was a war for which the country was ready. There was no excitement, no fever of the emotions; all sentiment had been drained a year earlier. . . . Britain went to war in 1939 rather than 1938, not merely because there was greater confidence in the armaments position, but because it was agreed that enough was enough.[31]

A brief account of the European diplomatic activity that preceded the war Chamberlain strove so hard to obviate was Christopher Thorne's *The Approach of War, 1938–1939*, published in 1967. Like many historians of the 1960s and since, Thorne alluded to the evident inadequacies of the old "Guilty Men" interpretation of British foreign policy, and he hoped to offer fresh insight into those events that so dominated the late 1930s. He perceived the messianic quality of Chamberlain's indefatigable efforts for peace, comparing them with the erratic brilliance of an earlier crusader, Woodrow Wilson.

> Appeasement became a mission. How many can believe in their mission whilst leaving unimpaired their judgement, their acceptance of criticism, their feelings for those impatiently trampled along the path to achievement? Woodrow Wilson for one had not been able to do so. Missions can corrupt as much as power, and Chamberlain, with his "inexhaustible vanity," found both to his liking.[32]

In the author's estimation, as events began to heat up in the ethnic cauldron that was Central Europe in 1938, Chamberlain preferred a dangerous optimism rather than a truthful assessment, which could well have hindered his appeasement efforts.

> As the urgency of the mission grew, one saw what one wished to see. Thus Hitler, whose government was for Chamberlain in May 1938 "utterly untrustworthy and dishonest" became four months later "a man who could be relied upon when he had given his word," . . . The testimony of Lord Swinton as to his Prime Minister's innermost thoughts at the time serves only to underline the hollowness of recent attempts to proclaim Munich an exercise in *Realpolitik*. To a far larger extent it was a study in self-delusion.[33]

Thorne pondered the actual physical toll of Munich on the Czechs, who had mistakenly believed that the high moral stance of their Western allies would protect them from German aggression, instead to discover to their great chagrin that morality mattered little in the face of impending military force.

> Altogether the country lost 11,000 square miles, 70 percent of its iron and steel capacity, 80 per cent of its textiles, 90 per cent of its porcelain, 86 per cent of its glass, 86 per cent of its chemicals, and 70 per cent of its electric power. It also lost, in this apparent triumph for self-determination, about 800,000 citizens of Czech origin.[34]

Thorne reflected on the "fiercest differences of opinion" engendered by the Munich settlement when he alluded to the resignation of Alfred Duff Cooper almost immediately after the Prime Minister's return and Winston Churchill's withering criticism of the entire affair. In a telling vignette, the author related an incident that took place in the House of Commons after Munich and was symbolic of the growing ambivalence of British public opinion:

> When it was announced that the Government were providing Prague with 10 million pounds to assist them to raise a loan of 30 million pounds, an opponent of appeasement in the Smoking Room of the House remarked on the changing values of betrayal since Judas Iscariot; he was knocked down by a supporter of Chamberlain.[35]

Opposition to appeasement could not coalesce, however, until the Nazi seizure of Prague in March 1939. Then Chamberlain would be obligated to make a dramatic volte-face and conclude a guarantee to Poland as a deterrent to future German belligerence in eastern Europe. This would be the end of "active appeasement." Thorne's monograph is an outstanding resource on Europe's inexorable descent into world war.

An account that utilized newly released Cabinet papers, which had been routinely subject to the thirty-year rule, was Roger Parkinson's *Peace for Our Time: Munich to Dunkirk—the Inside Story*, published in 1971. In his introduction, the author noted that he "had tried to avoid easy comparisons based on hindsight . . . and attempted to provide narration rather than presumptuous judgement,"[36] a manner of judgment that had been second nature to many accounts of the 1940s and 1950s. The author broke with much of the orthodox historical dogma over Munich, stressing that Chamberlain's initial trip to Germany set the real stage for the abandonment of the Czechs. By the end of September 1938 the die had long been cast.

> Berchtesgaden, not Munich, represents the pinnacle of appeasement. Events which followed were echoes of that first confrontation when the ex-house-painter decisively out-manoeuvred the Birmingham screw-manufacturer's son; It was at Hitler's mountain retreat that Chamberlain committed himself, in principle, to the handover of Sudetenland. . . . So Chamberlain's agreement "in principle" was not given on the grounds of justice, to revert the wrongs of Versailles; nor to prevent further Czech disintegration—by then the riots were firmly

under control. It was simply to preserve peace. . . . Peace had to be kept, at almost any price. Subsequent events merely set this price.[37]

At the conference itself, Parkinson alluded to a very embarrassing moment for the four powers that could have served as a harbinger of the bankruptcy of German promises. The author quoted an actual eyewitness of the Munich proceedings: "The final blow came at the moment of signature when it was discovered that the pompous inkstand contained no ink."[38]

Parkinson ruminated on the severe economic weaknesses that bedeviled Chamberlain in the wake of Munich, and he argued that although the Prime Minister had the best of intentions, he was unable and/or unwilling to transform Britain into a wartime economy for a war that he hoped would never be fought.

> Chamberlain has been fiercely criticized for not using adequately the extra, precious time he bought with Munich. But the Cabinet records make clear how anxious he was to increase the defence budget, and how completely economic and financial dictates prevented him. Only by switching the country at once to a wartime footing could more money have been found. . . . The resulting high taxes, restricted freedom, and bureaucratic impertinence would have created political upheaval—which would not have prepared Britain for war. Chamberlain had to balance the militants against the mood of the country—he dared not push too fast.[39]

This notion of finance as a "fourth arm of defence" has been developed in the chapter dealing with economics and rearmament. To someone who had spent much of his professional life either in business or directing the economy as the Chancellor of the Exchequer, those economic fears were that much more real to Chamberlain, and they served to hinder efforts to establish any form of rearmament program that might prove effective in the event of a European war. Parkinson discussed also the rather phenomenal popularity of Chamberlain after Munich, and the sad fact that the "man of peace" was hardly willing or able to prepare Britain for war; hence appeasement:

> Britain now needed a policy for the future. Appeasement and rearmament would preoccupy the Cabinet. Views would range from the realistic and far-sighted to the cowardly and blind. In Autumn 1938 Chamberlain had a powerful weapon in the overwhelming support of the people. An elected politician, he had conducted Britain's foreign affairs as they wanted him to do. . . . Chamberlain believed that if he

had "stood up to the dictators" in 1938, he would have been denied support from the electorate, from the powerful potential ally across the Atlantic, and from the Dominions. Churchill and his few colleagues would have been inadequate compensation; the voices for peace were still shouting down the cries for war.[40]

Of course the chorus of peace would be stilled in the wreckage of the Munich agreement in March 1939; the Prime Minister would be obligated to become a warrior, a state well-nigh anathema to his nature. Parkinson, like Thorne, chronicled the slippery slope down into war that occurred in spite of Chamberlain's nearly Herculean efforts to the contrary.

The 1972 publication of Corelli Barnett's *The Collapse of British Power* contains a valuable assessment of the consequences of Munich for Chamberlain, and is well worth review. Barnett's analysis of the Chamberlain plan for his personal intervention in the Czech crisis of late summer 1938 (Plan Z) attacked the Prime Minister's lack of strategic thinking on the possible, indeed, probable consequences of his diplomatic efforts. The hoary, well-worn cliché about Chamberlain's lack of a "sense of history" seems relevant to Barnett's reasoning:

> Chamberlain had unveiled both a course of action and a scheme for a settlement which demonstrate that even now he failed to see, or refused to see, the European situation in terms of conflict, strategy and the equilibrium of power. In the first place, by himself going to visit Hitler at his own suggestion he was only bringing to its climax that process of chasing after Germany which for so long had made that country a gift of the diplomatic upperhand. . . . In order to win a present respite, Chamberlain was now quite prepared to countenance the disappearance of a well-armed and well-organised Czechoslovakia from the European scene; to see forty divisions, and powerful defences, struck from the balance-sheet of "allied" strength, and their first-class equipment added instead to Germany's. He was prepared for these things to happen because, as the record makes clear, they held little importance for him. They were outside his system of political thought.[41]

Barnett alluded to Chamberlain's desperate letter to Berlin of 27 September 1938 ("I feel certain you can get all essentials without war, and without delay!") that suggested a Four-Power Conference that became Munich.[42] Although much of his Cabinet had rejected the humiliating Godesberg terms foisted upon the Czechs during Chamberlain's second mission to Germany, Barnett leveled his criticism at the Prime Minister's evident duplicity:

> The purpose of the proposed conference was therefore to avert war at all costs—and to do so by means which Chamberlain had been advocating since Godesberg, but to which half his Cabinet were now opposed: to wit, hand over the swag to the criminal in return for a due receipt, in order to save him the trouble of having to rob his victim.[43]

The Churchillian flavor of these comments represents an example of the author's estimation of Chamberlain's less-than-visionary if not overly optimistic policy toward Nazi Germany. If the Prime Minister had not won "peace for our time," at least he strongly felt Munich to be the initial step of an eventual European pacification. Barnett referred to a Chamberlain letter of 2 October to the Archbishop of Canterbury, which evidenced the ebullience of the P.M. just after Munich: "I sincerely believe that we have at last opened the way to that general appeasement which alone can save the world from chaos."[44]

This hopeful attitude was not enough to protect Chamberlain from the machinations of Nazi aggression in the coming months, but if there were to be trouble, as Barnett noted, it would not be of his doing:

> So strongly did Chamberlain wish to nurture the tender plant of mutual respect and amity which he believed to have germinated at Munich that he even wanted to discourage the Lord Mayor of London from opening a fund for Czechoslovakian refugees for fear that it "might have a bad effect on public opinion in Germany."[45]

Regrettably for Neville Chamberlain, his sordid antithesis in Berlin did not regard the "respect and amity" as reciprocal. As Barnett would clearly delineate, this imbalance between a man who lived for peace and one who only saw the world in terms of conquest would inevitably threaten the stability of Europe.

> Yet perhaps the most dangerous of all consequences of the Munich crisis was the total contempt in which Hitler now held Chamberlain. An English diplomat in the Berlin embassy was informed by reliable sources . . . that "Hitler regarded the Prime Minister as an impertinent busybody who spoke the ridiculous jargon of an outmoded democracy."[46]

Barnett's concluding judgment on the consequences of Munich was to be deferred until after the Nazi seizure of Prague forced Chamberlain's administration to scramble for a new policy amid the broken shards of appeasement's folly. Rather typically in view of his background, Barnett's perspective was of the military loss to the West, which was to surely follow the demise of Czech freedom:

> Chamberlain's surrender at Munich was thus finally consummated in the way that Churchill had foretold in October. The Czech army of forty divisions finally disappeared from the European balance, to provide equipment instead for forty new German divisions. It was a turnover of eighty divisions in Germany's favour. . . . And German troops now also stood on the border of Romania, a country rich in the oil resources necessary for the waging of modern war. Chamberlain in his well-meaning blindness had brought about the greatest of all the catastrophes which had befallen France and England since Hitler came to power.[47]

So much of Barnett's emphasis in his *Collapse of British Power* has to do with the economic weakness brought on Britain by two traumatic life and death struggles just a generation apart. The cruel irony of the economic situation was that the Premier had been correct all along: the economic dislocation caused by defense spending and total war served to weaken the country and the empire irrevocably. The only chance for Neville Chamberlain to preserve his beloved prewar Britain was to secure peace; we know now, in light of Nazi misdeeds, that save total British capitulation, which was never an option, Chamberlain never had a really viable chance for an overall European pacification.

A brief but valuable monograph that detailed the events from the *Anschluss* to the aftermath of Munich was Roy Douglas' *In the Year of Munich*, published in 1977. The initial chapter traced the failure of the Chamberlain administration to conclude a meaningful accord with the Italians in late 1937 and early 1938, which may well have placed a barrier in the way of the eventual *Anschluss* of March 1938. Douglas' sober recounting of the road to Munich dutifully attempted to eliminate some of the mythology that had evolved over forty years of hindsight. An example of one popular but mistaken perception was that Foreign Secretary Anthony Eden, who had resigned over the timing and conditions of Anglo-Italian discussions in February 1938, was an "implacable opponent of any understanding with dictators."[48] Douglas disagreed, and his arguments belied Eden's remembrances. He noted how even Alfred Duff Cooper, the only Cabinet member to resign in the wake of Munich, was an ardent supporter of Chamberlain's Italian initiative in February 1938, simply out of his greater fear of future German aggression and the need to obviate it with an Italian alliance.[49]

On the aftermath of the Munich Conference, Douglas argued that Chamberlain's most desperate hope—that the agreement would serve as the initial stage of an overall European pacification—was most probably illusory from the very beginning. His reasoned exposition of Munich's denouement followed:

> The overwhelming question which confronted Britain and the world was whether the Munich settlement could become the foundation of a new international order, based on reconciliation between the Powers. Probably this notion, on which Chamberlain in particular had set his heart, never really had a chance. Reconciliation presupposed not merely the mutual interest of the powers in averting war and reducing the universal burden of armaments; it also depended on genuine goodwill and trust in all major countries. This palpably did not exist. The British people—whether or not they regarded Munich as preferable to war—did not think of it as a just and equable settlement.[50]

In his analysis of the ramifications of the Munich settlement, Douglas insisted that the events of 1938 occurred in their respective order for significant reasons, in a pattern of cause and effect.

> Munich was a natural corollary of the *Anschluss*. The only possible way of preventing the *Anschluss* lay in getting on terms with Mussolini. . . . The sombre fact remains that this was the one slender chance to hold back Germany from her career of conquest without war which presented itself after Chamberlain had assumed the Premiership. Chamberlain's fault was not—as most critics have suggested—that he intruded in foreign policy, but that he allowed his first Foreign Secretary to have his head for much too long.[51]

Arguably Douglas' perspective gives too much weight to the hope in the sincerity and good faith of Il Duce, who was, after the Hoare-Laval fiasco, subject to mercurial flashes of petulance toward the West interspersed by periods of relative Anglo-Italian harmony. He was certainly not a figure to be trusted with the peace of Europe, a fact well known to Eden if obscured to his chief. In regard to the pejorative stigma attached to Chamberlain's pursuit of appeasement at Munich, Douglas queried why the Prime Minister's reputation had evolved into that "of a foolish and gullible old man, or even a wilful traitor to whom dictatorship was dearer than democracy?"[52] He attested to the "honourable manner" in which Chamberlain handled himself during the September crisis, offering a rationale for the heavy opprobrium later heaped upon the Premier:

> The most powerful arguments against Chamberlain do not really turn on the wisdom or unwisdom of the substantive measures which he took, but rather on the repeated indications that he believed Hitler to be speaking the truth. His declaration after Munich that he believed he had secured "peace in our time," and the profound trust which he evidently placed in the declaration he made along with Hitler just after the main Munich conference, are two famous indications of that state of mind.[53]

In reference to the failure of appeasement signified by the Nazi seizure of Prague and the inexorable war six months later, Roy Douglas concluded that Neville Chamberlain "failed because he attempted the impossible; but it does him no dishonour that he made the attempt."[54]

An insightful comparative study of appeasement in different periods of Britain's history was *Amiens and Munich*, written in 1978 by Ernst Presseisen. The author analyzed the similarities between the 1802 Treaty of Amiens, which halted eight years of war between Britain and Bonapartist France, and the September 1938 Munich agreement, which at that time avoided a war over the Sudeten Czech crisis between Britain and Nazi Germany. He noted that in 1802 as in 1938, Prime Ministers Henry Addington and Neville Chamberlain believed that they had brought back "peace with honor" from their respective peace conferences, only to have war erupt approximately a year later.[55] In both eras, Britain's leaders were faced with dangerous revolutionary situations, one arising as the byproduct of the destruction of feudal France, and the other an atavistic, reactionary, racist summons to Germans as the "master race," destined for conquest and control of Europe. Presseisen referred to the nature of appeasement when he alluded to a personal letter sent by Foreign Office official Orme Sargent to John Wheeler-Bennett in 1948, in which Sargent commented on the policy's complexity:

It becomes questionable as a method of negotiation only if it can be shown to be *immoral*; i.e., the appeaser sacrifices the rights and interests of a third party and not his own when making his concession; or if it is clearly *dangerous*, i.e., where the concession made seriously undermines the strength of the appeaser . . . and lastly when the whole process of appeasement is just ineffective.[56]

In retrospect, all of the above were true in relation to Munich, as the Czechs were betrayed, the Western allies weakened, and Chamberlain's dearest hopes shattered by Nazi duplicity in the six-month aftermath of the conference. Presseisen maintained that appeasement was a multilayered phenomenon that could not be readily understood without background information on its singular characteristics. He commented on one of the most significant elements of the policy:

What appears so striking about appeasement is first of all its lack of planning. Perhaps it would be better to call it a lack of foresight, since plans existed to negotiate a peace with France and a *detente* with Germany. Chamberlain wanted closer relations with Germany and had apparently laid down a series of steps to bring this about. Yet what happened in 1938 bore no relation to his plans. In fact, appeasement policies are almost always panic or impulse policies with visions that are very limited. The objective (peace) to be reached is so important that not much thought is given to events or policies in the following period. It is then that the lack of foresight becomes most apparent, and the implications of appeasement lead to disastrous results.[57]

Thus in the immediate aftermath of Munich Chamberlain continued to view events with a very roseate perspective, even as his policy of conciliation was beginning to collapse in the face of German misdeeds. Presseisen clearly delineated the dramatic variance in the meaning of Munich to both London and Berlin.

Did appeasement as a policy make England's enemies aware of her pacific intentions? It certainly did; it did all too well! The inadequacy of appeasement is the inadequacy to communicate clearly how far this policy would go. Thus, what was seen as the final concession on the one side was regarded as the first in a series of triumphs by the other.[58]

In conclusion, Presseisen expounded his opinions of the Munich agreement and of Neville Chamberlain, inextricably linked by destiny in an eternally pejorative fashion. His analysis, working across the centuries to illuminate foreign policy in both circumstances, outlined the deadly threats to British interests from both

Napoleonic and Nazi aggression, and highlighted what often occurs to men of peace in time of war.

> At Amiens, as at Munich, Great Britain obtained the peace she wanted so badly. Each time she paid for it with the territory of smaller states. The English lost nothing—except prestige. . . . Those who raised their voices against the settlements, Grenville and Windham, . . . Churchill and Duff Cooper, were rejected as extremists. Peace was reasonable, middle of the road and the public wanted no more heroics. Ultimately, Amiens and Munich have this in common: on the English side both settlements were the handiwork of moderate men in an immoderate age.[59]

And, regarding Chamberlain's legacy in the wake of Munich,

> Whatever his expectations were, and Chamberlain may not have been certain in his own mind what the future held, the outcome of appeasement was not peace so much as a period of watchful waiting. As an effective peace policy, then, appeasement never held much promise after the Munich pact. The gradual destruction of Czechoslovakia created more rather than less tension in central Europe. . . . Chamberlain always believed that the Munich agreement was right for its own sake, as the apogee of appeasement, rather than an instrument by which Britain gained valuable time. Chamberlain rejected the inevitability of war and the appeasement of Germany was to prevent conflict rather than delay it.[60]

His efforts placed the Chamberlain's government's perilous stance in regard to the Czech crisis in a continuum of British foreign policy going back to 1800, and in a compelling fashion.

One of the more relevant sources on Munich and its aftermath was written by Telford Taylor in 1979, *Munich: The Price of Peace*. Taylor was the chief American prosecutor at the Nuremberg Nazi war crimes trials, and his effort has long been regarded as one by which the standards were set. More than 1,000 pages long, it is magisterial in scope, voluminously covering the twenty years beginning in the wake of the Allied victory at Versailles, leading to the "unmitigated" diplomatic defeat of the West at Munich. Taylor insisted that he meant to discern the "lessons" of Munich, if there were any, from his scholarship. He offered a "fresh" assessment of the men and methods of Munich forty years after the fact.[61] His personal views of Neville Chamberlain and his historical legacy reflected the more sophisticated outlook of the "modern" era, which relied to a greater extent upon empirical evidence and documentation than the outrage and emotion of the "Guilty Men" years. Like Martin Gilbert nearly fifteen years before, Taylor sought not to judge the Prime Minister, but to understand:

> The character and motives of Neville Chamberlain, I believe, have been much distorted in the mirror of historical literature, in which his image is that of a timorous, bumbling, and naive old gentleman, waving an umbrella as a signal of cringing subservience to a bully. Nothing could be further from the truth. Chamberlain did what he did at Munich not because he thought he had to, but because he thought it right. For him, appeasement was a policy not of fear but of common and moral sense. In public life he was a dominant and often domineering man, profoundly convinced of the rightness of his own judgments, and skilled in bending others to his will. Sadly mistaken he may have been; cowardly or indecisive he was not, and for him Munich was no surrender, but a passionately moral act.[62]

Without doubt the avoidance of a European war would have been perceived as an act of high morality by most Englishmen in 1938, but it may well have been much more difficult to fathom the moral aspects from the perspective of Prague. The luckless Czechs would then soon be prostrate under the heel of the Gestapo, with questions of morality being among the least of their worries.

On the aftermath of the Munich conference, Taylor pondered the factors behind the German withdrawal from imminent war to a diplomatic settlement. He reasoned that the respective mobilizations of the Czech army and the British navy in the immediate days before Munich removed any element of surprise from German planning to invade Czechoslovakia. Taylor also alluded to the perception in Berlin of British and French weakness, which caused the Nazi tyrant to step up the diplomatic pressure in his search for a bloodless victory.

> It was plain to Hitler that Britain and France would go to great lengths to avoid war, and, once embarked on negotiations, he ruthlessly pressed his bargaining advantage. No doubt after Berchtesgaden he found it difficult to believe that Chamberlain would grant him the bulk of his demands but would go to war rather than yield to the new demands at Godesberg. In this he underestimated the strength of the British sense of order and fair play, as reflected by Halifax much more than Chamberlain. . . . Chamberlain's pertinacity had reaped its reward. He never gave up, and by following every failure with another effort, he finally pushed Hitler into a position in which no one—not

even Goering and Mussolini—would regard a refusal to compromise as rational.[63]

Taylor reserved some of his sternest criticism for the British and French behavior after Munich, in that the "guarantee" that putatively would have ensured the integrity of the remainder of the Czech state was as hollow as the earlier German proclamations of "no more territorial ambitions in Europe." He mused on the Chamberlain administration's abandonment of their pledged word, which abetted the Nazi effort to seize the Czech rump in March 1939. Appeasement had, at last, reached its nadir.

> The Munich Agreement, in the eyes of the British and French governments, was a cloak of respectability, . . . disclosure of the emptiness and futility of the commission and the guarantee would have torn gaping holes in the cloak. In retrospect, what is most offensive about the British Government's policy at and after Munich is that its leaders had no intention of effectively opposing whatever the Germans might insist on in execution of the agreement, while publicly proclaiming that the three-two "pro-Czech" majority in the commission and the international guarantee would give the Czechs justice and security. In this betrayal, Britain well deserved the Napoleonic epithet "perfidious Albion."[64]

In conclusion, Taylor offered his perspectives on the Munich Conference and its rather ironic denouement, namely a peace conference that served to accelerate the events leading to war, the conflict that Neville Chamberlain had so long feared.

> It is a safe conclusion that the chances of securing a stable European peace by ceding the Sudetenland were remote, both in fact and as viewed at the time by those involved in decision-making. Even Chamberlain, until the eve of the Munich conference, repeatedly revealed his doubts of such a prospect, in his private letters as well as in ministerial conclave. . . . It was not until the excitement of Plan Z, the naive belief that he had established a "personal influence" over Hitler, and the acclaim of the German crowds had inflated his hopes of emerging as the peacemaker of Europe, that he succumbed to the disastrous conviction that Munich had made war less likely, and therefore the rearmament program did not need to be expanded.[65]

Finally, the author stressed his belief that for many Britons, Munich was an opportunity to avoid the horrors of imminent war, and delay that catastrophe for an indefinite, hopefully extended period.

Munich was not, except in Chamberlain's autointoxicated phase, the product of a hope for an enduring European peace. Rather it was the result of a feckless procrastination on the part of some, and of a sincere conviction on the part of others, that the Allies could fight better in the future even with the loss of Czechoslovakia, that they could with her aid in September 1938.[66]

A book concerned with the military aspects of Munich and its aftermath was written by Williamson Murray in 1984, entitled *The Change in the European Balance of Power, 1938–1939*. Murray's effort reviewed the fateful events of 1938 that led to Munich, the seizure of Prague, and the outbreak of the wider war in September 1939. Murray's background as a military historian rendered insight on the complex parameters of the Czech crisis, and the actual readiness (if any!) of the respective adversaries to fight at the time of Munich. He commented on Chamberlain's diplomatic efforts between the Godesberg meeting of 22 September and the eventual Munich conclave on 29–30 September, and noted that he found them to be somewhat contrary to the Prime Minister's desire of a lasting European peace:

> There is a strange irony in Chamberlain's peacemaking efforts. He had hoped to keep Britain out of war by preventing a European conflict. But appeasement had not worked. The efforts to mediate between Czechs and Germans had increasingly involved Britain in the crisis. Chamberlain's peacemaking flights served above all to underline the mendaciousness of Nazi diplomacy. Hitler's brusque dismissal of the British efforts at Godesberg had revealed the real purposes of Nazi Germany. By the end of September, appeasement and the German reaction had persuaded much of the British public that Germany was again a menace that must be stopped—by war if necessary.[67]

The stiffening of British public opinion in the final weeks of September 1938 saw gas masks distributed and trenches dug in London's parks in readiness for an imminent war. This made the sense of relief among the British populace all the more profound when the Four-Power Conference reached its "successful" conclusion on 30 September. Murray offered a compelling analysis of Chamberlain's flawed policy of 1938:

> The essence of Chamberlain's tragedy was that, having pursued a course that revealed the nature of Nazi policy, he refused to recognize

that reality. From the *Anschluss* on, he rejected a strong, anti-German line. He was quite correct in his belief that a forceful policy would split the British nation and certainly the Conservative party, not to mention the dominions. . . . Ironically, the conciliatory nature of appeasement and the blatant, cynical Nazi response convinced the British that Hitler and his regime were malicious and dangerous. At Godesberg appeasement reached a dead end. Had Chamberlain recognized that fact, he would have had little difficulty in persuading his ministers and the country to resist. He did not and, in the end, threw everything away on the gamble that Hitler was trustworthy, that war would not come, and that Britain had no strategic interest in either Czechoslovakia or Southeastern Europe.[68]

Murray insisted that none of the participants were actually prepared to fight even a limited war at the time of Munich; conceivably, the Western allies would have been better off to seize the initiative in September 1938. This military effort, according to the author, "would have led to the eventual collapse of the Nazi regime at considerably less cost than the war that broke out the following September."[69] This statement is a facile piece of historical conjecture, if not a credible alternative to six years of torturous struggle. Murray noted that Chamberlain's statements after Munich, especially on rearmament, would haunt him later as appeasement was eventually discredited by events outside the Prime Minister's control.

In arguing for its policy over the summer, the government had stressed how unprepared for war the country was. Despite some attempts during the Munich debate to suggest that Britain had embarked on a "great program of rearmament," Chamberlain was caught in a web of his own making. If Britain was so ill-prepared, then the government must speed rearmament to repair the deficiencies, and, all protestations to the contrary, such a policy could only imply mistrust of German intentions. . . . In fact, Chamberlain had no intention of altering British rearmament policy. He indicated his real approach in linking British rearmament to a program of general European disarmament.[70]

Only the fall of Prague would ostensibly divert Chamberlain from active appeasement, and the rearmament campaign would palpably speed up as the Nazi mask was withdrawn to reveal a rapaciousness Chamberlain did not think possible among "civilized" men. The belated rearmament efforts allowed the the British to emerge victorious during the Blitz of 1940, but only on the razor's edge. If their deliverance was to come only by the slightest of margins during the Battle of Britain, how much worse could it have been if war had broken out in September 1938? Sadly for the Allies, the Germans did more in the period after Munich to strengthen their war machine than did the British, and tragedies such as Dunkirk and the fall of France were to be the unfortunate results. Murray discussed all of these compelling scenarios, and his work is a valued addition to the debate on appeasement and Munich.

A cogent contribution to the historiography is the work written in 1982 by Larry Fuchser, *Neville Chamberlain and Appeasement*. The author alluded to the historiographical debate over Neville Chamberlain's legacy, with the criticisms of the "Guilty Men" supporters opposed by the Chamberlain sympathizers, who felt he realistically and honorably addressed the problems that he faced as Premier, which were incidentally among the most daunting of this century. He also made mention of the "Munich analogy," which has been utilized by U.S. policy makers and their European counterparts whenever and wherever convenient, however flawed. Thus Korea, the 1956 Suez crisis, and Vietnam were all viewed as situations in which aggression, if left unchecked, could develop into another horrifying example of appeasement and truckling under to dictators. In Fuchser's estimation, any analysis of Neville Chamberlain had to rise above the partisan squabbling of the past to do justice to the man. His introductory synopsis of the Prime Minister was illustrative:

> In general, Chamberlain was a much more powerful leader, both in his control over domestic affairs and in foreign policy, than has heretofore been indicated either by his critics or his apologists. It is important to recognize from the outset that Chamberlain saw appeasement not as the diplomacy of capitulation but as a dramatically positive effort to achieve a settlement of all the intransient issues that had plagued European politics since the signing of the Versailles treaty in 1919. As such, it was a policy conceived in the classic manner of nineteenth-century European diplomacy, a gentlemanly agreement to redraw the political map of Europe. Unfortunately, at least one of the partners to that agreement was not a gentleman![71]

This notion of the continuity of British foreign policy from the nineteenth century to the Chamberlain years would become popular as the scholarship of the historiographical debate became more specialized in the 1970s and 1980s. Ironically, Chamberlain's businessman's orientation lacked what scholars have called a "sense of history," with its nonideological basis and ignorance of the notion of Britain's historical role vis-à-vis the European balance of power.

In regard to Munich itself, Fuchser stated that the signed agreement which was the "peace" of paper fluttering in the wind upon Chamberlain's triumphant return to England was, to the P.M., the crucial element of all of his peacemaking efforts.

> To Hitler, the agreement most likely appeared to be an innocuous document and signing it meant very little, but to Chamberlain it meant a great deal. What to Hitler was an insignificant afterthought to the Munich accord was to Chamberlain nothing less than the Anglo-German understanding which he had long hoped to achieve, the foundation on which a lasting structure of peace, the appeasement of Europe, could be erected. . . . While critics of Chamberlain have seen the fate of Czechoslovakia as the central issue decided at Munich, this was not the meaning attached to the conference by Chamberlain himself. To him, the triumph of Munich, the victory to which he attached the unfortunate phrase "peace in our time," lay not in the settlement of the Sudeten question but in the private accord he had reached with Hitler. It was this, not the four-power agreement on Czechoslovakia, which he waved to the cheering crowds at Heston airport on his return to London.[72]

The author alluded to a poignant letter written by Chamberlain to his stepmother more than a month after his diplomatic apogee at Munich. In it the Prime Minister made clear his optimism in the face of an ever perilous European scene, and Fuchser commented on the Premier's attitude in early November 1938:

> With the Munich agreement behind him, Chamberlain looked forward to better days ahead when the nations of the world could return to the period of mutual trust in which rearmament would be unnecessary and in which the business of improving the human condition would be paramount. These were clearly not the sentiments of a man who believed that he had merely succeeded in "buying time" in which to rearm in preparation for inevitable war, but of a man who believed that the nadir had been reached and that better things lay ahead.[73]

Certainly the events of late 1938, including the commencement of pogroms against German Jews and the fall of Prague in March 1939, forced Chamberlain to duly reconsider his attitudes in regard to Germany. Perhaps the greatest irony was that appeasement, as a policy meant to obviate a European war, only served to make a conflict more probable; the panic move that was the Polish guarantee was to be the vehicle which dragged Britain into a world war. Fuchser pondered the Prime Minister's motivations at Munich, criticizing his naivete as to the true intentions of the Nazi despot:

> Chamberlain did not sign an agreement which meant the end of Czechoslovak sovereignty because he wanted to buy time or because he felt Britain was too weak militarily to do otherwise, but because he believed that the dismemberment of Czechoslovakia was the price which had to be paid if another world war was to be avoided.[74]

This notion of an Anglo-German agreement for the pacification of European tension was, again, uppermost in Chamberlain's thoughts at Munich; only his lack of vision as to the iniquity of his adversaries would destroy both appeasement and his own historical reputation. Fuchser's account, supportive of that legacy so obscured by time and opprobrium, was important for its exposition of the extended appeasement debate.

One of the more dramatic ironies of appeasement historiography is that, fifty years after Munich, the debate has come full circle. The literary efforts of the late 1930s, 1940s, and 1950s, so filled with invective against the timorous "Guilty Men," were "weighed in the balance and found wanting" by the more detailed, empirical studies of the last quarter-century. The ideology and emotionalism that held such little weight with Neville Chamberlain and characterized the tone of the attacks against him, was abandoned by the clinical documentation of more recent scholarship. Insight into this critical epoch in British and European history could only benefit from a cessation of the personal rancor directed toward the Chamberlain legacy. Two recent efforts, however, have been characterized by a passion that hearkens back a half-century, when a simpler world seemed to offer moral absolutes and less ambiguity than today. This "recycling" of appeasement as a morality play is perhaps understandable in light of the formidable number of specialized studies during the past twenty-five years. Any attack or defense of Chamberlain in the present may be tenable only on an ideological level, since the detailed research into the complexities of appeasement as a policy has been so exhaustive in scope. The first of the two accounts from 1989 is British historian John Charmley's *Chamberlain and the Lost Peace*. The author attempted to "delineate Chamberlain's struggle to avert the inevitable consequences of war,"[75] in this case a war that would doubtless end Britain's claim to world-power status. Unlike many of his fellow historians, Charmley was not willing to view the Second World War in moral terms, solely of good triumphant over evil. In his words:

> Chamberlain saw no gains for Britain in another war, . . . it is by no means clear that the results of the Second World War were commensurate with the sacrifices it entailed. The old balance between the fascist and communist Powers on the continent was tipped decidedly in favour of the latter, whilst the economic and diplomatic foundations of the British Empire received a mortal blow.[76]

Charmley's rather amoral adherence to "peace at all costs," his reluctance to perceive Britain's fight as one in defense of all of Western civilization, was similar to much of Chamberlain's own perspective; that is, the Prime Minister's belief that he could deal with anyone to secure world peace, and that there was no reason why dictatorships and democracies could not coexist peacefully. Charmley alluded to the dramatic scene in the House of Commons on 28 September 1938, when Chamberlain publicly announced his acceptance of a third invitation to Germany in a desperate attempt to avoid war.

> For Chamberlain it was not only a tremendous (but unplanned) *coup de theatre*, it was a vindication of his policy towards Mussolini and of his patient hammering away at Hitler; of course it might yet all fail, but in his heart Chamberlain did not believe that it would, not now, not after such efforts and so many hopes.[77]

Charmley offered his analysis of the Munich agreement in the immediate wake of its signing; unlike many of his contemporary historians he was ebullient in regard to the potential for peace in central Europe.

> The Munich Agreement was, on paper, a considerable improvement on the Godesberg terms (as even Duff Cooper admitted) and bore a marked resemblance to the Anglo-French plan formulated after Berchtesgaden. . . . Much would, of course, depend upon the spirit in which Germany carried out her obligations but, given Hitler's surprising climb-down, there seemed reasons for confidence that he was not hell-bent on war.[78]

Why war indeed, when one could receive all the benefits of conquest without the risk of conflict? The critical danger was, of course, that one day the Western powers would call the Nazi bluff, with war as a result, as occurred in early September 1939. Charmley referred to Chamberlain's infamous pronouncement of 30 September 1938, when upon his return to London he pledged a belief that he had gained "peace for our time" at Munich: "Seldom have two sentences so blasted a reputation. It seems likely that the words were hardly out of his mouth before Chamberlain regretted them. . . . That he regarded Munich as providing an opening for better Anglo-German relations was the most he believed."[79] In Charmley's perspective, the Munich Agreement proved to be the high-water mark of the policy of appeasement. In rapid fashion, events out of the Prime Minister's control would intervene to shatter his hopes in the fateful five months after October 1938, the last being the brutal occupation of Prague on 15 March 1939. Charmley commented further on the consequences of Munich:

> The greatest lesson of the crisis was, in Halifax's view, the "unwisdom of having a foreign policy with insufficient armed strength." Defence policy had to relate to foreign policy, and Chamberlain had for some years tried to ensure that it did so. . . . But the crisis had other effects. It intensified that "return to Party politics" which Chamberlain's accession to the Premiership had brought; it invested a great deal of the Prime Minister's prestige in the success of his foreign policy; and it created a climate in which German intentions were now eagerly scrutinised—by Chamberlain's supporters looking for reasons for optimism, and by his opponents for signs to justify their pessimism.[80]

Although optimism was necessarily in short supply following the outrages perpetrated upon German Jewry during November 1938's *Kristallnacht*, Chamberlain was resolute in his determination to avoid another European war. Events would prove his efforts to be in vain; but in John Charmley's estimation, Chamberlain was to be heartily lauded for his devotion to his country, the cause of peace, and the good of mankind: "The venom of his opponents pursued him long, but his was the only policy which offered any hope of avoiding war—and of saving both lives and the British Empire."[81] Charmley's book clearly evidenced the ambiguity of the debate over Neville Chamberlain's legacy and his use of the policy of appeasement for the pacification of Europe in the late 1930s. That support for the Prime Minister could appear fifty years after his tenure of office and the tragic failure of his policy reflects the continued volatility of recent scholarship.

The second account, Richard Lamb's *The Drift to War, 1922–1939*, is of a far more critical nature than Charmley's effort. Lamb began with an analysis of the aftermath of Versailles and the reparations crisis, and delineated the baleful events of the 1930s up through the final desperate diplomatic initiatives to avoid "the abyss" of world war. In his introduction, Lamb stated unequivocally that the German threat at the time of Munich was less a physical danger and more a diplomatic bluff from Berlin than was realized in September 1938. "Hitler was bluffing at Munich because his armies were too weak to fight in the east and west simultaneously, but Chamberlain hoped that appeasing him would turn him into a peaceful animal. Such hopes were misplaced."[82] The irony is that for so recent an account, Lamb had characteristics similar to the "Guilty Men" genre in his personal venom for many of those responsible in the 1930s. He recounted that he had actually voted in the Oxford Union motion against war in February 1933, had supported the Peace Ballot, and had roundly condemned the Hoare-Laval Plan. Lamb intoned charges that might well have come out of a work fifty years earlier:

> The archives reveal clearly the cowardice and hesitations of most British politicians in the 1930s, apart from Winston Churchill, Leo Amery, Viscount Hailsham, Alfred Duff Cooper (Viscount Norwich), and Austen Chamberlain. It is a sad tale, from which few in high places in Britain emerge with credit.[83]

On the circumstances that led up to the Four-Power Conference at Munich, Lamb pondered just what might have been if the Prime Minister had decided to call Berlin's bluff after the fateful Godesberg meeting of 22 September. He cited a forceful Foreign Office press statement of 25 September, authorized by Foreign Secretary Halifax, to the effect that Britain would certainly support France in the event of a German invasion of Czechoslovakia. Lamb noted the significance of that statement:

> This was the high tide of Chamberlain's resistance to Hitler during the 1938 Czech crisis. At last an unequivocal commitment to support France if she went to war over Czechoslovakia had been given. . . . If Chamberlain had stuck to his guns Hitler would have been stopped dead in his tracks. He was too weak militarily to fight Czechoslovakia, Britain, France and Russia simultaneously, and he would have been

humiliated by having to call off his campaign for the Sudetenland after so much bombast.[84]

Lamb continued this theme when he referred to the events of 27 September, after the mobilization of the Royal Navy and the Prime Minister's fatuous speech referring to "a people of whom we know nothing." As the author related, Chamberlain's desperate communications with both of the European dictators to avoid the imminent war made the inevitable conflict that much tougher for the democracies when it did come.

> Thus at the moment when the British Cabinet and the French were about to call Hitler's bluff, Chamberlain sold the pass. If Britain had stayed firm Hitler would either have been defeated in the field or the German generals would have overthrown him. Hitler had staked his reputation on occupying Czechoslovakia by 1 October, and failure would have left him vulnerable.[85]

A weakness of Lamb's account is the continual repetition of these historical "what ifs" that have been rendered futile by a clear-eyed hindsight. History in this manner becomes counterfactual, where suppositions, never relevant to the actual events, become possible opportunities in the face of inexorable fate. Perhaps it is the quality of humanity, so evident in Chamberlain's makeup and so lacking in his Nazi adversary, that led a good man to leave no stone unturned in his attempt to avoid a second cruel apocalypse within a generation; perhaps historians also unconsciously try to obviate the terror of the past by supposing that at a certain time or place, things could have been different, for example, had Chamberlain stood fast at Munich. It is a tempting but sadly irrelevant course for scholarship.

Lamb stressed the respective gains garnered by Britain and Germany by the year's delay of war wrought by the Munich agreement. The breathing-space justification had always been a leitmotif of the Prime Minister's strongest supporters, although the languid pace of rearmament after Munich made the rationale somewhat illusory. In the author's estimation:

> There can be no doubt that the year's delay of the outbreak of war helped Germany and not Britain. The occupation of the Sudetenland made possible by the Munich agreement gave Germany a present of 1.5 million rifles, 750 aircraft, around 600 tanks, and over 2,000 field guns. Czech tanks and guns were superior to Germany's, and it has been estimated that every third tank used in the 1940 invasion of

France and the Low Countries was Czech-built. The arms production of the Skoda works at Pilzen between August 1938 and September 1939 was almost equal to the whole British weapons output.[86]

In conclusion, Lamb stressed the negative consequences of Munich for Britain; in his estimation, they were hardly in the same realm of Chamberlain's tenuous claim of "peace for our time":

> The archives reveal Munich was a disaster, because Hitler completely bluffed Neville Chamberlain over German military potential. If the British and French had declared war on Germany in October 1938 Russia would have joined them, and the result must have been an ignominious defeat for Germany.[87]

Such was the tone of *The Drift to War*, which though published in 1989, had a palpable Churchillian flavor in its criticisms of Chamberlain and his policy of appeasement. Much like John Charmley, who could, in 1989, applaud the Prime Minister for his attempts to steer clear of war fifty years after the fact, Richard Lamb, in 1989, would take Chamberlain to task for his failure to stand fast at Munich and so obviate the horrors of a second world conflagration. Two generations would pass, and the old arguments would still rage. In such a manner have we come full circle.

9

The Recent Past

FEW FOREIGN POLICIES OF THIS CENTURY HAVE BEEN SO WIDELY AND consistently excoriated as Neville Chamberlain's European appeasement of the dictator states. In a curious manner, appeasement's failure during Chamberlain's tenure became his personal tragedy, and, in truth, the man has been pilloried as brutally as the policy. The last quarter-century, however, has brought some semblance of historiographical balance to the continuing debate over appeasement's efficacy. In a very recent *Albion* book review, Professor R. J. Q. Adams alluded to a veritable flood tide of current appeasement offerings, with no perceptible ebb in the near future. Historians, ever aware of the significance of relevant anniversaries, had predicted a steady flow of publications to mark the half-century since appeasement's apogee at Munich, and the response has been more a river than a stream. Journalistic efforts and personal memoirs have appeared simultaneously with the efforts of career historians, with a fair bit of controversy perhaps reflective of the volatility of this field of British history.

I intend here to discuss a sizeable block of scholarship completed in late 1980s and early to mid-1990s and thus formulate a current perspective on appeasement, a notion on where the debate is headed after nearly six decades of contention.

An account specifically crafted for the fiftieth anniversary of the Munich agreement was Robert Kee's *Munich: The Eleventh Hour*. The book had its origins in a Thames television documentary on the Czech crisis, and while certainly not ahistorical in nature, was rather more journalistic than scholarly in tone. Historian John Charmley remarked in 1989 that Chamberlain's historical reputation was stronger than ever, and that the books published for Munich's fiftieth anniversary would be supportive of the Prime

Minister's legacy.[1] Kee's effort could easily be characterized as one that fit that description. Kee contemplated appeasement and Chamberlain's eventual failure to secure a lasting peace and attempted an explication:

> He appears in history as appeasement's "fall guy" only because, inheriting the policy as an enlightened one to which he felt sympathetic and to which he now contributed a personal enthusiasm of his own, he was too long temperamentally disinclined to recognise that it could turn to ashes while he espoused it. . . . "Munich" itself was to be nothing if not an attempt at a realistic treatment of Czechoslovakia's problems. He was just operating in a different dimension of realism from that of his opponent.[2]

The irony of the above is that no one had a clearer vision of realpolitik at Munich than Chamberlain, ever willing to sacrifice a "people of whom we know nothing" to save Europe from the abyss of civil war. Indeed, Kee debunked the mythology that Chamberlain had been outwitted at Munich because of his own stupidity or naivete, and he offered a defense of the embattled Prime Minister during the dramatic fortnight in September 1938:

> Nor was he a dupe in the sense that he did not realise what he was doing. He knew exactly what he was doing and over the next two weeks successfully accomplished exactly what he had set out to do. That this did not in the long run lead to the permanent result he had hoped for—that final appeasement of Europe in the era after Versailles for which British foreign policy had striven so long—must be assessed as his eventual failure. But this failure was a possibility he consciously took in his stride and it did not rule out the desirability of temporary success.[3]

For Neville Chamberlain, alas, the "success" of Munich was to be all too "temporary"; an agreement concluded between an honorable "man of peace" and those who "knew nothing" of honor would be swiftly violated by the events of March 1939. Robert Kee articulated his perspective of Chamberlain's failure, and his sympathetic tone lent credence to his belief that even though Chamberlain's efforts had been in vain, they had not been rendered any less valiant in nature: "The worst thing that can be said about him, judging him by his own lights, is that he was too ready to suppose that Hitler would act within his own (Chamberlain's) conventions because he so much wanted him to do so."[4]

An analysis published also in 1988 was Robert Shepherd's *A Class Divided: Appeasement and the Road to Munich, 1938.* Shepherd, much like Robert Kee, was more of a practicing journalist than historian in style, eschewing the usage of endnotes in his text. His main argument was that the failure of Chamberlain's appeasement of the dictators would lead to a decisive split in the Conservative Party ranks, thus assuring the Prime Minister's political downfall. In fact, at the time of Chamberlain's putative Munich triumph, vocal critics of appeasement were few and far between. Resistance to a popular and successful policy that avoided war was outright political suicide, as Alfred Duff Cooper acknowledged when he resigned following the Commons debate over Munich. It was, as Shepherd recounted, only the failure of the policy that caused significant opposition to coalesce against the government's course of action. Shepherd commented on the orientation of many of Britain's ruling elite in the 1930s:

> The governing class of the 1930s were the products of that suddenly distant late-Victorian and Edwardian era. . . . They had the same perspective on the world scene. Britain was a great power, which should maintain her position without risking another major war. But in the last resort Britain should "buy off" other countries thrusting for world power by making limited concessions, rather than face a showdown.[5]

Simply put, this was a major theme of Neville Chamberlain's appeasement. In the face of the implacable duplicity of Nazi Germany, however, a delicate pacification of Europe would be improbable at best. Shepherd noted that one of the few dissident groups in the Conservative Party during the Czech crisis was led loosely by Leo Amery and Winston Churchill, and that this group was ready to oppose the Prime Minister if war had come in September 1938. Among their many plans were a call for immediate war measures, even national service, and a "Grand Alliance" with the Soviet Union against the Nazis. Shepherd's opinion here is compelling:

> It seems remarkable that a gathering composed predominantly of Conservatives contemplated "conscription of capital" and getting "in touch with Russia." Chamberlain's determination to appease Germany was largely rooted in his opposition and the opposition of the vast bulk of Conservatives to radical proposals of this kind, since they would en-

tail a transformation of British society and a revolution in Britain's attitude towards the Soviet state.[6]

Of course, the rebel Conservatives could not act, as war was avoided with the signing of the Munich agreement on September 29–30, 1938. Chamberlain, despite his glorious diplomatic triumph, had an arduous task defending his policy in the Commons debate on Munich of 3–6 October. Shepherd described the Prime Minister's dilemma:

> Chamberlain had to present a convincing case both for the settlement with Hitler and for the continuation, even acceleration, of British rearmament. [Harold] Nicolson neatly summed up the quandary in which Chamberlain and his supporters found themselves, when he wrote: "It is difficult to say, 'This is the greatest diplomatic achievement in history: therefore we must redouble our armaments in order never again to be exposed to such humiliation.' "[7]

Sadly for the Prime Minister, events would soon spiral out of control. The difficulties inflicted upon him by Nazi misdeeds would climax with the German sack of Prague in March 1939. During that "Munich Winter," however, many remained adamant in support of Chamberlain. Shepherd referred to a November 1938 conversation between Foreign Office confreres Oliver Harvey and William Strang. As Shepherd put it:

> They agreed that "any war, whether we win or not, would destroy the rich idle classes and so they are for peace at any price." In Harvey's view, "The smug ones are the rich, the industrialists, the landowners, the idle, the party hacks—these still do not see that the Nazis will not save their dividends or their estates."[8]

Eventually the majority of Britons would realize the true nature of the regime in Berlin, and would comprehend the failure of appeasement, in Shepherd's words, as a "tragic misjudgment." Chamberlain, ill-equipped as a war leader, would be removed from authority in the aftermath of Britain's Norwegian debacle and because of the split in his own party. The events of May 1940 seemed an eternity away from the Munich triumph and "peace for our time," and Shepherd's analysis brought those days into focus in a dramatic fashion.

An intriguing analysis of interwar British public opinion was offered by Terrance Lewis in *A Climate for Appeasement?*, published in 1991. Lewis pondered whether the malaise of antiwar sentiment and disillusionment was a palpable catalyst for the widespread popularity of Chamberlain's appeasement efforts in the late 1930s. He reviewed many of the strains of British popular culture between the wars, including much of the significant literature of the "lost generation" that had been decimated in the squalor of four years in the trenches. In the realm of foreign policy in the 1930s, Lewis described the cruel paradox faced by Whitehall with an economy staggered by the worldwide depression.

> In short, Britain's military weaknesses and unwillingness to quickly rearm because of the poor health of the economy led to a "catch-22" situation. Britain could protect its interests, and itself, especially in the short term, only through some form of collective security or alliance system. Britain's weaknesses, however, caused doubt both overseas and at home about how much Britain could contribute, or would be willing to contribute, to any security arrangement. Why should any nation ally itself with Britain if Britain could not, or would not, be of assistance if needed?[9]

The reluctance of both Stanley Baldwin and then Neville Chamberlain to weaken Britain's economy by placing the nation on a more rapid rearmament program would place—to paraphrase Halifax—a heavy reliance on diplomacy, hence appeasement. Lewis characterized the various strands of thought relating to Britain's foreign policy in the 1930s, which may have led to the only viable alternative for Chamberlain in those dire circumstances:

> It is next to impossible to define and group together the foreign policies of the British Government during the 1930s. The guiding principle does not seem to have been a desire for peace as much as a great fear of war. This fear prevented the British from attempting any form of disarmament when universal disarmament might have had a slight chance for success. It also prevented them from using war as a threat, since war was the one thing to be avoided. It prevented both the age-old British concept of a Grand Alliance, as well as the new idea of collective security. Both pacifism and power politics were therefore impossible. Appeasement from weakness rather than from power was the only course open, other than open surrender.[10]

Lewis offered his opinion that the manifold problems facing Chamberlain in his quest for an overall pacification of Europe may have swirled out of his control during the Czech crisis of 1938. His analysis included one of the Prime Minister's favorite maxims: the inefficacy of international posturing in foreign policy without the resources to back up one's threats. In his dealings with the Nazis, Chamberlain would only view them as responsible statesmen, who, like him, would reject war as a policy. This would eventually prove a fatal misjudgment.

> Appeasement was not a set policy, unless the desire to avoid war at almost any price can be called a set policy. Rather, appeasement was a set of improvisations, some ill-timed and ill-conceived (such as the Hoare-Laval plan) and some which looked brilliant at the time (such as Chamberlain's first trip to Germany). Try as they sometimes did, the leaders of the National Government could not control events, since the only way, it turned out, they could have had any control over them would have been to acknowledge that the actions of the British Government would, in the end, have to be backed up by superior military power, and that the power would be used.[11]

To a "man of peace" like Chamberlain, another abattoir on the the scale of the Great War was anathema, and it is difficult to imagine him threatening the dictator states with violence in order to preserve the integrity of Central and Eastern Europe. Lewis concluded his account with a reasonable analysis of the effects of the disaster of 1914–1918 and its effects on public opinion in the gathering storm of 1938–1939.

> Although it cannot be shown to what extent the appeasers were affected by this general climate of disillusionment . . . it is certain that the appeasers were able to use the British fear of war—a fear caused, to a great extent, by the memories of the Great War—to ensure acquiescence on the part of much of the British public to the policies of appeasement.[12]

This overriding fear and many other contributing factors were to bolster support for appeasement until Nazi duplicity proved to be Chamberlain's undoing. Lewis' sophisticated analysis of the inter-war years added to the collective understanding of this critical epoch.

An account that chronicled Britain's appeasement of the dictator states was William Rock's *Chamberlain and Roosevelt: British Foreign Policy and the United States, 1937–1940*, published in

1988. Rock had, through the late 1960s and 1970s, written several monographs on Chamberlain and appeasement. His most recent effort reflected the relationship between the heads of the two great democracies in the face of persistent aggression from Germany and Italy preceding the outbreak of war. Rock outlined the meaning of Chamberlain's "magnificent obsession" of a European appeasement:

> Any effort Britain could make to remove legitimate grievances and promote harmony among the nations would bring its own reward, if it made a contribution to the general welfare. Herein lay the essence, and the motivation, for the policy of appeasement with which his name has become synonymous—and all the other motives that have been attributed to him by a wide range of friends and foes alike were either secondary at best or largely rationalizations concocted after the event to serve a particular purpose.[13]

In regard to Roosevelt's January 1938 diplomatic initiative, (which would, at worst, have placed the prestige and power of the United States that much closer to "Europe's quarrel"), Rock commented on Chamberlain's rather brusque rejoinder:

> Considering the strength of his own commitment to appeasement, Chamberlain naturally resented anything that might interfere with its pursuit. This posture involved some vanity, of which Chamberlain was clearly victim . . . . He may not have been anti-American, but his attitude toward Americans generally, and Roosevelt in particular, was condescending and arrogant. Inclined to judge plans in the short run, . . . he did not appear to look beyond the Roosevelt plan itself (which might well have failed) to salutary consequences that might have sprung from it even in failure.[14]

This puzzling episode, combined with the amazing contretemps between Chamberlain and Foreign Secretary Eden over the timing of Anglo-Italian conversations, would foreshadow Eden's sudden resignation from the Cabinet in late February 1938. The *Anschluss* would soon follow, and six months later Chamberlain met his date with destiny at Munich. Roosevelt was to have a very limited influence on the events of September 1938, and Rock related how the fluidity of international events had altered Chamberlain's perspective of the European situation:

> The fact is that Chamberlain's outlook had changed upon his assumption of leadership. Whereas previously he had said that only force would influence Germany, he now began to believe that timely conces-

sions to meet legitimate German grievances—appeasement—
constituted the most effective approach for dealing with the German
danger. . . . The shift is better explained in terms of the weight of responsibility, which now rested on his shoulders alone, and his growing
confidence in his own ability—indeed, his sense of mission—to resolve
the problems threatening Europe and thus ensure peace for the Continent.[15]

In his conclusion, Rock articulated his perceptions on Chamberlain and his Munich settlement. The agreement was initially regarded very favorably by Roosevelt, until Nazi excesses in the five
months leading to Prague shattered the faith of most of the appeasers, and presaged the terrible war that was to follow.

> Chamberlain's own appraisal of Munich is difficult to determine.
> Clearly his "peace in our time" statement was made in a moment of
> high emotion and did not represent his settled judgment about what
> had been accomplished. Yet it is equally evident that he was hopeful,
> if not genuinely optimistic, about the future possibilities of
> appeasement. . . . But with Chamberlain hope was a major component
> of personality, and it sometimes led him to impose a construction on
> events that did not correspond with reality.[16]

Ironically, the wartime "partnership" between Roosevelt and the
new Prime Minister, Churchill, would be as intimate as Chamberlain and Roosevelt's had been strained.

A sophisticated analysis of Chamberlain's foreign policy published on the fiftieth anniversary of the Munich agreement was
Keith Robbins' *Appeasement*. Robbins had written one of the
more significant works on the events of September 1938 twenty
years before, namely *Munich 1938*. In it he had described Munich
and its aftermath as the "necessary purgatory" that Britain was
forced to endure in order to emerge victorious from another world
war. In his more recent effort Robbins offered several intriguing
perspectives on interwar foreign policy, linking it with Britain's inexorable decline after the scourge of the Great War: "It might be
possible at least to understand appeasement better if it were seen
as a central episode in a protracted retreat from an untenable
"world power" status. Appeasement, on such an analysis, was neither stupid nor wicked: it was merely inevitable."[17] Robbins
stressed that this slippage from a position of international domi-

nance was far more readily apparent to Britain's potential enemies than to most Britons themselves, save those in power who could grasp the grim realities of the situation. This dilemma of the "greatness" of Britain would continue to bedevil Whitehall well after the defeat of Germany and Japan, indeed, well into the 1950s.

> To employ a useful distinction, the British position in the world rested upon an acceptance of Britain's authority rather than Britain's power. What characterized the 1930s as opposed to the 1920s was the growing willingness of certain other states to challenge that authority, supposing that the power always necessary to underpin authority was in fact ebbing away.[18]

Robbins balked at the legendary portrayal of Neville Chamberlain as a naive and cringing political lightweight who, as fate would have it, happened to be at the wrong place at the wrong time. This pejorative reputation is easily belied by the record of Chamberlain's indefatigable toil at both the Ministry of Health and the Exchequer in the two decades prior to his ascent to the summit of British politics in May 1937. In Robbins' estimation:

> For many writers, he is the man of appeasement *par excellence* and it remains difficult to put his career into focus. Few Prime Ministers have been subject to such widely varying assessments. . . . Recent writing has had little patience with the simple stereotypes which once dominated the field. Chamberlain was not an ignorant meddler in matters in which he had no experience. When he became Prime Minister he seemed at the time to be the only man for the job.[19]

The factor of British public opinion cannot be ignored in any analysis of appeasement, and Keith Robbins judged the antiwar sentiments of most Britons as a spur to Chamberlain's policy. As Terrance Lewis would later elucidate, the "climate" was there for appeasement, and its failure, in hindsight, was to become Chamberlain's failure. Robbins was reluctant to condemn Chamberlain out of hand for a policy that had been so overwhelmingly popular at the time.

> The standard complaint against the practitioners of appeasement is that concessions were made from a position of weakness, or perceived weakness, which should only have been contemplated from a position of strength. . . . A substantial section of British opinion had no wish to accept the priorities which would have been required to achieve the necessary image of strength. The problem of how a peaceloving de-

mocracy can be persuaded to prepare for war is an enduring one to which there is no easy answer.[20]

Much like his earlier effort, Robbins' *Appeasement* addressed the varied factors that led to the formation of British foreign policy in the late 1930s in an illuminating fashion.

We turn now to the final five works in our review of the most recent appeasement historiography, all published in 1993. Indeed, the fortunate circumstance of the ink hardly being dry on these efforts allows us all, as scholars of European history, to examine the very latest tendencies in the long-running historiographical debate. An effort that must be addressed, if in passing, for its controversial aspects is John Charmley's *Churchill: The End of Glory*. The natural successor to his earlier *Chamberlain and the Lost Peace*, Charmley's account enraged many in Britain and the United States when he suggested that a 1940 accommodation with Berlin would have enabled Britain to keep both its empire and great-power status intact through the war. He reasoned that even though the defeat of Germany secured British liberty, the exertions of a six-year war left the British little future save that of a satellite of the United States. On appeasement, Charmley drew the contrast between Chamberlain and Churchill:

> Churchill still saw Britain as a Great Power, able to weld together a grand coalition in defence of civilisation. Chamberlain saw the weaknesses of the foundations upon which British power rested. He did not suppose that even a "successful" war would leave that power intact, so in that sense Britain could not gain anything from a war.[21]

In Charmley's estimation, the failure of appeasement made the war inevitable, and with the war came the final diminution of Britain as an independent world power, the true end of glory.

Our next appeasement offering is a concise and engaging account by R. J. Q. Adams, entitled *British Politics and Foreign Policy in the Age of Appeasement, 1935–1939*. Professor Adams stressed in his introduction his desire to tie together many of the strands of appeasement's micro-history, splintered as it was through the intense specialization of recent scholarship, into an "appeasement primer." Suffice it to say, his exertions were not in vain. His description of Neville Chamberlain, much-maligned and certainly misunderstood by many historians, is compelling.

> Chamberlain is one of those figures whom the conventional wisdom, regardless of the pleas of many historians, is determined to see as an archetype. He is described as weak, when one of his greatest failings was his remarkable strength as a leader: future Prime Ministers like Churchill, Eden, and Macmillan were crushed when they opposed him, and he dominated his Cabinet as few others have done. He is described as irresolute, when his remarkable self-confidence was such that he ruthlessly pursued his own vision of what was best for his nation in the face of all counter-arguments and all who opposed him.[22]

These personality traits hardly dovetail with the "cringing appeaser" opprobrium of the immediate postwar era, when truth seemed of secondary consequence to righteous indignation and emotional condemnation. Adams quite perceptively grasped the significance of appeasement as a policy driven by the strength of Chamberlain's will:

> Chamberlain was not the only appeaser, and neither credit nor blame was his alone. But as Prime Minister he gave direction, shape and voice to the policy as no other man could and used the power of his office to silence and condemn his critics. His determination to save the nation and the world in his own way divided him from his detractors in and outside of his own party. This singular vision raised him briefly to dizzying heights of popularity and threw him down again, but he never ceased to believe in it.[23]

Adams pondered the significance of the fabled "piece of paper," the agreement signed by the British Prime Minister and the Nazi dictator in the wake of Munich on 30 September 1938.

> It was this which became infamous as the "piece of paper" which Chamberlain held up after alighting from his airplane in London later that same day. To him it was nothing less than an insurance policy for hope. It was the high point, the finest product of active appeasement and represented to him the firm commitment on the part of the greatest potential peace-breaker in Europe that disagreements and disappointments could, and would, be settled through peaceful means rather than by war.[24]

To the Birmingham businessman whose personal word had always been his bond, a new "golden age" of European peace may well have appeared possible. In retrospect, had Chamberlain recognized the actual villainy of his rivals, he may have been able to grasp the hopelessness of his situation. In his conclusion, Adams offered salient perspectives on Neville Chamberlain and his legacy, still viewed pejoratively by many after a half-century of debate.

> He sought to drag the civilized world away from the precipice of destruction, and particularly, to save Britain from that which he hated most—the mindless destruction of another World War. He judged himself a supreme realist, the superior to his colleagues, his opponents and to the dictators whom he sought to quieten with his reasonable settlements. . . . His goal was a comprehensive peace, not merely the avoidance of war now in the hope of making more effective war later. . . . It must always be remembered that the appeasers did not pursue a course which led to such tragic results because they were weak or cowardly or stupid or wicked: whatever the reasons, what they were was wrong.[25]

British historian R. A. C. Parker stressed that his latest effort called to task those revisionist historical perspectives that have attempted to expiate Chamberlain's guilt for the the failure of appeasement. *Chamberlain and Appeasement: British Policy and the Coming of the Second World War* stated that

> The balance of evidence points to counter-revisionist interpretations. Chamberlain led the government in 1938 and 1939, particularly in the months after Munich, into rejecting the option of a close Franco-British alliance. . . . Chamberlain's powerful, obstinate personality and his skill in debate probably stifled serious chances of preventing the Second World War.[26]

In the same vein, Parker amplified his indictment of the Prime Minister's actions in those perilous days, actions that while obviously meant to avoid war ironically made it all the more inevitable.

> Chamberlain and his colleagues made choices among alternative possibilities and that so far as Chamberlain decided them . . . they were choices for conciliation rather than resistance. Whenever the British government had to decide between resistance to German ambitions and compromise with them, Chamberlain led the way to compromise.[27]

Parker's work reflected a sophistication that many of the early ap-peasement critiques clearly lacked. While on the one hand he hec-tored the Prime Minister for his wrongheaded policy, Parker also acknowledged the unfair, reckless charges that had sullied Cham-berlain's historical reputation in the last half-century. He com-mented on the earliest of these, which, incidentally, were from the pen of the greatest British icon of the twentieth century, Winston Churchill.

> Posthumous libels have destroyed Chamberlain's reputation and falsi-fied historical interpretation. Churchill began it. In conversation, dur-ing the war, he described Chamberlain as "the narrowest, most ignorant, most ungenerous of men." . . . This depreciation is mislead-ing; Chamberlain was not like that. Narrowness of mind, ignorance of Europe are not the explanations of what he did. . . . The coming of war was more complicated than Churchill claimed and Chamberlain's errors are less simply explained than by his alleged ignorance and stu-pidity.[28]

Parker offered a number of intriguing insights into Chamberlain's *mentalite* in the immediate aftermath of Munich, and in the wake of the Nazi seizure of Prague in March 1939. In regard to his ill-starred "peace in our time" statement, Parker stressed that the Premier knew the realities of the situation, especially in relation to British public opinion.

> Chamberlain knew that his policy of peace through conciliation of Hit-ler and Mussolini was less popular than he thought it should have been. He knew that most of those who had applauded Munich did so because they thought he had bought time to enable the United King-dom to grow militarily stronger and to be able to resist threats of vio-lence, not because they thought it the first in a series of agreements with the European dictators.[29]

Parker pondered Chamberlain's puzzling continuity of policy even after the fall of Prague on 15 March 1939, and claimed what has been widely believed for generations, that Chamberlain's re-nowned Birmingham speech of St. Patrick's Day 1939 had been motivated by a near mutiny among his Conservatives.

> The German occupation of Prague did not change Chamberlain's pol-icy but it made it much more difficult for him to put it into effect. Many members of Parliament, some of his own Cabinet, Foreign Office offi-cials, even some times Halifax himself, favored sabre-rattling threats.

Chamberlain's continued struggle for peace involved combativeness at home as an essential part of the process of curbing it abroad.[30]

As we know in retrospect, the Polish and Rumanian guarantees of spring 1939 were concluded, in Chamberlain's estimation, much more for their deterrent effect than for any palpable military assistance Britain might give these countries if they were violated by Nazi Germany. R. A. C. Parker highlighted the complexities of appeasement and, as Professor Adams had, saw Chamberlain as the power behind the policy. He noted, in conclusion, the difficulty of ignoring the clear evidence of "Chamberlain's supremacy in the making of British policy in those years . . . he chose the policy and he was not the mere puppet of circumstantial constraints."[31]

A complex, multifaceted review of many of the problems facing Britain's leadership in the mid-1930s was written by Gaines Post, Jr., entitled *Dilemmas of Appeasement: British Deterrence and Defense, 1934–1937*. Post offered as his central theme the notion that Britain's machinery of foreign policy and process of policy-making during the 1930s caused much wailing and gnashing of teeth in Whitehall as the decade progressed, and the war clouds hovering over Europe grew ever more menacing:

> The machinery's confusion and irresolution, more pronounced for long-term planning than for responding to international crises, muddled deterrence and lost time. The machinery's defects also helped create the illusion that Chamberlain's more decisive style of policymaking could save Britain's worsening strategic dilemma once he became prime minister.[32]

That vexing dilemma, of course, was the simultaneous threat of aggression aimed at the British Empire from Germany, Italy, and Japan. Post alluded to the often mean-spirited rivalries between the Foreign Office and the Treasury, among others, in the formulation of a workable policy in the mid-1930s.

> In the ensuing debate over how to buy time, the weight of argument began to shift toward appeasement, with the pejorative meaning of surrender that has haunted the word since the late 1930s. During the fall and winter of 1936–37, the Foreign Office lost prestige because of its internal dissension and its failure to reduce the number of Britain's potential enemies. . . . Chamberlain thought Britain must extend time,

not deterrence. He and the Treasury began to formulate the doctrine that economic stability is an arm of defense with great deterrent power.[33]

Because of the perilous international situation and what the then-Chancellor characterized as the "dangerous drift" of foreign policy under Stanley Baldwin, Chamberlain began to envision his future role as an activist prime minister who would save the peace of Europe through a two-pronged plan of gradual rearmament and political appeasement. He would employ the prestige and power of Britain, albeit on the decline, to revive British foreign policy from the ennui of Baldwin's declining years. Post delineated Chamberlain's desiderata and the illusory hopes that fueled his dreams of a peaceful future.

> Chamberlain was certain that he could clearly define national policy and bring order to it. He would increase the opportunities for conciliation, reduce the international and strategic options for deterrence, . . . systematize British defense policy with a logical plan based on air power and finance, and prevent war. . . . Events of 1937–39 would reveal how delusionary was the idea that a fundamental change in leadership and planning could prevent war with Germany or give Britain much prospect for winning.[34]

In the face of a revanchist Germany intent upon establishing hegemony over Central Europe, Chamberlain would be, in his three-year tenure as prime minister, obligated to assume a reactive posture. His inability to control events, to truly "bring order" to Europe, would mean the eventual doom of appeasement and his historical reputation. Post commented on his domination of the machinery of policy, noting that even as Chancellor of the Exchequer he was *primus inter pares* in the Baldwin Cabinet, the unchallenged heir apparent for the the somnolent Premier, and as fate would have it, as authoritarian a leader as Britain would see in the twentieth century.

> A man whose conceit was as extraordinary as his ability, Chamberlain worked harder than any of his colleagues and knew more about the work of departments besides his own. He considered the machinery of policy efficient insofar as it deduced congenial conclusions from his general assumptions, produced evidence to substantiate those assumptions, eliminated inconsistencies and waste, and confirmed his own decisiveness.[35]

In the fateful days of autumn 1938, when the Czech crisis made war seem imminent, Chamberlain and his "inner circle" of advisors would brook little criticism of their policies, and this rigidity would be a weakness in the face of the rapidly deteriorating situation.

In conclusion, Gaines Post credited Chamberlain as the indisputable driving force behind appeasement, but indicated that although the future Prime Minister bore the great weight of a half-century of historical opprobrium for its failure, the policy had been almost universally supported at every level of Whitehall.

> From 1934 to 1937, Whitehall weighed alternative policies for their deterrent value. As Chancellor, Chamberlain identified flexibility with disorder, and argued against it for economic, strategic, and political reasons. He found support for his views—if not for every detail of his design—in the Cabinet, Treasury, Foreign Office, Chiefs of Staff, and Secretariat, all of which had grown frustrated with difficulties that they blamed increasingly on inefficient policymaking and weak leadership at the top. . . . The search for a coherent strategy of deterrence was Whitehall's, not only Chamberlain's, and the policy of appeasing Germany without risking war was British, not simply personal.[36]

The final selection from our collection of recent historiography is actually a chapter from an edited collection of articles on Winston Churchill and his legacy. *Churchill* was edited by Robert Blake and William Roger Lewis, and our relevant chapter, written by arguably the worldwide authority on appeasement, Donald Cameron Watt, is entitled "Churchill and Appeasement." Watt lamented the fact that the Churchillian critique of appeasement had been employed rather disastrously in the postwar world, specifically in relation to Korea, the Suez crisis of 1956, and the Persian Gulf war. The flawed usage of the "Munich analogy" to deter aggression led to conflicts that lacked the desperate circumstances of the late 1930s, but the "lessons of Munich" were to be heeded, often at great cost. Watt offered several intriguing thoughts on the Churchillian critique of appeasement:

> While purporting to be an argument about political realism, it is in fact one which is about morality. The term "appeasement" itself has lost its original meaning of the defusing of conflict and taken on the meaning of purchasing peace for one's own interests by sacrificing the interests of others. It is only where such a policy is unsuccessful, where it

has fired the appetite of the acquisitive and encouraged the bully to believe he lacks serious opposition, that it is called "appeasement." . . . Appeasement, like treason, has to be unsuccessful to be both immoral and unrealistic.[37]

One need only recall the dizzying heights of euphoria surrounding Neville Chamberlain's return from Munich on 30 September 1938 to fathom fully Watt's penetrating analysis. While the policy was successful in avoiding war, it was also representative of British popular opinion. Only with the "double jeopardy" of the fall of Prague and, later, the invasion of Poland, would the British people turn their eyes and hearts from appeasement, and prepare for the horrible maelstrom of world war. In a like manner and with an almost eerie coincidence, while peace still had some chance, through the months of the *Sitzkrieg*, Chamberlain remained at the levers of power. Only with the German strike against Western Europe would the real shooting war begin, and the "man of peace" be forsaken. Another startling irony existed in that the individual that Britain would turn to for deliverance was a man truly scorned during the halcyon days of appeasement, Winston Churchill.

Watt traced Churchill's beliefs in regard to deterrence through a faster rate of rearmament, the possible formulation of a Grand Alliance including the Soviet Union, and the chances of an anti-Nazi revolt among the German general staff. He stated that much of Churchill's information on these topics was faulty, especially in regard to the relative strength of the Luftwaffe, the sincerity of Soviet intentions, and the reality of the anti-Nazi resistance. Watt cited some crucial differences in perspective between Churchill and Chamberlain in regard to the Berlin regime:

From 1936 onwards Churchill seems to have accepted the views of the Germanophobes within the administration and seen Hitler as a new Napoleon of unrestricted ambitions and drive. Chamberlain and Halifax, wishing to avoid war, believing or hoping a stage would arrive when British rearmament would make the hazards of further expansion unacceptable to Hitler, were unwilling to accept so black and white, so pessimistic a view of Hitler, until events forced it upon them. For Churchill, further appeasement of Germany only increased the dangers the expansion of German power represented.[38]

In many ways, the legacy of Churchill's perspective of appeasement relates to the hoary cliche about "only the victors write history." With a righteous sense of postwar hindsight, Churchill was willing and able to color history to his desired hue in his indictment of the "cringing appeasers."[39] Had the policy of appeasement been successful and war been avoided, Churchill may well have remained in the "wilderness," and Neville Chamberlain's would be an honored name in British history. Watt's final analysis confirmed the stark reality, that both Chamberlain and Churchill, in their respective fashions, were mistaken about appeasement's efficacy. " 'Appeasement' and 'Munich' acquired a pejorative association with the ignominious surrender of principle and the purchase of peace by the sacrifice of the interests of the weak and the defenceless, which they will never lose."[40] And, finally: "The dismissal of all policy options save conflict as 'appeasement' and the constant reiteration of the adage 'appeasement never pays,' are together one of the legacies of the Churchillian legend."[41]

The sophisticated scholarship of the present day has only succeeded in promoting a greater sense of ambiguity in the mind of the scholar of appeasement. Long gone are the days of certainty, when moral absolutes rendered debate unnecessary, and vitriol rather than empiricism was the fashion of the day. The plethora of problems facing Neville Chamberlain may well have daunted a man of lesser confidence in the perilous years of 1938 and 1939. The literary efforts of the past ten years have, as have many before them, helped to balance the scales of historical judgment on less of a moral level in regard to appeasement, and have placed it on more of an intellectual one. Perhaps the ambiguity of the modern-day historiographical debate was correctly envisioned by a *Times Literary Supplement* review of Keith Feiling's *Life of Neville Chamberlain* from 14 December 1946. Allow this, then, to be our final word on Chamberlain's legacy: "The book, therefore, should enable the reader to make his own estimate of a man who is no more likely to get a unanimous verdict from a jury of historians looking back on his life 200 years hence than from his own contemporaries."[42]

Epilogue

THE AMBIGUITY OF THE HISTORIOGRAPHICAL DEBATE OVER APPEASE-
ment has been a dramatically salient characteristic of recent scholarship. Sixty years after Munich Neville Chamberlain and his
"inner circle" can be lauded for their tireless attempts to avoid a
second apocalypse within a generation. In stark contrast, a half-
century after the end of the Second World War the efficacy of
peacemaking efforts in the face of systematic aggression is under
fire, as it was in the aftermath of Munich, in regard to the human
tragedy unfolding in present-day Bosnia. Humanity yearns for
quick and definitive answers to insoluble problems. As in the late
1930s, the moral conundrum over diplomatic parley versus military resistance retains its Gordian knot status for the luckless
statesmen who, like Chamberlain, must deal with a number of
dangerous variables on an ever-volatile world stage. John F. Kennedy, the quintessential Cold Warrior who solemnly vowed to
"bear any burden" for the survival and success of liberty, doubtless had the Chamberlain experience in mind when he intoned,
"let us never negotiate out of fear, but let us never fear to negotiate."[1] In his best-selling analysis of the Chamberlain years, *Why
England Slept*, we can grasp his telling insight on the appeasement
debate, even from 1940. Kennedy, ever the detached pragmatist,
insisted that Chamberlain had no other alternative but appeasement in view of his military weakness at the time of Munich. It
is significant, however, that Kennedy also decried the tendency of
democratic states to blame figures like Chamberlain too heavily for
their failures, which were in many ways more institutional in nature than the fault of any individual.

In a similar vein, I believe that the cliche of "history being written by the victors" should not be applicable in the study of appeasement in the 1930s. The notion of that period as a sort of
morality play, where Chamberlain and his "Guilty Men" were attacked on a political and personal basis as cowardly, traitorous
crypto-Fascists leading Britain to ruin because of their own weaknesses is fallacious. Furthermore, it does little justice to the honest

efforts of the Prime Minister to avoid another abattoir on the horrific scale of the Great War. In an ironic twist, the deification of
Winston Churchill as the faultless icon of Britain's "finest hour"
(that emerged simultaneously out of Chamberlain's condemnation) bears faint resemblance to the reality of Churchill's often
flawed but always inspiring character. No scholar can spend any
extended amount of time perusing the University of Birmingham's
Chamberlain collection of letters, diaries, and documentation
without a sober realization that this austere Victorian businessman was far from a lightweight in any of his life's activities. By a
strange process of history, the failure of Neville Chamberlain's
policy of appeasement became, through the years, his *personal*
failure as a human being. This process was doubtless abetted by
the flood of condemnatory works, whether justified or not, which
began with Churchill's formidable account, *The Gathering Storm*.
In other, similar cases, failures of policy down through history
have not resulted in the destruction of an individual's personal
reputation. Two which come readily to mind are Napoleon Bonaparte and Confederate General Robert E. Lee, whose birthday was
still recently celebrated in many Southern states in lieu of Abra-
ham Lincoln's! The indefatigable Chamberlain, so very often portrayed as spineless and cringing in the face of aggression, was in
truth as formidable a parliamentary leader as Britain has seen in
the twentieth century. The fact that he was able to persevere at the
levers of power fourteen months after his appeasement policy had
collapsed in March 1939 duly signified the depth of his authoritarian capabilities. His six years at the Exchequer were combined
with a de facto premiership from 1935 on, as the ailing Baldwin
had no longer any spirit for the job. Chamberlain's concept of a
robust economy as a "fourth arm of defence" spoke dramatically
in regard to his motivations and his insistence upon standing fast
with appeasement. Nonetheless, he may well be questioned in reference to foresight in foreign affairs: his lack of a "sense of history," his noncomprehension of the actual nature of his
adversaries.

I laud the courage and vision of historians such as A. J. P. Taylor
and Donald C. Watt, who, in the early 1960s, emerging from the
stifling repression of the Fifties, called for an end to the condemnation of the past. Simultaneously they challenged historians to provide a more detailed scholarship vis-à-vis the multiplicity of factors
that influenced the Prime Minister's foreign policy. Perhaps this
clarion call for understanding reflected Taylor and Watt's worth to
the profession. By putting their reputations on the line they illus-

trated the grave need for an overall reassessment of the appeasement debate. The specialization of various fields relevant to the
formation of Britain's foreign policy in the 1930s would thus eventually result, and the historiography of appeasement could only
benefit in a switch from emotionalism to empiricism. In the preceding pages I have attempted to illuminate many of the various
perspectives and arguments central to the appeasement debate
through over one-half century of historiography. It may well be
best to conclude this exercise with a final clash of opinions that,
in their respective eloquence, serve to capture the essence of two
diametrically opposed positions, which have been hotly debated
since the 1930s.

> This is the real reason why appeasement was damned by the best at
> the time and has remained accursed ever since. It is undyingly associ-
> ated with the decadence of a ruling order which oscillated between il-
> lusory hopes and exaggerated fears. It is only at this level that we can
> explain the enormous sense of relief of all the active elements in con-
> ventional British politics when Chamberlain, suicidal even in his bold-
> ness, made his decisions for war in March and September 1939. They
> sensed that parliamentary democracy could only survive through war,
> however terrible the cost, because only war would give it the sinews
> and the will to rejuvenate itself and create a world that was worth liv-
> ing in.[2]

And, in contrast, the other extreme:

> Chamberlain had feared that history, written by those who had re-
> placed him, might judge him harshly, and he was correct. But not even
> the edifice erected by Churchill could survive unscathed that opening
> of the records which, Chamberlain hoped, would explain his policy.
> The "Guilty Men" syndrome has run its course, and Chamberlain's
> reputation stands better now than it has ever done—and the flood of
> books which will mark the fiftieth anniversary of 1939 will revive it
> still more.[3]

Over one-half century after the descent into war, the respective
supporters and critics of Neville Chamberlain's foreign policy of
appeasing the dictators remain at odds. The probability of some
sort of historical consensus is, in my estimation, not promising.
Those supporters who insist the Prime Minister did only what he
could have done at Munich in the midst of very dire constraints
have defensible arguments that have stood the test of sixty years
of opprobrium. Keith Robbins utilized the metaphor of "the purga-

tory of Munich" that served to unite the country for the coming struggle. Chamberlain correctly perceived his beloved Victorian Britain would disappear should war ensue from appeasement's failure. No country as badly bludgeoned by two world wars and a depression could have retained great-power status in Britain's dolorous post-1945 circumstances. In contrast, critics can rightfully claim the breathing-space of eleven months gained by the truncation of Czechoslovakia aided the German rearmament much more than Britain's; thus the argument that the Western democracies should have fought Germany in September 1938 before the fledgling Wehrmacht became a juggernaut. This position is certainly arguable in the light of Britain's horrific losses in the maelstrom of a six-year war. Furthermore, opponents of appeasement cite the "blinders mentality" of Chamberlain's businessman's orientation; his crucial failure to understand the true motivations of Nazi Germany and to employ the centuries-old British policy of securing a European balance of power through strategic alliances. Like oil and water, which when mixed create an emulsion, the differing opinions in the appeasement debate cannot coalesce into consensus. The sixty years of documentation and vitriol over appeasement have at times altered the parameters of the discussion, but in my estimation, to borrow from Kipling, "never the twain shall meet." Assuredly the historiographical debate must roll on, as long as historians continue to plunge into the depths of the interwar years for insight into the path taken by British foreign policy up to the outbreak of world history's most destructive war, the defining event of the twentieth century.

Notes

INTRODUCTION

1. British Broadcasting Corporation Television Production, "God Bless You, Mr. Chamberlain," first aired September 1988.

2. Robert Skidelsky, "Going to War with Germany," *Encounter* 39, 2 (July 1972): 56–65. I wish to clearly avoid the syllogism that the Goethe quote on revisionism implies that I will conduct a careful examination of all of the multifarious economic, political, and social forces of the 1960s and 1970s that led historians to revise their perceptions on appeasement. That would require a much longer manuscript, and perhaps is a battle to be fought another day. This will remain a review of the relevant historiography of appeasement rather than any extended discussion of the postwar historical zeitgeist.

CHAPTER 1. BEGINNINGS OF CONFLICT, 1938–1940

1. Neville Chamberlain, *In Search of Peace* (New York, G. P. Putnam's, 1939), 175.

2. CATO, *Guilty Men* (London: Victor Gollancz, Ltd., 1940), 110.

3. Ibid., 19.

4. Ibid., 45.

5. Ibid., 100.

6. Ibid., 124.

7. Ibid., 124–25.

8. K. Zilliacus, *Can the Tories Win the Peace?* (London, V. Gollancz Publishers 1945), frontispiece.

9. Sidney Aster, "Guilty Men: The Case of Neville Chamberlain," in *Paths to War: New Essays on the Origins of the Second World War*, ed. Robert Boyce and Esmonde Robertson (London, Macmillan, 1989), 235.

10. Simon Haxey, *England's Money Lords, Tory M.P.* (New York: Harrison-Hilton Books, 1939), 17.

11. Ibid., 171.

12. Ibid., 248.

13. Ibid., 59.

14. Ibid., 24.

15. Ibid., 209.

16. Ibid., 220.

17. Ibid., 221–22.

18. Ibid., 224.

19. Ibid., 235.

20. Ibid., 245.

21. *The Times Literary Supplement* (29 July 1939), 458–59.

22. Steven Macgregor, *Truth and Mr. Chamberlain* (London: Fore Publications, Ltd., 1939), 13.

23. Ibid.

24. Ibid., 57.

25. Ibid., 49.

26. Ibid., 59.

27. Ibid.

28. R. W. Seton-Watson, *From Munich to Danzig* (London: Methuen & Co. Ltd., 1939), xi.

29. Ibid., 169.

30. Ibid., 172.

31. Ibid., 171.

32. Ibid., 169 (Seton-Watson's italics).

33. Harold Oxbury, *Great Britons: Twentieth-Century Lives* (Oxford, Oxford Univ. Press, 1985), 7.

34. Sir Norman Angell, *For What Do We Fight?* (London: Hamish Hamilton Ltd., 1939), 92.

35. Ibid., 93.

36. Ibid., 95–96.

37. Hubert Ripka, *Munich: Before and After* (London: Victor Gollancz Ltd., 1939), 111.

38. Ibid., 25.

39. Ibid., 236.

40. Ibid., 473.

41. Eleanor Rathbone, *War Can Be Averted* (London: Victor Gollancz Ltd., 1938), v.

42. Ibid., 20.

43. Ibid., 70.

44. Ibid., 192–93.

45. Derek Walker-Smith, *Neville Chamberlain: Man of Peace* (London: R. Hale Publishers, 1940), 288.

46. Ibid., 318–19.

47. Neville Chamberlain Papers, University of Birmingham Library, NC 18/1/1066 to Ida Chamberlain, 3 September 1938.

48. Walker-Smith, *Man of Peace*, 403.

49. Duncan Keith-Shaw, *Prime Minister Neville Chamberlain* (London: Wells Gardner, Darton & Co., 1939), 3.

50. Ibid. (Keith-Shaw's italics.)

51. Ibid., 83.

52. Ibid., 117.

53. Ibid., 190.

54. Ibid., 210.

55. Stuart Hodgson, *The Man Who Made the Peace: Neville Chamberlain* (New York: E. P. Dutton and Company, 1938), 122.

56. Ibid., 133.

57. Ibid., 70.

58. Ibid., 137.

59. E. H. Carr, *Britain: A Study of Foreign Policy from the Versailles Treaty to the Outbreak of War* (London: Longmans, Green and Co., 1939), 17.

60. Ibid., 27.
61. Ibid., 195–96.
62. Ibid., 176.
63. Ibid., 195–96.
64. Martin Gilbert and Richard Gott, *The Appeasers* (Boston: Houghton Mifflin Company, 1963), 11–12.
65. Marquess of Londonderry, *Ourselves and Germany* (London: R. Hale Publishers, 1938). 13.
66. Ibid., 24.
67. Ibid., 68.
68. Ibid., 176.
69. John F. Kennedy, *Why England Slept* (New York: W. Funk and Company, 1940), xvi. (For more background on the authenticity of Kennedy's magnum opus, see Thomas Reeves, *JFK: A Question of Character* [New York, *Free Press*, 1991], 49–50.)
70. Ibid., 156–57.
71. Ibid., 184.
72. Ibid., 192.
73. Ibid., 215–16.
74. Sir Charles Petrie, *The Chamberlain Tradition* (New York: Stokes and Company, 1938), 296.
75. Ibid., 340.

CHAPTER 2. THE FEILING AND MACLEOD BIOGRAPHIES

1. Neville Chamberlain Papers, University of Birmingham Library, NC 11/15/43, G. Dawson to Mrs. A. Chamberlain, 14 January 1941.
2. Ibid.
3. Neville Chamberlain Papers, NC 11/15/129, K. Feiling to H. Wilson, 31 July 1941; see John F. Naylor, *A Man and an Institution* (Cambridge: Cambridge University Press, 1984), 234–35, for a record of Feiling's failure to gain access to official Cabinet papers.
4. Neville Chamberlain Papers, NC 11/15/129, K. Feiling to H. Wilson, 31 July 1941.
5. Neville Chamberlain Papers, NC 11/15/137, H. Wilson to Mrs. A. Chamberlain, 30 December 1943.
6. Neville Chamberlain Papers, NC 11/15/3, K. Feiling to Mrs. A. Chamberlain, 30 September 1944.
7. Neville Chamberlain Papers, NC 11/15/4 K. Feiling to Mrs. A. Chamberlain, 22 March 1945.
8. Ibid.
9. Ibid.
10. Keith Feiling, *The Life of Neville Chamberlain* (London: Macmillan and Co. Ltd., 1946), 30.
11. Ibid., 123–24.
12. Ibid., 63. For more on Chamberlain's desire to set right his reputation after his failure at National Service, see L. S. Amery, *The Unforgiving Years* (London: Hutchinson and Co., 1955), 225, and A. L. Rowse, *Appeasement: A Study in Political Decline, 1933–1939* (New York: W. W. Norton and Co., 1961), 80.
13. Feiling, *Life of Chamberlain*, 65.

14. Ibid.
15. Neville Chamberlain Papers, NC 18/1/969, Neville to Hilda Chamberlain, 11 July 1936.
16. Feiling, *Life of Chamberlain*, 313.
17. Ibid., 321.
18. Ibid., 333.
19. Ibid., 359.
20. Ibid.
21. Ibid., 360.
22. Ibid., 398.
23. Ibid., 402.
24. Ibid., 403.
25. Ibid., 404.
26. Ibid., 445.
27. Ibid., 446.
28. Ibid., 456n.
29. Ibid., 458.
30. Thomas Jones, "Neville Chamberlain: Minister of 'Appeasement' in the Gathering Storm," *London Times* (10 December 1946).
31. Ibid.
32. *Time and Tide* review, from the Neville Chamberlain Papers, NC 11/15A/1, Richard Law, "Notes on the Way" (1 February 1947).
33. Ibid.
34. Ibid.
35. Ibid.
36. Iain Macleod, *Neville Chamberlain* (London: Frederich Muller Ltd., 1961), 13.
37. "The Man of Munich," *Times Literary Supplement* (1 December 1961), 857.
38. Macleod, *Neville Chamberlain*, 164.
39. Ibid., 178.
40. Ibid., 193.
41. Ibid., 258.
42. Ibid., 206.
43. Ibid., 176; quoted from Neville Chamberlain Papers, Neville to Hilda Chamberlain, 28 July 1934.
44. Macleod, *Neville Chamberlain*, 202.
45. Ibid., 203.
46. Ibid., 222.
47. Ibid., 209, as quoted from Viscount Templewood, *Nine Troubled Years* (London: Collins Publishers, 1954), 375.
48. Macleod, *Neville Chamberlain*, 209.
49. Ibid., 261. This question of a one year's breathing-space had been one of the main justifications of Munich by Chamberlain's supporters from the beginning. As early as 1940 John F. Kennedy had alluded to it in *Why England Slept*. A. J. P. Taylor would refute it in his 1961 review of Macleod's biography, and later research would point toward the languid pace of British rearmament after Munich as a powerfully damning denial of the breathing-space thesis.
50. Ibid., 266–67.
51. Ibid., 282–83. See Feiling, *Life of Neville Chamberlain*, 445, for Neville's personal corroboration of this viewpoint, as well as a possible rationale for his continuance in office during the "phony war."

52. Macleod, *Neville Chamberlain*, 297.
53. "The Man of Munich," *Times Literary Supplement* (1 December 1961), 858.
54. Ibid.
55. Ibid.
56. A. J. P. Taylor, "Unlucky Find," *New Statesman* (1 December 1961), 833.
57. Ibid., 834.
58. Ibid.

CHAPTER 3. CHURCHILL AND THE "GUILTY MEN" GENRE

1. Winston S. Churchill, *The Gathering Storm* (Boston: Houghton Mifflin and Co., 1948), iv.
2. David Cannadine, ed., *Blood, Toil, Tears and Sweat: The Speeches of Winston Churchill* (Boston, Houghton Mifflin, 1989), 195.
3. Churchill, *Gathering Storm*, 222.
4. Ibid., 248, For corroboration of these sentiments, see Anthony Eden, *Facing the Dictators* (Boston: Houghton Mifflin Company, 1962), 532.
5. The phrase is from Frank Freidel's *Franklin D. Roosevelt: A Rendezvous with Destiny* (Boston, Little, Brown & Co., 1990), 294. A more specific account of the Rooseveltian initiative of January 1938 can be found in William Rock's *Chamberlain and Roosevelt: British Foreign Policy and the United States, 1937–1940* (Columbus: Ohio State University Press, 1988), 55–58.
6. Churchill, *Gathering Storm*, 255.
7. Ibid., 274.
8. Ibid., as quoted from Feiling, 347–48.
9. Churchill, *Gathering Storm*, 275.
10. Ibid., 305.
11. Ibid.
12. Ibid., 334.
13. Ibid., 339.
14. Ibid., 319.
15. Ibid., 344. See Hugh Dalton, *The Fateful Years: 1931–1945* (London, Muller & Co., 1957), 198, for a slightly different Churchillian commentary on Chamberlain's "hard core," something akin to "abject surrender."
16. Churchill, *Gathering Storm*, 346.
17. Ibid., 347.
18. Ibid.
19. Ibid., 347–48.
20. Eden, *Facing the Dictators*, 488–89.
21. Ibid., 510.
22. Ibid., 511.
23. Ibid., 532. The same subject is referred to in detail in Churchill, *Gathering Storm*, 248.
24. Viscount Templewood, *Nine Troubled Years* (London: Collins Publishers, 1954), 258.
25. Eden, *Facing the Dictators*, 570.
26. Ibid., 590.
27. Ibid., 629.
28. Ibid., 635.

29. Ibid., 645.
30. Ibid., 683.
31. For a more detailed analysis of the Conservative opposition to appeasement in the House of Commons see Neville Thompson, *The Anti-Appeasers* (Oxford: Oxford University Press, 1971).
32. Leopold Amery, *The Unforgiving Years, 1929–1940* (London: Hutchinson and Co., 1955), 280. For an interesting commentary on how this particular event was skillfully "stage-managed" by Chamberlain and his inner circle, see Naomi Black, "Decision-Making and the Munich Crisis," *British Journal of International Studies* 6, 3 (October 1980): 298.
33. Amery, *Unforgiving Years*, 228–29.
34. Ibid., 293–94.
35. Ibid., 398.
36. Ibid., 292–93.
37. Alfred Duff Cooper, *Old Men Forget* (London, Rupert Hart-Davis Publishers, 1954). As fate would have it, Duff Cooper became Viscount Norwich upon his entrance into the House of Lords in 1952.
38. Ibid., 200.
39. Ibid., 210. Allowing for Duff Cooper's overly-optimistic view on this point, the rather nebulous content of the President's offer makes the total avoidance of the European war a bit of conjecture stretched to the limit, in my opinion.
40. Ibid., 246.
41. Ibid., 248.
42. Sir Robert Boothby, *I Fight to Live* (London: Victor Gollancz Ltd., 1947), 141.
43. Ibid., 148–49.
44. Ibid., 178.
45. Ibid., 178–79.
46. Ibid., 178.
47. Ibid., 185–86.
48. Ibid., 186. A curious argument, this "world domination" concept, as opposed to "European domination," but singularly difficult to prove, especially under duress.
49. Ibid., 219.

Chapter 4. Chamberlain's Support vs. the Foreign office

1. Viscount Maugham, *The Truth About the Munich Crisis* (London: William Heinemann Ltd., 1944), 3.
2. Ibid., 35.
3. Ibid.
4. Ibid., 54–55.
5. Ibid., 63.
6. Ibid., 68–70. Maugham's last statement is in direct contrast with CATO's thesis, in which the disaster at Dunkirk was clearly related to the casual pace of the rearmament efforts.
7. Sir John Simon, *Retrospect: The Memoirs of Sir John Simon* (London: Hutchinson and Company, 1952), 232.
8. Ibid., 238–39.
9. Ibid., 253–54.

10. Viscount Templewood, *Nine Troubled Years* (London: Collins Publishers, 1954), 373–374.

11. Ibid., 375.

12. Ibid., 378–79.

13. Ibid., 381.

14. Ibid., 377.

15. Ibid., 370. See W. N. Medlicott, *British Foreign Policy Since Versailles* (London: Methuen and Company Ltd.), 207–11, for more or less the same analysis of the Anglo-Soviet talks of summer 1939.

16. Templewood, *Nine Troubled Years*, 388.

17. Edward Halifax, *Fulness of Days* (New York: Dodd, Mead and Company, 1957), 236–37.

18. Ibid., 233.

19. Ibid., 199.

20. Ibid., 200.

21. Ibid., 200–01.

22. Ibid., 201.

23. Anthony Eden, *Facing the Dictators* (Boston: Houghton Mifflin Company, 1962), 510–11.

24. Neville Chamberlain Papers, University of Birmingham Library, NC 18/1/1025, Neville to Hilda Chamberlain, 24 October 1937.

25. Neville Chamberlain Papers, University of Birmingham Library, NC 18/1/1027, Neville to Hilda Chamberlain, 6 November 1937.

26. Neville Chamberlain Papers, University of Birmingham Library, NC 18/1/1031, Neville to Ida Chamberlain, 12 December 1937. Vansittart's judgment of Chamberlain, seemingly much more generous in nature, can be found in his *The Mist Procession* (London, Hutchinson & Co. 1958), 429–30. A sampling of Vansittart's analysis found him regarding Chamberlain as "a good man, unlucky in appeasement's sudden change of meaning from virtuous endeavour to craven immorality."

27. David Dilks, ed., *The Diaries of Sir Alexander Cadogan, 1938–1945* (London: Cassell and Company, 1971), 53–54.

28. Ibid., 54; quoted from a letter of of Cadogan to Birkenhead, 12 October 1964. This notion of "honourable conduct" would evidence a pathetic variance between Czech and British perspectives in the aftermath of the Sudeten crisis.

29. Ibid., 69–70.

30. Ibid., 103–4.

31. Ibid., 105.

32. Ibid., 161.

33. John Harvey, ed., *The Diplomatic Diaries of Oliver Harvey, 1937–1940* (London: Collins Publishers, 1970), 71.

34. Ibid., 75–76. For additional background on the mysterious Sir Horace, who in accordance with his laconic nature never wrote his memoirs, see Martin Gilbert, "Horace Wilson: Man of Munich?" *History Today* 32 (October 1982): 3–9.

35. Harvey, *Diplomatic Diaries*, 109.

36. Ibid., 148–49.

37. Ibid., 208.

38. Ibid., 210.

39. William Strang, *Home and Abroad* (London: Andre Deutsch Ltd., 1956), 124.

40. Ibid., 125.
41. Ibid., 125–26.
42. Ibid., 126.
43. Ibid., 146.
44. Ibid., 152.
45. Ibid., 182.
46. Ibid., 152–53.
47. Nevile Henderson, *Failure of a Mission* (New York: G. P. Putnam's Sons, 1940), 7.
48. Ibid., 17.
49. Ibid., 27–28.
50. Ibid., 173.

CHAPTER 5. THE SIXTIES—DECADE OF CHANGE

1. A. L. Rowse, *Appeasement: A Study in Political Decline, 1933–1939* (New York: W. W. Norton and Company, 1961), 19–20.
2. Ibid., 57.
3. Ibid., 63.
4. Ibid., 65–66. This prose seems almost identical to certain portions of *The Gathering Storm* in spite of the nearly fifteen-year gap between publication dates. This is clear evidence of the overarching predominance of the antiappeasers in the postwar years, in that the Labour Party supporter Rowse's views on appeasement could dovetail with those of Churchill, a sworn antagonist of socialism.
5. Ibid., 104–5 (Rowse's italics).
6. Ibid., 118.
7. A. J. P. Taylor, *The Origins of the Second World War* (London: Hamish Hamilton Ltd., 1961, 1963), xxii–xxiii.
8. Ibid., 134–135.
9. Ibid., 136.
10. Ibid., 170.
11. Ibid., 184.
12. Ibid., 191.
13. Ibid., 205. Templewood quoted from *Nine Troubled Years*, 377.
14. Taylor, *Origins of the Second World War*, 243–44.
15. M. Gilbert and R. Gott, *The Appeasers* (Boston: Houghton Mifflin Company, 1963), ix.
16. Ibid., xii–xiii.
17. Ibid., 9.
18. Ibid., 26.
19. Ibid., 48.
20. Ibid., 147.
21. Ibid., 180; quoted from Bruce Lockhart, *Friends, Foes, and Foreigners*, 196.
22. Gilbert and Gott, *The Appeasers*, 180; quoted by the authors from the H. A. L. Fisher Papers, Bodleian Library, Oxford, Box A.
23. Gilbert and Gott, *The Appeasers*, 234; quoted from Hansard, *House of Commons Debates* (15 March 1939).
24. Gilbert and Gott, *The Appeasers*, 317.

25. D. C. Watt, "Appeasement: the Rise of a Revisionist School?" *Political Quarterly* 36, 2 (April–June 1965): 191–213.

26. Ibid., 192. For a somewhat updated version of Dr. Watt's perceptions, see his "The Historiography of Appeasement," *Crisis and Controversy: Essays in Honour of A. J. P. Taylor*, eds. Alan Sked and Chris Cook (New York, St. Martin's Press 1976), 110–29.

27. Watt, "Appeasement," 193–94.

28. Ibid., 194–95.

29. Ibid., 196.

30. As early as 1940 William Norton Medlicott had made clear that his work would be characterized by empiricism rather than the customary vitriol. His *British Foreign Policy Since Versailles* (London: Methuen and Company Ltd., 1940), was arguably more scholarly and objective than the accounts of his contemporaries. This foresight served only to enhance his reputation when the parameters of the debate underwent so much change in the 1960s.

31. Watt, "Appeasement," 208–9.

32. Ibid., 210.

33. Ibid. For a thoroughgoing analysis of the Labour Party's stand on the policy of appeasement, see John F. Naylor, *Labour's International Policy: The Labour Party in the 1930s* (Cambridge: Cambridge University Press, 1969), 214–259; as for the Conservative Party's position, see Neville Thompson's aptly titled account, *The Anti-Appeasers: Consevative Opposition to Appeasement in the 1930s* (Oxford, 1971). As regarding rearmament, see Ch. 7 of Thompson for insights into the relevant historiography.

34. Watt, "Appeasement," 213.

35. Martin Gilbert, *The Roots of Appeasement* (London: Weidenfeld and Nicolson, 1966), xi.

36. Ibid., xiii.

37. Ibid., 9.

38. Ibid., 54–55.

39. Ibid., 165–66.

40. Ibid., 167.

41. Ibid., 175.

42. Ibid., 177, Ostensibly Gilbert is not here alluding to the French, who had bona-fide pledges to assist the Czech state. His assessment is more moderate than his earlier opprobrium, characterized by the "decayed serving men" analogy.

43. Ibid., 185.

44. Keith Middlemas, *The Strategy of Appeasement: The British Government and Germany, 1937–1939* (Chicago: Quadrangle Books, 1972), 5–6.

45. Ibid., 8n.

46. Ibid., 47.

47. Ibid., 59.

48. Ibid., 108–9. Cited by Middlemas from the Chamberlain Papers, University of Birmingham Library, letter of 5 June 1938.

49. Ibid., 56. Robert Shay, in his *British Rearmament in the Thirties: Politics and Profits* (Princeton: Princeton University Press, 1977), credited Middlemas' study as being the first "to consider the impact that rearmament had on British foreign policy in the 1930s," see 170(ff).

50. Middlemas, *Strategy of Appeasement*, 128.

51. Ibid., 132. Cited by the author from the Chamberlain Papers, NC 18/1/1020, Neville to Hilda Chamberlain, 12 September 1939.

52. Ibid., 154 (italics are Middlemas').
53. Ibid., 447.
54. Ibid.
55. Ibid., 448–49.
56. Ibid., 449.
57. Ian Colvin, *The Chamberlain Cabinet* (New York: Taplinger Publishing, 1971), 10.
58. Ibid., 14.
59. Ibid., 64.
60. Ibid., 105–6.
61. Ibid., 109; quoted from the Foreign Policy Committee Papers, CAB 27/623, 164.
62. Colvin, *The Chamberlain Cabinet*, 124.
63. Ibid., 142.
64. Ibid., 168 (Colvin inteview of Lord Swinton).
65. Ibid., 173 (brackets are Colvin's).
66. Ibid., 186.
67. Ibid., 261.
68. Ibid., 263.

CHAPTER 6. ECONOMICS, REARMAMENT, AND APPEASEMENT

1. Martin Gilbert, *The Roots of Appeasement* (London: Weidenfeld and Nicolson, 1966), 67.
2. Ibid., 65.
3. John Maynard Keynes, *The Economic Consequences of the Peace* (London and New York: Harcourt, Brace, Jovanovich, 1920, 1988), 146.
4. Ibid., 225.
5. Ibid, 268.
6. Basil Liddell Hart, *The Defence of Britain* (London, 1939), 44. Indeed, this quotation is a direct paraphrase of a statement in an earlier Liddell Hart work, *The British Way in Warfare* (London, 1932), 16. Suffice it to say, this notion of "limited liability" was characteristic of the entire decade of the 1930s, and not solely created in 1939.
7. Neville Chamberlain Papers, University of Birmingham Library, NC 18/1/949 to Hilda Chamberlain on 9 February 1936; this missive bore witness to the fact that well over a year before his accession to the premiership, before the Rhineland crisis, Chamberlain was pondering the ideas that surrounded the doctrine of "limited liability." See Wiiliamson Murray, *The Change in the European Balance of Power, 1938–1939* (Princeton: Princeton University Press, 1984), 86–87, for insight into Liddell Hart's ideas and Chamberlain's utilization of "limited liability" to try to obviate the buildup of a British continental force.
8. Neville Chamberlain Papers, University of Birmingham Library, NC 18/1/1108, Neville to Ida Chamberlain, 23 July 1939, and NC 18/1/1122, Neville to Ida Chamberlain, 23 September 1939.
9. Liddell Hart, *The Defence of Britain*, 25.
10. For corroboration on the notion that the danger engendered by Munich caused a dramatic alteration in the course of Britain's rearmament, see William Hancock and M. M. Gowing, *British War Economy* (London, 1949), 68.
11. Liddell Hart, *The Defence of Britain*, 46.

12. M. M. Postan, *British War Production* (London: HMSO, 1952), 1.

13. Ibid.

14. Ibid., 10.

15. Ibid., 13. Hancock and Gowing, in *British War Economy*, corroborated this notion of a "fourth arm of defence" in a paragraph alluding to a late 1936 address by the Minister for the Co-Ordination of Defence, Thomas Inskip. To the Commons, he opined, "Remember that we depend upon the resources of finance for the successful fighting of a war as much as upon the production of munitions," 69 (my insert).

16. Brian Bond, *British Military Policy Between the Two World Wars* (Oxford: Clarendon Press, 1980), 218 (quoted from the Pownall diary, 27 January 1936). For a good deal more background on Lieutenant General Pownall and his opinions, see Brian Bond, ed., *Chief of Staff: The Diaries of Sir Henry Pownall*, vol. 1 (London, 1973).

17. Bond, *British Military Policy*, 243; quoted originally from Inskip's Interim Report on Defence Expenditure in Future Years, 15 December 1937, CAB24/273.

18. Ibid., 284.

19. Robert Shay, *British Rearmament in the Thirties: Politics and Profits* (Princeton: Princeton University Press, 1977), 3.

20. Ibid., 174.

21. George Peden, *British Rearmament and the Treasury, 1932–1939* (Edinburgh: Scottish Academy Press, 1979), 181, made the cogent point that the £1.5 billion figure was illusory in its very conservative level for a five year estimate. Peden placed the eventual totals at £382 million for 1938, and £642 million for 1939, a total of over £1 billion pounds for just two years.

22. Shay, *British Rearmament*, 191; quoted from CAB 63/53, 14 January 1938, Hankey to Inskip.

23. Shay, *British Rearmament*, 195–96.

24. Ibid., 227. See Martin Gilbert, *The Roots of Appeasement* (London: Weidenfeld and Nicolson, 1966), 177, for corroboration on this theme of courage versus cowardice. (Italics and insertion mine.)

25. Shay, *British Rearmament*, 285–86.

26. Ibid., 287–88.

27. Ibid., 288.

28. Brian Bond, *British Military Policy Between the Two World Wars*, 371(ff).

29. Peden, *British Rearmament*, 14.

30. Ibid., 15.

31. Ibid., 39.

32. Ibid., 63.

33. Ibid., 65.

34. Ibid., 105; quoted by Peden from CAB 23/95, Cabinet minutes, 3 October 1938, 304. Telford Taylor's authoritative *Munich: The Price of Peace* (Garden City, N.Y.: Doubleday & Company, 1979), insisted of Chamberlain and rearmament: "Energetic and dedicated to the public good as he was, Chamberlain must be held primarily responsible for the parlous state of British arms in 1938 and 1939" (998).

35. Peden, *British Rearmament*, 160. See page 205 for an illustrative table of expenditures for all three services from 1932 to 1939.

36. Ibid., 178.

37. Ibid., 184.

38. Brian Bond review, *Journal of Strategic Studies* 2, 3, (1979): 362–63.

39. Gustav Schmidt, *The Politics and Economics of Appeasement: British Foreign Policy in the 1930s* (Leamington Spa: Berg Publishers, 1986), 21 (Schmidt's italics).

40. Ibid., 25–26.

41. Ibid., 253.

42. Ibid., 390.

43. Ibid., 370–71.

44. Michael Howard, *The Continental Commitment: The Dilemma of British Defence Policy in the Era of the Two World Wars* (London: Temple Smith Ltd., 1972), 114, See Peden, *British Rearmament*, 125, for a refutation of Howard's stance on Chamberlain's attitude.

45. Howard, *Continental Commitment*, 128.

46. Ibid., 130.

47. Ibid., 134.

48. Ibid., 135.

49. B. E. V. Sabine, *British Budgets in Peace and War: 1932–1945* (London: George Allen and Unwin, Ltd., 1970), 95.

50. Ibid., 101.

51. Ibid., 103.

52. Ibid., 102.

53. Uri Bialer, *The Shadow of the Bomber: the Fear of Air Attack and British Politics, 1932–1939* (London: Royal Historical Society Press, 1980), 4–5.

54. Ibid., 127. Benny Morris, *The Roots of Appeasement: The British Weekly Press and Nazi Germany During the 1930s* (London, 1991), offered the notion the the abject "air fear" of German bomber potential was one of the main motivations behind the widespread acceptance of appeasement as a policy: of course the weekly periodicals such as the *New Statesman* and *The Economist* reflected this dread.

55. Bialer, *The Shadow of the Bomber*, 146.

56. Ibid., 158, quoted from Harold Macmillan, *Winds of Change* (London, 1966), 522 (Bialer's italics).

57. Paul Kennedy, "Appeasement and British Defence Policy in the Interwar Years," *British Journal of International Studies* 4 (July 1978): 163.

58. Norman Gibbs, *Grand Strategy*, vol. I, *Rearmament Policy* (London: HMSO, 1976), 284; quoted from Cabinet Conclusions, CAB 23, 48(37)9 and 49(37)1.

59. Ibid., 294–95, quoted from Cabinet Conclusions, CAB 23, 16 February 1938.

60. Ibid., 315, quoted from Cabinet Conclusions, CAB 23, 15(38).

61. Ibid., 296, In spite of earlier rhetoric calling for a quick and vigorous rearmament, it was not until the war scare of late September 1938 that Britain really began taking rearmament seriously. M. M. Postan, *British War Production* (London, 1952), insisted that until late 1938 and early 1939, national efforts to rearm "remained on a peacetime scale" (10).

62. Gibbs, *Grand Strategy*, 809.

63. Wesley Wark, *The Ultimate Enemy: British Intelligence and Nazi Germany, 1933–1939* (Ithaca: Cornell University Press, 1985), 19.

64. Bialer, *The Shadow of the Bomber*, 157.

65. Wark, *The Ultimate Enemy*, 122, Certainly the "air fear," personified by

Baldwin's 1932 dictum that "the bomber would always get through" (originally attributed to Giulio Douhet) had much to do with the widespread dread of war among Britons.

66. Ibid., 122–23.
67. Ibid., 157.
68. Ibid., 169.
69. Ibid., 170; quoted from a Morton letter to A. J. Nicholls, 25 January 1938.
70. Wark, *The Ultimate Enemy*, 171–72.
71. Ibid., 211.
72. Ibid., 231. The same track was pursued by Churchill in his *Gathering Storm*, e.g., that Britain would have fared much better if she had stood for war in September 1938 before the Nazi war machine had been fully girded for conquest.
73. F. Coghlan, "Armaments, Economic Policy, and Appeasement: Background to British Foreign Policy, 1931–1937," *History*, 57, 90, (June 1972): 208.
74. Ibid., 209.
75. Ibid., 211.
76. Ibid., 214; quoted from *Political Quarterly* (1937): 268.
77. Coghlan, 216.
78. George Peden, "A Matter of Timing: The Economic Background to British Foreign Policy, 1937–1939" *History* 69, 225 (February 1984): 15.
79. Ibid., 25.
80. Ibid., 26.
81. Ibid., 27–28.

Chapter 7: Appeasement and the British Print Media

1. Keith Middlemas, *The Strategy of Appeasement* (Chicago: Quadrangle Books, 1972), 102, ascribed "quality" status to the following papers in 1937–1938: *The Times, Daily Telegraph, Manchester Guardian, Observer, Sunday Times,* and the provincial *Birmingham Post, Yorkshire Post, Glasgow Herald,* and *Scotsman.*
2. Stanley Morison, ed., *The History of The Times, The 150th Anniversary and Beyond, 1912–1948,* part II, chapters XIII–XXIV, *1921–1948* (New York: Macmillan Company, 1952), 882.
3. Ibid.
4. Ibid., 907–8; quoted from a G. Dawson letter of 23 May 1937 to H. G. Daniels.
5. Ibid. See pages 904–5 for an analysis by Morison that pointed out the ignorance of both Dawson and Barrington-Ward in regard to European affairs, and their necessary reliance on "certain personal sources"; thus, the "foreign policy pursued by *The Times* after the crucial year of 1936 became increasingly indebted . . . upon the editor's ministerial friends, Baldwin, Chamberlain, and Halifax." What effect this had on the paper's independence and integrity of thought is certainly debatable.
6. Ibid., 936–37.
7. Ibid., 947–48.
8. John E. Wrench, *Geoffrey Dawson and Our Times* (London: Hutchison and Company, 1955), 362–63.
9. Ibid., 363, As a matter of fact, according to Benny Morris in *The Roots of Appeasement: The British Weekly Press and Nazi Germany During the 1930s*

(London: Frank Cass and Company, 1991), 14, Wrench himself was a lifelong "Germanophile," who often contributed to the weekly journal *The Spectator*, was a staunch supporter of appeasement in the 1930s, and wrote a memoir of sorts in 1940 entitled *I Loved Germany*.

10. Ibid., 373.

11. Ibid., 376, on the same page Wrench commented on Dawson's sincere belief that Britain's dominions were in no way ready to fight over the Sudetenland, and that Dawson was "certainly influenced" by the notion that Nazi Germany might serve as a barrier to the spread of Soviet Communism in the West.

12. Ibid., 381.

13. Ibid., 395–96.

14. Ibid., 430.

15. Donald McLachlan, *In the Chair: Barrington-Ward of the Times, 1927–1948* (London, 1971), 99.

16. Ibid., 133.

17. Ibid., 104.

18. Ibid., 109–100. Similar viewpoints were held tenaciously by Neville Chamberlain all through his tenure as prime minister, which offers added testimony to the nearly unshakeable unanimity of purpose shared by the authors of *The Times* and the Chamberlain administration.

19. Franklin R. Gannon, *The British Press and Germany, 1936–1939* (Oxford: Clarendon Press, 1971), 2.

20. Ibid., 4–5.

21. Ibid., 36.

22. Ibid., 41–42. Perhaps Wells had this prediction dead right; certainly the next six years would prove his prescience.

23. Ibid., 42; quoted from *Documents on German Foreign Policy* 3rd series, vol. IV, document 300.

24. Gannon, *The British Press and Germany*, 44.

25. Ibid., 49; quoted from Gannon's private information.

26. Ibid.

27. Ibid., 51. See Morris, *The Roots of Appeasement*, 32, for a different interpretation of Garvin's attitude toward the Czechs, an effusive and heartfelt tribute on the occasion of Czech founder Thomas Masaryk's eighty-second birthday in 1932.

28. Gannon, *The British Press and Germany*, 52.

29. Ibid.

30. Ibid., 55; quoted from R. C. K. Ensor's entry on Sidebotham in *Dictionary of National Biography, 1931–1940* (London, 1949), 810–811.

31. Gannon, *The British Press and Germany*, 55.

32. Ibid., 65. Gannon recommended checking the original source for more detail, that being *The Week* 8 (14 September 1938).

33. Ibid., 70. Gannon's point of view would certainly come under fire in the 1970s and 1980s; an excellent example can be found in Richard Cockett, *Twilight of Truth: Chamberlain, Appeasement and the Manipulation of the Press* (London, 1989), 12–13.

34. Gannon, *The British Press and Germany*, 74.

35. Ibid., 76.

36. Ibid., 83.

37. Ibid., 87–88.

38. James Margach, *The Abuse of Power: The War Between Downing Street*

and the Media from Lloyd George to Callaghan (London,: W. H. Allen and Company, 1978), 50.

39. Ibid., 54.
40. Ibid., 60.
41. Ibid., 62.
42. Stephen Koss, *The Rise and Fall of the Political Press in Britain*, vol. II, *The Twentieth Century* (Chapel Hill: University of North Carolina Press, 1984), p.542.
43. Ibid., 544.
44. Ibid., 576.
45. Ibid., 575.
46. Richard Cockett, *Twilight of Truth: Chamberlain, Appeasement and the Manipulation of the Press* (London: Weidenfeld and Nicolson, 1989), 1–2.
47. Ibid., 7–8.
48. Ibid., 12–13.
49. Ibid., 78. For corroboration of the author's statement on the tight-fisted control of information by Whitehall, see Anthony Adamthwaite, "The British Government and the Media, 1937–1938," *Journal of Contemporary History* 18, 2 (April 1983): 281–97. Adamthwaite specifically enumerated his belief that "the government restricted public debate and limited the ventilation of alternative views," and that, "arguably, if more had been known about the issues, resistance would have been greater" (282).
50. Cockett, *Twilight of Truth*, 79.
51. Ibid., 80.
52. Ibid., 83.
53. Ibid., 97.
54. Ibid., 97–98, from *Yorkshire Post* leader (8 December 1938).
55. Cockett, *Twilight of Truth*, 98–99.
56. Ibid., 122.
57. Ibid., 189.
58. Morris, *The Roots of Appeasement* 1.
59. Ibid., 11–12.
60. Ibid., 14.
61. Ibid.
62. Ibid., 17.
63. Ibid., 19.
64. Ibid., 20. This sense of "unreserved condemnation" of Nazism belied the behavior of Sir Walter Layton on 30 September 1938, when he suppressed a negative analysis of the just completed Munich agreement offered by *News Chronicle* correspondent Vernon Bartlett, to the anguish of many on his own staff.
65. Ibid., 29.
66. Ibid., 30.
67. See Cockett, *Twilight of Truth*, 183, for a bit more background on Ball's erratic behavior after Chamberlain's fall in May 1940. A brief excerpt here reveals that Ball, according to Cockett, meant to "use *Truth* to propagate the struggle against their enemies, which meant anyone or anything that had crossed Chamberlain's path, be it Churchill, Eden, the Russians or the Jews," and that Ball's obsessional devotion to Neville Chamberlain now "bordered on hysterical fanaticism."
68. Morris, *The Roots of Appeasement* 24.
69. Ibid., 25.

70. Ibid.
71. Ibid., 26.
72. Ibid., 27.
73. Ibid., 35.
74. Ibid.
75. Ibid., 36.
76. Ibid.
77. Margach, *The Abuse of Power*, 51.

CHAPTER 8. MUNICH: AN OVERVIEW

1. Paul Kennedy, "Appeasement," *History Today* 32 (October 1982): 51–53.
2. Ibid., 53.
3. Neville Chamberlain, *In Search of Peace* (New York, 1939), p.98.
4. Neville Chamberlain Papers, University of Birmingham Library, NC 18/1/ 1069, Neville to Ida Chamberlain, 18 September 1938.
5. Ibid.
6. Neville Chamberlain Papers, University of Birmingham Library, NC/18/1/ 1070, Neville to Hilda Chamberlain, 2 October 1938. For an intriguing opinion that offered that the whole episode in the House that day was orchestrated for dramatic effect, see Naomi Black, "Decision-Making and the Munich Crisis," *British Journal of International Studies* 6, 3 (October 1980): 278–309, in which Black insisted that the Prime Minister knew of the fateful invitation three to four hours before his House of Commons address.
7. Chamberlain, *In Search of Peace*, 215.
8. Ibid., 230, this statement is quite a far piece from the Churchillian perspective of Munich as a "total and unmitigated defeat," and perhaps can be employed as a metaphor to dramatize how very different were the respective worldviews of these two political strongmen.
9. Ibid., 232–33.
10. A. J. P. Taylor was one of the first to offer that Chamberlain wanted more than just to buy time for rearmament at Munich, that he desperately wanted appeasement to succeed in the wholesale pacification of Europe. See Taylor's *New Statesman* article of 1 December 1961, a critique of Ian Macleod's new biography of Chamberlain (alluded to in chapter 2 of this work). It is without question true that many more have embraced this notion since Taylor, especially those critical of the Prime Minister's conduct.
11. Eduard Benes, *Memoirs of Dr. Eduard Benes: From Munich to New War and New Victory* (Boston: Houghton Mifflin Company, 1954), 33.
12. Ibid., 43 (Benes' italics).
13. Ibid., 59–60 (Benes' italics).
14. Soviet Foreign Ministry, *Documents and Materials Relating to the Eve of the Second World War*, vol. I, *November 1937–December 1938* (New York, 1948), 236.
15. Ibid., 239.
16. Ibid., 267.
17. Ibid.
18. Ibid., 269–270.
19. John Wheeler-Bennett, *Munich: Prologue to Tragedy* (New York: Duell, Sloan and Pearce, 1948), 293.

20. Keith Eubank, *Munich* (Norman: University of Oklahoma Press, 1963), 17.

21. Ibid., 214.

22. Ibid., 221.

23. Ibid.

24. Ibid., 264, from Chamberlain, *In Search of Peace*, 269–75.

25. Eubank, *Munich*, 278–79.

26. Ibid., 286–87.

27. Keith Robbins, *Munich 1938* (London: Cassell and Company, 1968), 3. For several corroborating perspectives on the continuity of British foreign policy, see Paul Schroeder, "Munich and the British Tradition," *Historical Journal* 19, 1 (1976): 223–43, and Paul Kennedy, "The Tradition of Appeasement in British Foreign Policy, 1865–1939," *British Journal of International Studies* 2, 3 (October 1976): 195–215.

28. Robbins, *Munich 1938*, 4.

29. Ibid., 328.

30. Ibid., 331–32.

31. Ibid., 335.

32. Christopher Thorne, *The Approach of War, 1938–1939* (London: Macmillan and Company, 1967), 20.

33. Ibid., 21, from Keith Feiling, *The Life of Neville Chamberlain* (London: Macmillan and Company, 1946), 354 and 367. The Swinton comment was from Ian Colvin, *Vansittart in Office* (London, 1965), 276.

34. Thorne, *The Approach of War*, 86.

35. Ibid., quoted from CATO, *Guilty Men* (London: Victor Gollancz Ltd., 1940), 55–56.

36. Roger Parkinson, *Peace for Our Time: Munich to Dunkirk—The Inside Story* (London: Rupert Hart-Davis, Ltd., 1971), xix.

37. Ibid., 27–28. See Churchill's speech in the House of Commons Munich debate, 3–6 October 1938, where he used the "pistol's point" metaphor to set the price for a tenuous peace; also, Telford Taylor's expansive *Munich: The Price of Peace* (Garden City, N.Y.: Doubleday & Company, 1979), xv, in which Taylor heartily agreed with the thesis that Chamberlain's first trip to Germany was more critical than the Munich meeting where the cession of the Sudetenland was already a fait accompli.

38. Parkinson, *Peace for Our Time*, 59, from Ivone Kirkpatrick, *The Inner Circle* (London, 1959), 128–29.

39. Parkinson, *Peace for Our Time*, 65.

40. Ibid., 66 (author's italics).

41. Corelli Barnett, *The Collapse of British Power* (New York: William Morrow and Company, 1972) 525. Barnett's view of the stout Czech defenses and the top-rate quality of their army, to be fair to the Prime Minister, has been challenged as excessive by several of the author's contemporaries in the field of military history.

42. Ibid., 545.

43. Ibid.

44. Ibid., 551.

45. Ibid.; quoted from Cabinet Conclusions, CAB/23/95, 48(38).

46. Barnett, *The Collapse of British Power*, 550. Perhaps any sort of condemnation coming from this onetime house painter and failed artist should have made Chamberlain proud in view of the old adage that "you can tell a lot about a

man from viewing a list of his enemies." It is to Chamberlain's credit that he had at long last discerned the type of cur he had been dealing with even though it was not in time to salvage his own historical reputation.

47. Ibid., 556.

48. Roy Douglas, *In the Year of Munich* (New York: St. Martin's Press, 1977), 15.

49. Ibid., 15–16.

50. Ibid., 79.

51. Ibid., 130–31.

52. Ibid., 129.

53. Ibid.

54. Ibid., 134.

55. Ernst Presseisen, *Amiens and Munich: Comparisons in Appeasement* (The Hague: Martinus Nijhoff, 1978), 3.

56. Ibid., 11. Originally from the Orme Sargent letter, which can be found in Appendix 5 of Martin Gilbert's *Roots of Appeasement* (London: Weidenfeld and Nicolson, 1966), 220–23. (Sargent's italics in the quote.)

57. Presseisen, *Amiens and Munich*, 13.

58. Ibid., 25.

59. Ibid., 62–63.

60. Ibid., 130–31. This analysis corroborates the earlier efforts of A. J. P. Taylor, who had refuted the "one year of breathing-space for rearmament" thesis as early as 1961.

61. T. Taylor, *Munich: The Price of Peace*, xvi.

62. Ibid., xiv–xv. See Gilbert, *The Roots of Appeasement*, passim, for a very similar analysis of Neville Chamberlain's motivations.

63. T. Taylor, *Munich: The Price of Peace*, 896–97.

64. Ibid., 924.

65. Ibid., 983. Because the Prime Minister felt so strongly about Munich as the first step to the eventual pacification of Europe he perceived no great need to radically alter the speed of Britain's rearmament efforts in light of the war scare brought on by the Czech crisis. He also faced a plethora of economic concerns at the time and was unwilling to place Britain on a war footing for a conflict that might never occur.

66. Ibid., 984.

67. Williamson Murray, *The Change in the European Balance of Power, 1938–1939* (Princeton: Princeton University Press, 1984), 213.

68. Ibid., 214.

69. Ibid., 263.

70. Ibid., 271; quoted from Hansard, *Parliamentary Debates*, 5th Series, vol. 339, columns 49–50.

71. Larry Fuchser, *Neville Chamberlain and Appeasement* (New York: W. W. Norton and Company, 1982), x. Ernst Presseisen had also envisioned the continuity of appeasement as a policy whose roots stemmed from the nineteenth century, in his provocative *Amiens and Munich*.

72. Fuchser, *Neville Chamberlain and Appeasement*, 163–64.

73. Ibid., 166.

74. Ibid., 197.

75. John Charmley, *Chamberlain and the Lost Peace* (London: Hodder and Stoughton, 1989), xiv.

76. Ibid. This thesis works well aided by fifty years of hindsight, but to ignore

the overriding moral issues of those perilous years can lead to critical historical misjudgments, i.e., that Britain had any alternative to war on 3 September 1939.

77. Ibid., 137. Recently historians have begun to take issue with the "unplanned" status of Chamberlain's surprise announcement. For an example, see Naomi Black, "Decision-Making and the Munich Crisis" *British Journal of International Studies* 6, 3 (October 1980).

78. Charmley, *Chamberlain and the Lost Peace*, 139.

79. Ibid., 140–41.

80. Ibid., 144–45.

81. Ibid., 212. Charmley's perception that an accommodation with Nazi Germany would have avoided war and saved the British Empire is hopeful conjecture, to say the least. The fate of 27 million Soviet dead is a mute testament to those who would have faith in the tender mercies of Berlin.

82. Richard Lamb, *The Drift To War, 1922–1939* (London: W. H. Allen and Company, 1989), ix.

83. Ibid., x. One can better understand Lamb's orientation by realizing that he achieved maturity in the 1930s, hence the "Guilty Men" tone of his work. However, to have it published in 1989, well after the refutation of the "cringing appeasers" genre, testifies to the fluidity of the historiographic debate.

84. Ibid., 254. In spite of Lamb's analysis and to Chamberlain's credit, there is still scant evidence to reinforce the scenario that either France or the Soviet Union would have been either willing or able to place effective forces in the field at the time of Munich, despite the litany of solemn Russian vows to the contrary. Indeed, Moscow was to later employ the so-called sellout of the Czechs as a justification for their duplicity of summer 1939, which led to the Nazi-Soviet Pact and the dual invasion of Poland.

85. Ibid., 258. Once again, in spite of the persuasive accounts of Churchill's *Gathering Storm* and Walter Goerlitz's *History of the German General Staff* (N.Y.: Praeger Publishers, 1953), there is little conclusive evidence to support the notion of a revolt among the German generals. Little doubt exists that a noble service to mankind would have performed had these men moved to decapitate the Nazi high command. Perhaps the most sanguine account of the possibilities of a military coup at the time of Munich can be found in the work of Peter Hoffmann, *The History of the German Resistance, 1933–1945* (Cambridge, Mass., MIT Press, 1977).

86. Lamb, *The Drift to War*, 265.

87. Ibid., 269. Admittedly one must take Soviet pledges of that time with an attitude of cum grano salis, lest we read more into the probability and quality of their contribution as a prospective ally of the West. This is mentioned only in light of Stalin's decimation of the Soviet officer corps in the prewar purges. According to a reliable source (R. Conquest) the total liquidated was 43,000, the cream of the Red Army.

CHAPTER 9. THE RECENT PAST

1. John Charmley, *Chamberlain and the Lost Peace* (London: Hodder and Stoughton, 1989), p.212.

2. Robert Kee, *Munich: The Eleventh Hour* (London: Hamish Hamilton, 1988), 107.

3. Ibid., 154.

4. Ibid., 210.

5. Robert Shepherd, *A Class Divided: Appeasement and the Road to Munich, 1938* (London: Macmillan Publishers, 1988), 18. See E. H. Carr's *Britain: A Study of Foreign Policy from the Versailles Treaty to the Outbreak of War* (London: Longmans, Green and Co., 1939), 27, for a similar analysis of Britain's status as a "satiated" rather than "expansionist" power in the first half of the twentieth century.

6. Shepherd, *A Class Divided*, 205–6. With all due respect to Shepherd, to ignore the Prime Minister's raison d'etre, namely, his lifelong belief in the inefficacy of war as an instrument of national policy, is, in my estimation, to miss the point of Chamberlain's core orientation. I might add that anti-Communism and "economics as a fourth arm of defense" were significant issues, albeit ancillary ones.

7. Ibid., 231 (brackets are mine).

8. Ibid., 274.

9. Terrance Lewis, *A Climate for Appeasement?* (New York: Peter Lang Publishing, 1991), 175.

10. Ibid., 194.

11. Ibid., 214.

12. Ibid., 233.

13. William Rock, *Chamberlain and Roosevelt: British Foreign Policy and the United States, 1937–1940* (Columbus: Ohio State University Press, 1988), 8–9.

14. Ibid., 70–71. A similar analysis was set forth by Eden in his *Facing the Dictators* (Boston: Houghton Mifflin Publishers, 1962), 645, written a quarter-century after the event.

15. Rock, *Chamberlain and Roosevelt*, 295.

16. Ibid., 299.

17. Keith Robbins, *Appeasement* (London: Basil Blackwell, 1988), 6.

18. Ibid., 26.

19. Ibid., 60.

20. Ibid., 81.

21. John Charmley, *Churchill: The End of Glory* (New York: Harcourt Brace, 1993), 325.

22. R. J. Q. Adams, *British Politics and Foreign Policy in the Age of Appeasement, 1935–1939* (Stanford, Calif.: Stanford University Press, 1993), 65.

23. Ibid., 77.

24. Ibid., 126. A corroboration of this perspective can be found in Larry W. Fuchser's *Neville Chamberlain and Appeasement* (New York: W. W. Norton and Company, 1982), 163–164, which in many ways speaks to the level of Chamberlain's self-delusion in regard to Berlin's future behavior.

25. Adams, *British Politics and Foreign Policy*, 159–160.

26. R. A. C. Parker, *Chamberlain and Appeasement: British Policy and the Coming of the Second World War* (New York: St. Martin's Press, 1993), 347.

27. Ibid., 343.

28. Ibid., 10. See Neville Chamberlain Papers, University of Birmingham Library, NC 7/9/80, for a personal letter of 10 May 1940 from Churchill to Chamberlain in which the new Prime Minister opined that "to a very large extent—I am in your hands—and I feel no fear of that." Had he lived, Chamberlain would have had ample justification to fear for the fate of his own historical reputation, in the hands, as it was, of Churchill and his *Gathering Storm*.

29. Parker, *Chamberlain and Appeasement*, 186.

30. Ibid., 203. See Charmley's controversial effort, *Churchill: The End of Glory*, 359, for a similar opinion, i.e., that the fall of Prague did little to alter Chamberlain's deep-seated faith in the efficacy of appeasement.

31. Parker, *Chamberlain and Appeasement*, 364.

32. Gaines Post, Jr., *Dilemmas of Appeasement: British Deterrence and Defense, 1934–1937* (Ithaca: Cornell University Press, 1993), 3.

33. Ibid., 19.

34. Ibid., 21–22.

35. Ibid., 68. This self-confidence bordering on hubris gave Winston Churchill pause as early as 1948, when in the *Gathering Storm* he was left "breathless with amazement" at the Prime Minister's refusal to accept the proffered hand of assistance from Franklin Roosevelt in January 1938.

36. Post, *Dilemmas of Appeasement*, 342–43.

37. Donald Cameron Watt, "Churchill and Appeasement," in *Churchill*, ed. Robert Blake and William Roger Lewis (Oxford: Oxford University Press, 1993), 199–200.

38. Ibid., 213.

39. See the intriguing work of Frederick Woods on Churchill's literary style, *Artillery of Words: the Writings of Sir Winston Churchill* (London, Cooper Publ., 1992), 121, where Woods quotes from Maurice Ashley, *Churchill as Historian* (London, Scribner 1968), 18, on the Churchillian hubris toward history: "Give me the facts, and I will twist them the way I want to suit my argument."

40. Watt, "Churchill and Appeasement," 214.

41. Ibid.

42. *Times Literary Supplement* (14 December 1946): 609.

EPILOGUE

1. John F. Kennedy, *Inaugural Address*, 20 January 1961. Another remarkable irony exists in that the newly elected President, so eager to subscribe to the evils of the "Munich analogy," (in this circumstance Communism taking the place of Nazism), was the progeny of one of the most supine appeasers of the twentieth century, Ambassador Joseph Kennedy, who understandably was quite reviled by the British by the end of his tenure at the Court of St. James in late 1940. For a compelling vignette that testified to the depth of Kennedy's bitterness toward the British after his recall, see the British Foreign Office General Correspondence (F.O. 371), File 339, 21 February 1941.

2. Robert Skidelsky, "Going to War with Germany," *Encounter* 39, 2 (July 1972): 65.

3. John Charmley, *Chamberlain and the Lost Peace* (London: Hodder and Stoughton, 1989) 212.

Bibliography

Primary Sources

Public Record Office, London

CAB 23/92–100. Cabinet Minutes and Conclusions. February 1938–September 1939.
CAB 24. Memoranda for Cabinet Meetings, 1938–1939.
F.O. 371. Foreign Office General Correspondence, 1938–1941.

Private Collections

Heslop Room, University of Birmingham (U.K.) Library.
Neville Chamberlain Papers, Letters, Diaries, and Correspondence.

Published Sources

PARLIAMENTARY PAPERS

Hansard: Parliamentary Debates (Commons), Fifth Series (October 1938). Vol. 339, 3–373.
Neville Chamberlain. *In Search of Peace*. New York: 1939.

COLLECTED DOCUMENTS

Germany, Foreign Ministry Archives

Documents on German Foreign Policy, 1918–1945. Series D (1937–1945). Vol. IV, The Aftermath of Munich, October 1938–March 1939.

Woodward, E. L., and Rohan Butler

Documents on British Foreign Policy, 1919–1939. Third Series, Vols. II (1938) and III (1938–39). London: His Majesty's Stationery Office, 1950.

U.S. Department of State

Foreign Relations of the United States: Diplomatic Papers, 1938 and 1939. Vol. I (General). Washington: U.S. Government Printing Office, 1956.

Soviet Union, The Ministry of Foreign Affairs

Documents and Materials Relating to the Eve of the Second World War. Vol. I, November 1937–1938. Vol. II, Dirksen Papers (1938–1939). New York: International Publishers, 1948.

EDITED DIARIES

Dilks, Donald. *The Diaries of Sir Alexander Cadogan, 1938–1945.* London: Cassell and Company, 1971.

Harvey, John. *The Diplomatic Diaries of Oliver Harvey, 1937–1940.* London: Collins Publishers, 1970.

NEWSPAPERS

The Times, The Times Literary Supplement

SECONDARY SOURCES

Important Works Cited

Adams, R. J. Q. *British Politics and Foreign Policy in the Age of Appeasement, 1935–1939.* Stanford: Stanford University Press, 1993.

Amery, Leopold. *My Political Life,* Vol. III, *The Unforgiving Years, 1929–1940.* London: Hutchinson and Co., 1955.

Angell, Sir Norman. *For What Do We Fight?* London: Hamish Hamilton Ltd., 1939.

Barnett, Corelli. *The Collapse of British Power.* New York: William Morrow and Company, 1972.

Benes, Eduard. *Memoirs of Dr. Eduard Benes: From Munich to New War and New Victory.* Boston: Houghton Mifflin Company, 1954.

Bialer, Uri. *The Shadow of the Bomber: The Fear of Air Attack in British Politics, 1932–1939.* London: Royal Historical Society Press, 1980.

Bond, Brian. *British Military Policy Between the Two World Wars.* Oxford: Clarendon Press, 1980.

Boothby, Robert. *I Fight to Live.* London: Victor Gollancz Ltd., 1947.

Carr, E. H. *Britain: A Study of Foreign Policy from the Versailles Treaty to the Outbreak of War.* London: Longmans, Green and Co., 1939.

CATO. *Guilty Men.* London: Victor Gollancz Ltd., 1940.

Charmley, John. *Chamberlain and the Lost Peace.* London: Hodder and Stoughton, 1989.

———. *Churchill: The End of Glory.* New York: Harcourt Brace, 1993.

Churchill, Winston. *The Gathering Storm.* Boston: Houghton Mifflin and Co., 1948.

Cockett, Richard. *Twilight of Truth: Chamberlain, Appeasement and the Manipulation of the Press.* London: Weidenfeld and Nicolson, 1989.

Coghlan, F. "Armaments, Economic Policy and Appeasement, Background to British Foreign Policy, 1931–1937." *History* 57, 190 (June 1972).

Colvin, Ian. *The Chamberlain Cabinet*. New York: Taplinger Publishing, 1971.

Douglas, Roy. *In the Year of Munich*. New York: St. Martin's Press, 1977.

Duff Cooper, Alfred. *Old Men Forget*. London: Rupert Hart-Davis Publishers, 1955.

Eden, Anthony. *Facing the Dictators*. Boston: Houghton Mifflin Company, 1962.

Eubank, Keith. *Munich*. Norman: University of Oklahoma Press, 1963.

Feiling, Keith. *The Life of Neville Chamberlain*. London: Macmillan and Company Ltd., 1946.

Fuchser, Larry W. *Neville Chamberlain and Appeasement: A Study in the Politics of History*. New York: W.W. Norton and Company, 1982.

Gannon, Franklin R. *The British Press and Germany, 1936–1939*. Oxford: Clarendon Press, 1971.

Gibbs, Norman. *Grand Strategy:* Volume 1, *Rearmament Policy*. London: HMSO, 1976.

Gilbert, Martin. *The Roots of Appeasement*. London: Weidenfeld and Nicolson, 1966.

―――― and Richard Gott. *The Appeasers*. Boston: Houghton Mifflin Company, 1963.

Halifax, Edward. *Fulness of Days*. New York: Dodd, Mead and Company, 1957.

Haxey, Simon. *England's Money Lords—Tory M.P.* New York: Harrison-Hilton Books, 1939.

Henderson, Nevile. *Failure of a Mission, Berlin 1937–1939*. New York: G.P. Putnam's Sons, 1940.

Hodgson, Stuart. *The Man Who Made the Peace: Neville Chamberlain*. New York: E.P. Dutton and Company, 1938.

Howard, Michael. *The Continental Commitment*. London: Temple Smith Ltd., 1972.

Kee, Robert. *Munich: The Eleventh Hour*. London: Hamish Hamilton, Ltd., 1988.

Keith-Shaw, Duncan. *Prime Minister Neville Chamberlain*. London: Wells Gardner, Darton & Co., 1939.

Kennedy, John F. *Why England Slept*. New York: W. Funk and Company, 1940.

Keynes, J. M. *The Economic Consequences of the Peace*. London and New York: Harcourt, Brace, Jovanovich, 1920 and 1988.

Koss, Stephen. *The Rise and Fall of the Political Press in Britain*. Volume II. *The Twentieth Century*. Chapel Hill: University of North Carolina Press, 1984.

Lamb, Richard. *The Drift to War, 1922–1939*. London: W.H. Allen and Company, 1989.

Lewis, Terrance. *A Climate for Appeasement?* New York: Peter Lang Publishing, 1991.

Liddell Hart, Basil. *The Defence of Britain*. London: Faber and Faber, 1939.

Londonderry, Lord. *Ourselves and Germany*. London: R. Hale Publishers, 1938.

Macgregor, Steven. *Truth and Mr. Chamberlain*. London: Fore Publications, Ltd., 1939.

Macleod, Iain. *Neville Chamberlain*. London: Frederick Muller Ltd., 1961.

Margach, James. *The Abuse of Power: The War Between Downing Street and the Media from Lloyd George to Callaghan*. London: W.H. Allen and Company, Ltd., 1978.

Maugham, Viscount. *The Truth About the Munich Crisis*. London: William Heinemann Ltd., 1944.

McLachlan, Donald. *In the Chair: Barrington-Ward of the Times, 1927–1948*. London: Weidenfeld and Nicolson, 1971.

Medlicott, W. N. *British Foreign Policy Since Versailles, 1919–1939*. London: Methuen and Company Ltd., 1940.

Middlemas, Keith. *The Strategy of Appeasement: The British Government and Germany, 1937–1939*. Chicago: Quadrangle Books, 1972.

Morison, Stanley, ed. *The History of The Times*. Volume IV. *The 150th Anniversary and Beyond, 1912–1948, Part II, 1921–1948*. New York: The Macmillan Company, 1952.

Morris, Benny. *The Roots of Appeasement: The British Weekly Press and Nazi Germany During the 1930s*. London: Frank Cass and Company, 1991.

Murray, Williamson. *The Change in the European Balance of Power, 1938–1939*. Princeton: Princeton University Press, 1984.

Parker, R. A. C. *Chamberlain and Appeasement: British Policy and the Coming of the Second World War*. New York: St. Martin's Press, 1993.

Parkinson, Roger. *Peace for Our Time: Munich to Dunkirk—The Inside Story*. London: Rupert Hart-Davis, Ltd., 1971.

Peden, George. *British Rearmament and the Treasury, 1932–1939*. Edinburgh: Scottish Academic Press, 1979.

———. "A Matter of Timing, the Economic Background to British Foreign Policy, 1937–1939." *History* 69, 225 (February 1984).

Petrie, Sir Charles. *The Chamberlain Tradition*. New York: Stokes and Company, 1938.

Post, Gaines. *Dilemmas of Appeasement: British Deterrence and Defense, 1934–1937*. Ithaca: Cornell University Press, 1993.

Postan, M. M. *British War Production*. London: HMSO, 1952.

Presseisen, Ernst. *Amiens and Munich: Comparisons in Appeasement*. The Hague: Martinus Nijhoff, 1978.

Rathbone, Eleanor. *War Can Be Averted*. London: Victor Gollancz Ltd., 1938.

Ripka, Hubert. *Munich: Before and After*. London: Victor Gollancz Ltd., 1939.

Robbins, Keith. *Appeasement*. London: Basil Blackwell, 1988.

———. *Munich 1938*. London: Cassell and Company, Ltd., 1968.

Rock, William. *Chamberlain and Roosevelt: British Foreign Policy and the United States, 1937–1940*. Columbus: Ohio State University Press, 1988.

Rowse, A. L. *Appeasement: A Study in Political Decline, 1933–1939*. New York: W.W. Norton and Company, 1961.

Sabine, B. E. V. *British Budgets in Peace and War, 1932–1945*. London: George Allen and Unwin, Ltd., 1970.

Schmidt, Gustav. *The Politics and Economics of Appeasement*. Leamington Spa: Berg Publishers, 1986.

Seton-Watson, R. W. *From Munich to Danzig*. London: Methuen & Co. Ltd., 1939.

Shay, Robert P. *British Rearmament in the Thirties: Politics and Profits*. Princeton: Princeton University Press, 1977.

Shepherd, Robert. *A Class Divided: Appeasement and the Road to Munich, 1938*. London: Macmillan Publishers, 1988.

Simon, Sir John. Retrospect: The Memoirs of Sir John Simon. London: Hutchinson and Company, 1952.

Strang, Lord. *Home and Abroad*. London: Andre Deutsch Ltd., 1956.

Taylor, A. J. P. *Origins of the Second World War*. London: Hamish Hamilton Ltd., 1961 and 1963.

Taylor, Telford. *Munich: The Price of Peace*. Garden City, N.Y.: Doubleday & Company, 1979.

Templewood, Viscount. *Nine Troubled Years*. London: Collins Publishers, 1954.

Thorne, Christopher. *The Approach of War, 1938–1939*. London: Macmillan and Company Ltd., 1967.

Walker-Smith, Derek. *Neville Chamberlain: Man of Peace*. London: R. Hale Publishers, 1940.

Wark, Wesley. *The Ultimate Enemy: British Intelligence and Nazi Germany, 1933–1939*. Ithaca: Cornell University Press, 1985.

Watt, Donald C. "Appeasement: A Case for Revision." *Political Quarterly* (April–June 1965).

———. "Churchill and Appeasement." *Churchill*. Edited by Robert Blake and William Roger Lewis. Oxford: Oxford University Press, 1993.

Wheeler-Bennett, Sir John. *Munich: Prologue to Tragedy*. New York: Duell, Sloan and Pearce, 1948.

Wrench, John E. *Geoffrey Dawson and Our Times*. London: Hutchinson and Company, 1955.

Background Sources

Bruegel, Johann. *Czechoslovakia Before Munich*. London: Cambridge University Press, 1973.

George, Margaret. *The Warped Vision: British Foreign Policy, 1933–1939*. Pittsburgh, Pa.: University of Pittsburgh Press, 1965.

Gilbert, Martin. *Winston S. Churchill*. Volume V. *The Prophet of Truth, 1932–1939*. Boston: Houghton Mifflin Company, 1977.

Hill, Christopher. *Cabinet Decisions on Foreign Policy*. Cambridge: Cambridge University Press, 1991.

Hyde, H. Montgomery. *Neville Chamberlain*. London: Weidenfeld and Nicolson, 1976.

Ismay, Hastings. *The Memoirs of General Lord Ismay*. New York: Viking Press, 1960.

Jones, Thomas. *A Diary with Letters, 1931–1950*. London: Oxford University Press, 1954.

Kennan, George. *From Prague After Munich: Diplomatic Papers 1938–1940*. Princeton: Princeton University Press, 1968.

Kennedy, Paul. *The Realities Behind Diplomacy: Background Influences in British External Policy (1865–1980)*. London: George Allen and Unwin, 1981.

Kirkpatrick, Ivone. *The Inner Circle*. London: Macmillan and Company, Ltd., 1959.

MacDonald, C. A. *The United States, Britain, and Appeasement, 1936–1939*. London: Macmillan Press, Ltd., 1981.

Mackintosh, John, ed. *British Prime Ministers in the Twentieth Century*. Volume 1. *Balfour to Chamberlain*. New York: St.Martin's Press, 1977.

Minney, R. J.. *The Private Papers of Hore-Belisha*. London: Collins Press, 1960.

Mommsen, Wolfgang, and Lothar Kettenacker. *The Fascist Challenge and the Policy of Appeasement*. London: George Allen and Unwin, 1983.

Naylor, John F. *A Man and An Institution: Sir Maurice Hankey, the Cabinet Secretariat, and the Custody of Cabinet Secrecy*. Cambridge: Cambridge University Press, 1984.

Ovendale, Ritchie. *"Appeasement" and the English Speaking World*. Cardiff: University of Wales Press, 1975.

Reynolds, P. A. *British Foreign Policy in the Inter-War Years*. London: Longmans, Green and Company, 1954.

Strang, Lord. *The Moscow Negotiations, 1939*. Cambridge: Leeds University Press, 1968.

Thompson, Laurence. *The Greatest Treason: The Untold Story of Munich*. New York: William Morrow and Company, 1968.

Thompson, Neville. *The Anti-Appeasers: Conservative Opposition to Appeasement in the 1930s*. Oxford: Oxford University Press, 1971.

Vansittart, Robert. *The Mist Procession*. London: Hutchinson and Company, Ltd., 1958.

Unpublished Dissertations

Hachey, Thomas. *Neville Chamberlain vs. Anthony Eden: Britain's Policy of Appeasement from May 1937 to February 1938*. New York: St. John's University, 1965.

Kelly, Thomas L. *Appeasement: The Ploy that Failed: Henderson, Chamberlain, The Foreign Office and Anglo-German Relations, 1937–1939*. Tuscaloosa: The University of Alabama, 1979.

Myers, Walter K. *A Rationale for Appeasement: A Study of British Efforts to Conciliate Germany in the 1930s*. Baltimore: Johns Hopkins University, 1972.

Vieth, Jane K. *Joseph P. Kennedy: Ambassador to the Court of St. James, 1938–1940*. Volumes I–II. Columbus: Ohio State University, 1975.

Index

Krofta, Kamil, Munich Conference report, 183–84

Labour Party: Chamberlain animosity, 46–47, 106; rearmament support, 20. *See also* Conservative Party
Lacroix, (French Minister), 183
Lamb, Richard *(The Drift to War, 1922–1939)*, 209–11
Law, Richard, 43
Layton, Sir Walter, 167, 170–71
leadership, war: Macleod on NC, 48; NC's self-assessment, 41–42
League of Nations, 22, 170, 181
Left Book Club, 16
Leger, Alexis, 183
Lewis, Terrance *(A Climate for Appeasement?)*, 216–17, 220
Lewis, William Roger, 227
Liddell Hart, Basil *(Defence of Britain)*, 118–19
Life of Neville Chamberlain, The (Feiling): assessment of NC, 37–41; author authorization, 34–36; influence of, 44; reviews of, 42–43, 229
limited liability policy: Bialer's discussion, 136–37; Bond's discussion, 121–23; Liddell Hart's advocacy, 118–19; Pownall's opposition, 121
Litvinov, Maxim, 54, 62
Lloyd George, David, 38, 102, 159, 174
Londonderry, Lord (Charles Stuart): Haxey's accusations, 19; memoirs, 30–32
Luce, Henry, 32

MacDonald, Ramsay, 16–17, 102
Macgregor, Steven *(Truth and Mr. Chamberlain)*, 20–21
Macleod, Ian, 44, 45. See also *Neville Chamberlain* (Macleod)
Macmillan, Harold, 137
Manchester Guardian, 161–62
Mann, Arthur, 168
Man Who Made the Peace, The: Neville Chamberlain (Hodgson), 28–29
Margach, James *(The Abuse of Power: The War Between Downing Street and the Media from Lloyd George to Callaghan)*, 162–64, 173–74

Masarik, Hubert, 183
Masaryk, Thomas, 180
"Matter of Timing, A: The Economic Background to British Foreign Policy, 1937–1939" (Peden), 146–47
Maugham, Viscount Frederick *(The Truth About the Munich Crisis)*, 68–70
McLachlan, Donald *(In the Chair: Barrington-Ward of the Times)*, 155–57
Medlicott, W. N. *(The Coming of War)*, 100, 101
Memories of Dr. Eduard Benes: From Munich to New War and New Victory (Benes), 179–81
Middlemarch, NC's marked passage, 42
Middlemas, Keith *(The Strategy of Appeasement: The British Government and Germany, 1937–1939)*, 105–9
Molotov, V. M., 85
Morison, Stanley *(The History of the Times: The 150th Anniversary and Beyond, 1912–1948)*, 149–52
Morning Post, 159
Morris, Benny *(The Roots of Appeasement: The British Weekly Press and Nazi Germany During the 1930s)*, 169–73
Morton, Desmond, 142
Mount Temple, Lord, 19
Mowat, Charles, 100
Munich: Before and After (Ripka), 23–24
Munich: The Eleventh Hour (Kee), 212–13
Munich: The Price of Peace (Taylor), 199–202
Munich: Prologue to Tragedy (Wheeler-Bennett), 184
Munich Agreement (1938): Amery's criticism, 62–63; Anglo-German Fellowship letter, 18; Barnett's assessment, 194–95; Boothby's criticism, 65–66; Charmley's criticism, 207–8; Churchill's discussion, 54–55; Czech leadership response, 23–24, 180–81, 183–84; Douglas' discussion, 196; Duff Cooper's criticism,